ABOUT THIS PUBLICATION

FOR SERVICE ASSISTANCE

Customer Service
1.704.898.0770

North Carolina General Statues is published by The Muliti-Media Group of Greater Charlotte in Charlotte, North Carolina. Copyright 2015 by the Multi-Media Group of Greater Charlotte. This book or parts thereof may not be reproduced in any form, stored in a retrieval system, or transmitted in any form by any means—electronic, mechanical, photocopy, recording or otherwise—without prior written permission of the publisher, except as provided by United States of America copyright law.

The records required by U.S. Code 2257(a) through (c) and the pertinent regulations 28 C.F.R. Cli. 1, Part 75 with respect to this publication and all materials associated with such records are maintained by The Multi-Media Group of Greater Charlotte, Publisher and available for review by Attorney General.

www.visionbooks.org

Copyright © 2015 by MMGGC
All rights reserved!

TID: 5064369
ISBN (10) digit: 1502933985
ISBN (13) digit: 978-1502933980

123-4-56789-01239-Paperback
123-4-56789-01239-Hardback

First Edition

090520140547

Printed in the United States of America

2015 EDITION

North Carolina Criminal Law And Procedure-Pamphlet # 55

Printed In conjunction with the Administration of the Courts

North Carolina Criminal Law and Procedure
Pamphlet Reference Guide

Chapters	Pamphlet
Chapter 1 Civil Procedure	1
Chapter 1 Civil Procedure (Continue)	2
Chapter 1A Rules of Civil Procedure	2
Chapter 1B Contribution.	2
Chapter 1C Enforcement of Judgments.	2
Chapter 1D Punitive Damages.	2
Chapter 1E Eastern Band of Cherokee Indians.	2
Chapter 1F North Carolina Uniform Interstate Depositions and Discovery Act.	2
Chapter 2 - Clerk of Superior Court [Repealed and Transferred.]	3
Chapter 3 - Commissioners of Affidavits and Deeds [Repealed.]	3
Chapter 4 - Common Law	3
Chapter 5 - Contempt [Repealed.]	3
Chapter 5A - Contempt	3
Chapter 6 - Liability for Court Costs	3
Chapter 7 - Courts [Repealed and Transferred.]	3
Chapter 7A – Judicial Department	3
Chapter 7A – Continuation (Judicial Department)	4
Chapter 7A – Continuation (Judicial Department)	5
Chapter 7B - Juvenile Code	5
Chapter 8 - Evidence	6
Chapter 8A - Interpreters for Deaf Persons [Recodified.]	6
Chapter 8B - Interpreters for Deaf Persons	6
Chapter 8C - Evidence Code	6
Chapter 9 - Jurors	6
Chapter 10 - Notaries [Repealed.]	6
Chapter 10A - Notaries [Recodified.]	6
Chapter 10B - Notaries	6
Chapter 11 - Oaths	6
Chapter 12 - Statutory Construction	6
Chapter 13 - Citizenship Restored	6
Chapter 14 - Criminal Law	7
Chapter 14 –Criminal Law (Continuation)	8
Chapter 15 - Criminal Procedure	9

Chapter 15A - Criminal Procedure Act (Continuation)	10
Chapter 15A - Criminal Procedure Act (Continuation)	11
Chapter 15B - Victims Compensation	11
Chapter 15C - Address Confidentiality Program	11
Chapter 16 - Gaming Contracts and Futures	11
Chapter 17 - Habeas Corpus	11
Chapter 17A - Law-Enforcement Officers [Recodified.]	11
Chapter 17B - North Carolina Criminal Justice Education and Training System [Recodified.] Chapter 17C - North Carolina Criminal Justice Education and Training Standards Commission	11
Chapter 17D - North Carolina Justice Academy	11
Chapter 17E - North Carolina Sheriffs' Education and Training Standards Commission	11
Chapter 18 - Regulation of Intoxicating Liquors [Repealed.]	12
Chapter 18A - Regulation of Intoxicating Liquors [Repealed.]	12
Chapter 18B - Regulation of Alcoholic Beverages	12
Chapter 18C - North Carolina State Lottery	12
Chapter 19 - Offenses against Public Morals	12
Chapter 19A - Protection of Animals	12
Chapter 20 - Motor Vehicles	13
Chapter 20 - Motor Vehicles (Continuation)	14
Chapter 20 - Motor Vehicles (Continuation)	15
Chapter 20 - Motor Vehicles (Continuation)	16
Chapter 21 - Bills of Lading	17
Chapter 22 - Contracts Requiring Writing	17
Chapter 22A - Signatures	17
Chapter 22B - Contracts Against Public Policy	17
Chapter 22C - Payments to Subcontractors	17
Chapter 23 - Debtor and Creditor	17
Chapter 24 – Interest	17
Chapter 25 – Uniform Commercial Code	18
Chapter 25 – Uniform Commercial Code (Continuation)	19
Chapter 25A – Retail Installment Sales Act	20
Chapter 25B - Credit	20
Chapter 25C - Sales of Artwork	20
Chapter 26 - Suretyship	20
Chapter 27 - Warehouse Receipts [Repealed.]	20
Chapter 28 - Administration [Repealed.]	20
Chapter 28A - Administration of Decedents' Estates	20
Chapter 28B - Estates of Absentees in Military Service	20
Chapter 28C - Estates of Missing Persons	20
Chapter 29 - Intestate Succession	21
Chapter 30 - Surviving Spouses	21
Chapter 31 - Wills	21
Chapter 31A - Acts Barring Property Rights	21
Chapter 31B - Renunciation of Property and Renunciation of	

Fiduciary Powers Act	21
Chapter 31C - Uniform Disposition of Community Property Rights at Death Act	21
Chapter 32 - Fiduciaries	21
Chapter 32A - Powers of Attorney	21
Chapter 33 - Guardian and Ward [Repealed and Recodified.]	21
Chapter 33A - North Carolina Uniform Transfers to Minors Act	21
Chapter 33B - North Carolina Uniform Custodial Trust Act	21
Chapter 34 - Veterans' Guardianship Act	22
Chapter 35 - Sterilization Procedures	22
Chapter 35A - Incompetency and Guardianship	22
Chapter 36 - Trusts and Trustees [Repealed.]	22
Chapter 36A - Trusts and Trustees	22
Chapter 36B - Uniform Management of Institutional Funds Act [Repealed.]	22
Chapter 36C - North Carolina Uniform Trust Code	22
Chapter 36D - North Carolina Community Third Party Trusts, Pooled Trusts	23
Chapter 36E - Uniform Prudent Management of Institutional Funds Act	23
Chapter 37 - Allocation of Principal and Income [Repealed.]	23
Chapter 37A - Uniform Principal and Income Act	23
Chapter 38 - Boundaries	23
Chapter 38A - Landowner Liability	23
Chapter 39 - Conveyances	23
Chapter 39A - Transfer Fee Covenants Prohibited	23
Chapter 40 - Eminent Domain [Repealed.]	23
Chapter 40A - Eminent Domain	23
Chapter 41 - Estates	23
Chapter 41A - State Fair Housing Act	23
Chapter 42 - Landlord and Tenant	23
Chapter 42A - Vacation Rental Act	23
Chapter 43 - Land Registration	23
Chapter 44 - Liens	24
Chapter 44A - Statutory Liens and Charges	24
Chapter 45 - Mortgages and Deeds of Trust	24
Chapter 45A - Good Funds Settlement Act	24
Chapter 46 - Partition	24
Chapter 47 - Probate and Registration	25
Chapter 47A - Unit Ownership	25
Chapter 47B - Real Property Marketable Title Act	25
Chapter 47C - North Carolina Condominium Act	25
Chapter 47D - Notice of Settlement Act [Expired.]	25
Chapter 47E - Residential Property Disclosure Act	25
Chapter 47F - North Carolina Planned Community Act	25
Chapter 47G - Option to Purchase Contracts	25
Chapter 47H - Contracts for Deed	25

Chapter 48 - Adoptions +	26
Chapter 48A - Minors	26
Chapter 49 - Bastardy	26
Chapter 49A - Rights of Children	26
Chapter 50 - Divorce and Alimony	26
Chapter 50A - Uniform Child-Custody Jurisdiction and Enforcement Act	26
Chapter 50B - Domestic Violence	26
Chapter 50C - Civil No-Contact Orders	26
Chapter 51 - Marriage	26
Chapter 52 - Powers and Liabilities of Married Persons	27
Chapter 52A - Uniform Reciprocal Enforcement of Support Act [Repealed.]	27
Chapter 52B - Uniform Premarital Agreement Act	27
Chapter 52C - Uniform Interstate Family Support Act	27
Chapter 53 - Banks	27
Chapter 53A - Business Development Corporations and North Carolina Capital Resource Corporations	28
Chapter 53B - Financial Privacy Act	28
Chapter 54 - Cooperative Organizations	28
Chapter 54A - Capital Stock Savings and Loan Associations [Repealed.]	28
Chapter 54B - Savings and Loan Associations	29
Chapter 54C - Savings Banks	29
Chapter 55 - North Carolina Business Corporation Act	30
Chapter 55A - North Carolina Nonprofit Corporation Act	31
Chapter 55B - Professional Corporation Act	31
Chapter 55C - Foreign Trade Zones	31
Chapter 55D - Filings, Names, and Registered Agents for Corporations, Nonprofit Corporations, and Partnerships	31
Chapter 56 - Electric, Telegraph and Power Companies [Repealed.]	31
Chapter 57 - Hospital, Medical and Dental Service Corporations [Recodified.]	31
Chapter 57A - Health Maintenance Organization Act [Recodified.]	31
Chapter 57B - Health Maintenance Organization Act [Recodified.]	31
Chapter 57C - North Carolina Limited Liability Company Act.	31
Chapter 58 - Insurance.	32
Chapter 58 - Insurance (Continuation)	33
Chapter 58 - Insurance (Continuation)	34
Chapter 58 - Insurance (Continuation)	35
Chapter 58 - Insurance (Continuation)	36
Chapter 58 - Insurance (Continuation)	37
Chapter 58 - Insurance (Continuation)	38
Chapter 58A - North Carolina Health Insurance Trust	

Commission [Recodified.]	38
Chapter 59 - Partnership.	39
Chapter 59B - Uniform Unincorporated Nonprofit Association Act.	39
Chapter 60 - Railroads and Other Carriers [Repealed and Transferred.]	39
Chapter 61 - Religious Societies	39
Chapter 62 - Public Utilities	39
Chapter 62 - Public Utilities (Continuation)	40
Chapter 62A - Public Safety Telephone Service And Wireless Telephone Service	40
Chapter 63 - Aeronautics	40
Chapter 63A - North Carolina Global TransPark Authority	40
Chapter 64 - Aliens	40
Chapter 65 – Cemeteries	40
Chapter 66 - Commerce and Business	41
Chapter 67 - Dogs	41
Chapter 68 - Fences and Stock Law	41
Chapter 69 - Fire Protection	41
Chapter 70 - Indian Antiquities, Archaeological Resources and Unmarked Human Skeletal Remains Protection	42
Chapter 71 - Indians [Repealed.]	42
Chapter 71A - Indians	42
Chapter 72 - Inns, Hotels and Restaurants	42
Chapter 73 - Mills	42
Chapter 74 - Mines and Quarries	42
Chapter 74A - Company Police [Repealed.]	42
Chapter 74B - Private Protective Services Act [Repealed.]	42
Chapter 74C - Private Protective Services	42
Chapter 74D - Alarm Systems	42
Chapter 74E - Company Police Act	42
Chapter 74F - Locksmith Licensing Act	42
Chapter 74G - Campus Police Act	42
Chapter 75 - Monopolies, Trusts and Consumer Protection	42
Chapter 75A - Boating and Water Safety	43
Chapter 75B - Discrimination in Business	43
Chapter 75C - Motion Picture Fair Competition Act	43
Chapter 75D - Racketeer Influenced and Corrupt Organizations	43
Chapter 75E - Unlawful Activities in Connection With Certain Corporate Transactions	43
Chapter 76 - Navigation	43
Chapter 76A - Navigation and Pilotage Commissions	43
Chapter 77 - Rivers, Creeks, and Coastal Waters	43
Chapter 78 - Securities Law [Repealed.]	43
Chapter 78A - North Carolina Securities Act	43
Chapter 78B - Tender Offer Disclosure Act [Repealed.]	43
Chapter 78C - Investment Advisers	43
Chapter 78D - Commodities Act	43

Chapter 79 - Strays [Repealed]	43
Chapter 80 - Trademarks, Brands, etc.	44
Chapter 81 - Weights and Measures [Recodified]	44
Chapter 81A - Weights and Measures Act of 1975.	44
Chapter 82 - Wrecks [Repealed]	44
Chapter 83 - Architects [Recodified]	44
Chapter 83A - Architects	44
Chapter 84 - Attorneys-at-Law	44
Chapter 84A - Foreign Legal Consultants	44
Chapter 85 - Auctions and Auctioneers [Repealed]	44
Chapter 85A - Bail Bondsmen and Runners [Recodified]	44
Chapter 85B - Auctions and Auctioneers	44
Chapter 85C - Bail Bondsmen and Runners [Recodified]	44
Chapter 86 - Barbers [Recodified]	44
Chapter 86A - Barbers	44
Chapter 87 - Contractors	44
Chapter 88 - Cosmetic Art [Repealed]	44
Chapter 88A - Electrolysis Practice Act	44
Chapter 88B - Cosmetic Art	45
Chapter 89 - Engineering and Land Surveying [Recodified]	45
Chapter 89A - Landscape Architects	45
Chapter 89B - Foresters	45
Chapter 89C - Engineering and Land Surveying	45
Chapter 89D - Landscape Contractors	45
Chapter 89E - Geologists Licensing Act	45
Chapter 89F - North Carolina Soil Scientist Licensing Act	45
Chapter 89G - Irrigation Contractors	45
Chapter 90 - Medicine and Allied Occupations	45
Chapter 90 - Medicine and Allied Occupations (Continuation)	46
Chapter 90 - Medicine and Allied Occupations (Continuation)	47
Chapter 90 - Medicine and Allied Occupations (Continuation)	48
Chapter 90A - Sanitarians and Water and Wastewater Treatment Facility Operators	48
Chapter 90B - Social Worker Certification and Licensure Act	48
Chapter 90C - North Carolina Recreational Therapy Licensure Act	48
Chapter 90D - Interpreters and Transliterators	48
Chapter 91 - Pawnbrokers [Repealed]	48
Chapter 91A - Pawnbrokers Modernization Act of 1989	48
Chapter 92 - Photographers [Deleted]	48
Chapter 93 - Certified Public Accountants	48
Chapter 93A - Real Estate License Law	49
Chapter 93B - Occupational Licensing Boards	49
Chapter 93C - Watchmakers [Repealed]	49
Chapter 93D - North Carolina State Hearing Aid Dealers and Fitters Board.	49
Chapter 93E - North Carolina Appraisers Act	49

Chapter 94 - Apprenticeship	49
Chapter 95 - Department of Labor and Labor Regulations	49
Chapter 95 - Department of Labor and Labor Regulations (Continuation)	50
Chapter 96 - Employment Security	50
Chapter 97 - Workers' Compensation Act	50
Chapter 97 - Workers' Compensation Act (Continuation)	51
Chapter 98 - Burnt and Lost Records	51
Chapter 99 - Libel and Slander	51
Chapter 99A - Civil Remedies for Criminal Actions	51
Chapter 99B - Products Liability	51
Chapter 99C - Actions Relating to Winter Sports Safety and Accidents	51
Chapter 99D - Civil Rights	51
Chapter 99E - Special Liability Provisions	51
Chapter 100 - Monuments, Memorials and Parks	51
Chapter 101 - Names of Persons	51
Chapter 102 - Official Survey Base	51
Chapter 103 - Sundays, Holidays and Special Days	51
Chapter 104 - United States Lands	51
Chapter 104A - Degrees of Kinship	51
Chapter 104B - Hurricanes or Other Acts of Nature	51
Chapter 104C - Atomic Energy, Radioactivity and Ionizing Radiation [Repealed and Recodified.]	51
Chapter 104D - Southern States Energy Compact	51
Chapter 104E - North Carolina Radiation Protection Act	51
Chapter 104F - Southeast Interstate Low-Level Radioactive Waste Management Compact [Repealed]	51
Chapter 104G - North Carolina Low-Level Radioactive Waste Management Authority Act of 1987 [Repealed]	51
Chapter 105 - Taxation	51
Chapter 105 - Taxation (Continuation)	52
Chapter 105 - Taxation (Continuation)	53
Chapter 105 - Taxation (Continuation)	54
Chapter 105A - Setoff Debt Collection Act	55
Chapter 105B - Defaulted Student Loan Recovery Act	55
Chapter 106 - Agriculture	55
Chapter 106 - Agriculture (Continue)	56
Chapter 106 - Agriculture (Continue)	57
Chapter 107 - Agricultural Development Districts [Repealed.]	57
Chapter 108 - Social Services [Repealed and Recodified.]	57
Chapter 108A - Social Services	57
Chapter 108B - Community Action Programs	58
Chapter 108C Medicaid and Health Choice Provider Requirements.	58
Chapter 108D Medicaid Managed Care for Behavioral Health Services.	58
Chapter 109 - Bonds [Recodified.]	58

Chapter 110 - Child Welfare	58
Chapter 111 - Aid to the Blind	58
Chapter 112 - Confederate Homes and Pensions [Repealed.]	58
Chapter 113 - Conservation and Development	58
Chapter 113 - Conservation and Development (Continuation)	59
Chapter 113A - Pollution Control and Environment	59
Chapter 113A - Pollution Control and Environment (Continuation)	60
Chapter 113B - North Carolina Energy Policy Act of 1975	60
Chapter 114 - Department of Justice	60
Chapter 115 - Elementary and Secondary Education [Repealed.]	60
Chapter 115A - Community Colleges, Technical Institutes, and Industrial Education Centers [Repealed.]	60
Chapter 115B - Tuition and Fee Waivers	60
Chapter 115C - Elementary and Secondary Education	60
Chapter 115C - Elementary and Secondary Education (Continuation)	61
Chapter 115C - Elementary and Secondary Education (Continuation)	62
Chapter 115C - Elementary and Secondary Education (Continuation)	63
Chapter 115D - Community Colleges	63
Chapter 115E - Private Educational Facilities Finance Act [Recodified]	63
Chapter 116 - Higher Education	63
Chapter 116 - Higher Education (Continuation)	63
Chapter 116A - Escheats and Abandoned Property [Repealed.]	64
Chapter 116B - Escheats and Abandoned Property	64
Chapter 116C - Continuum of Education Programs	64
Chapter 116D - Higher Education Bonds	64
Chapter 117 - Electrification	64
Chapter 118 - Firemen's and Rescue Squad Workers' Relief and Pension Funds [Recodified.]	64
Chapter 118A - Firemen's Death Benefit Act [Repealed.]	64
Chapter 118B - Members of a Rescue Squad Death Benefit Act [Repealed.]	64
Chapter 119 - Gasoline and Oil Inspection and Regulation	64
Chapter 120 - General Assembly	65
Chapter 120 - General Assembly (Continuation)	66
Chapter 120 - General Assembly (Continuation)	67
Chapter 120C - Lobbying	67
Chapter 121 - Archives and History	67
Chapter 122 - Hospitals for the Mentally Disordered [Repealed.]	67
Chapter 122A - North Carolina Housing Finance Agency	67
Chapter 122B - North Carolina Agricultural Facilities	

Finance Act [Repealed.]	67
Chapter 122C - Mental Health, Developmental Disabilities, and Substance Abuse Act of 1985	67
Chapter 122C - Mental Health, Developmental Disabilities, and Substance Abuse Act of 1985 (Continuation)	68
Chapter 122D - North Carolina Agricultural Finance Act	68
Chapter 122E - North Carolina Housing Trust and Oil Overcharge Act	68
Chapter 123 - Impeachment	69
Chapter 123A - Industrial Development [Repealed.]	69
Chapter 124 - Internal Improvements	69
Chapter 125 - Libraries	69
Chapter 126 - State Personnel System	69
Chapter 127 - Militia [Repealed.]	69
Chapter 127A - Militia	69
Chapter 127B - Military Affairs	69
Chapter 127C - Advisory Commission on Military Affairs	69
Chapter 128 - Offices and Public Officers	69
Chapter 128 - Offices and Public Officers (Continuation)	70
Chapter 129 - Public Buildings and Grounds	70
Chapter 130 - Public Health [Repealed.]	70
Chapter 130A - Public Health	70
Chapter 130A - Public Health (Continuation)	71
Chapter 130A - Public Health (Continuation)	72
Chapter 130B - Hazardous Waste Management Commission [Repealed.]	72
Chapter 131 - Public Hospitals [Repealed.]	72
Chapter 131A - Health Care Facilities Finance Act	72
Chapter 131B - Licensing of Ambulatory Surgical Facilities [Repealed.]	72
Chapter 131C - Charitable Solicitation Licensure Act [Repealed.]	72
Chapter 131D - Inspection and Licensing of Facilities	72
Chapter 131E - Health Care Facilities and Services	72
Chapter 131E - Health Care Facilities and Services (Continuation)	73
Chapter 131F - Solicitation of Contributions	73
Chapter 132 - Public Records	73
Chapter 133 - Public Works	74
Chapter 134 - Youth Development [Recodified.]	74
Chapter 134A - Youth Services [Repealed.]	74
Chapter 135 - Retirement System for Teachers and State Employees; Social Security; Health Insurance Program for Children	74
Chapter 135 - Retirement System for Teachers and State Employees; Social Security; Health Insurance Program for Children	75

Chapter 136 - Transportation	75
Chapter 136 - Transportation (Continuation)	76
Chapter 137 - Rural Rehabilitation [Repealed.]	76
Chapter 138 - Salaries, Fees and Allowances	76
Chapter 138A - State Government Ethics Act	76
Chapter 139 - Soil and Water Conservation Districts	76
Chapter 140 - State Art Museum; Symphony and Art Societies	76
Chapter 140A - State Awards System	76
Chapter 141 - State Boundaries	76
Chapter 142 - State Debt	76
Chapter 143 - State Departments, Institutions, and Commissions	77
Chapter 143 - State Departments, Institutions, and Commissions (Continuation)	78
Chapter 143 - State Departments, Institutions, and Commissions (Continuation)	79
Chapter 143 - State Departments, Institutions, and Commissions (Continuation)	80
Chapter 143A - State Government Reorganization	80
Chapter 143B - Executive Organization Act of 1973	80
Chapter 143B - Executive Organization Act of 1973 (Continuation)	81
Chapter 143B - Executive Organization Act of 1973 (Continuation)	82
Chapter 143C - State Budget Act	83
Chapter 143D - The State Governmental Accountability and Internal Control Act	83
Chapter 144 - State Flag, Official Governmental Flags, Motto, and Colors	83
Chapter 145 - State Symbols and Other Official Adoptions.	83
Chapter 146 - State Lands	83
Chapter 147 - State Officers	83
Chapter 148 - State Prison System	84
Chapter 149 - State Song and Toast	84
Chapter 150 - Uniform Revocation of Licenses [Repealed.]	84
Chapter 150A - Administrative Procedure Act [Recodified.]	84
Chapter 150B - Administrative Procedure Act	84
Chapter 151 - Constables [Repealed.]	84
Chapter 152 - Coroners	84
Chapter 152A - County Medical Examiner [Repealed.]	84
Chapter 152A - County Medical Examiner [Repealed.] (Continuation)	85
Chapter 153 - Counties and County Commissioners [Repealed.]	85
Chapter 153A - Counties	85

Chapter 153B - Mountain Resources Planning Act	85
Chapter 153C - Uwharrie Regional Resources Act	85
Chapter 154 - County Surveyor [Repealed.]	85
Chapter 155 - County Treasurer [Repealed.]	85
Chapter 156 - Drainage	85
Chapter 156 – Drainage (Continuation)	86
Chapter 157 - Housing Authorities and Projects	86
Chapter 157A - Historic Properties Commissions [Transferred.]	86
Chapter 158 - Local Development	86
Chapter 159 - Local Government Finance	86
Chapter 159 - Local Government Finance (Continuation)	87
Chapter 159A - Pollution Abatement and Industrial Facilities Financing Act [Unconstitutional.]	87
Chapter 159B - Joint Municipal Electric Power and Energy Act	87
Chapter 159C - Industrial and Pollution Control Facilities Financing Act	87
Chapter 159D - The North Carolina Capital Facilities Financing Act	87
Chapter 159E - Registered Public Obligations Act	87
Chapter 159F - North Carolina Energy Development Authority [Repealed.]	87
Chapter 159G - Water Infrastructure	87
Chapter 159H - [Reserved.]	87
Chapter 159I - Solid Waste Management Loan Program and Local Government Special Obligation Bonds	87
Chapter 160 - Municipal Corporations [Repealed And Transferred.]	87
Chapter 160A - Cities and Towns	88
Chapter 160A - Cities and Towns (Continuation)	89
Chapter 160B - Consolidated City-County Act	89
Chapter 160C - Baseball Park Districts [Repealed.]	90
Chapter 161 - Register of Deeds	90
Chapter 162 - Sheriff	90
Chapter 162A - Water and Sewer Systems	90
Chapter 162B Continuity of Local Government in Emergency.	90
Chapter 163 Elections and Election Laws.	90
Chapter 163 Elections and Election Laws. (Continuation)	91
Chapter 164 Concerning the General Statutes of North Carolina.	92
Chapter 165 Veterans.	92
Chapter 166 Civil Preparedness Agencies [Repealed.]	92
Chapter 166A North Carolina Emergency Management Act.	92
Chapter 167 State Civil Air Patrol [Repealed.]	92
Chapter 168 Persons with Disabilities.	92
Chapter 168A Persons With Disabilities Protection Act.	92

Chapter 105A.

Setoff Debt Collection Act.

Article 1.
In General.

§ 105A-1. Purposes.

The purpose of this Chapter is to establish as policy that all claimant agencies and the Department of Revenue shall cooperate in identifying debtors who owe money to the State or to a local government through their various agencies and who qualify for refunds from the Department of Revenue. It is also the intent of this Chapter that procedures be established for setting off against any refund the sum of any debt owed to the State or to a local government. Furthermore, it is the legislative intent that this Chapter be liberally construed so as to effectuate these purposes as far as legally and practically possible. (1979, c. 801, s. 94; 1997-490, s. 1.)

§ 105A-2. Definitions.

The following definitions apply in this Chapter:

(1) Claimant agency. - Either of the following:

a. A State agency.

b. A local agency acting through a clearinghouse or an organization pursuant to G.S. 105A-3(b1).

(2) Debt. - Any of the following:

a. A sum owed to a claimant agency that has accrued through contract, subrogation, tort, operation of law, or any other legal theory regardless of whether there is an outstanding judgment for the sum.

b. A sum a claimant agency is authorized or required by law to collect, such as child support payments collectible under Title IV, Part D of the Social Security Act.

c. A sum owed as a result of an intentional program violation or a violation due to inadvertent household error under the Food and Nutrition Services Program enabled by Part 5 of Article 2 of Chapter 108A of the General Statutes.

d. Reserved for future codification purposes.

e. A sum owed as a result of having obtained public assistance payments under any of the following programs through an intentional false statement, intentional misrepresentation, intentional failure to disclose a material fact, or inadvertent household error:

1. The Work First Program provided in Article 2 of Chapter 108A of the General Statutes.

2. The State-County Special Assistance Program enabled by Part 3 of Article 2 of Chapter 108A of the General Statutes.

3. A successor program of one of these programs.

(3) Debtor. - A person who owes a debt.

(4) Department. - The Department of Revenue.

(5) Reserved.

(6) Local agency. - Any of the following:

a. A county, to the extent it is not considered a State agency.

b. A municipality.

c. A water and sewer authority created under Article 1 of Chapter 162A of the General Statutes.

d. A regional joint agency created by interlocal agreement under Article 20 of Chapter 160A of the General Statutes between two or more counties, cities, or both.

e. A public health authority created under Part 1B of Article 2 of Chapter 130A of the General Statutes or other authorizing legislation.

f. A metropolitan sewerage district created under Article 5 of Chapter 162A of the General Statutes.

g. A sanitary district created under Part 2 of Article 2 of Chapter 130A of the General Statutes.

h. A housing authority created under Chapter 157 of the General Statutes, provided that the debt owed to a housing authority has been reduced to a final judgment in favor of the housing authority.

i. A regional solid waste management authority created under Article 22 of Chapter 153A of the General Statutes.

(7) Net proceeds collected. - Gross proceeds collected through setoff against a debtor's refund minus the collection assistance fees provided in G.S. 105A-13.

(8) Refund. - A debtor's North Carolina tax refund.

(9) State agency. - Any of the following:

a. A unit of the executive, legislative, or judicial branch of State government, except for the following:

1. Any school of medicine, clinical program, facility, or practice affiliated with one of the constituent institutions of The University of North Carolina that provides medical care to the general public.

2. The University of North Carolina Health Care System and other persons or entities affiliated with or under the control of The University of North Carolina Health Care System.

b. A local agency, to the extent it administers a program supervised by the Department of Health and Human Services or it operates a Child Support Enforcement Program, enabled by Chapter 110, Article 9, and Title IV, Part D of the Social Security Act.

c. A community college. (1979, c. 801, s. 94; 1981, c. 724; 1983, c. 922, s. 21.11; 1983 (Reg. Sess., 1984), c. 1034, s. 10.2; 1985, c. 589, s. 33; c. 649, s. 6; c. 747; 1985 (Reg. Sess., 1986), c. 1014, s. 63(e), (f); 1987, c. 564, s. 18; c.

578, ss. 1, 2; c. 856, s. 12; 1989, c. 141, s. 2; c. 539, s. 1; c. 699; c. 727, s. 30; c. 770, s. 75.2; 1993 (Reg. Sess., 1994), c. 735, s. 1; 1995, c. 227, s. 1; 1996, 2nd Ex. Sess., c. 18, s. 24.30(d); 1997-433, ss. 3.3, 11.3; 1997-443, ss. 11A.118(a), 11A.119(a), 11A.122, 12.26; 1997-490, s. 1; 1998-17, s. 1; 1998-98, s. 38(a); 2002-156, s. 5(a); 2003-333, s. 1; 2004-138, s. 1; 2005-326, s. 1; 2006-259, s. 20; 2007-97, s. 2; 2010-31, ss. 10.19A(a), 31.8(d); 2011-365, s. 1; 2012-88, s. 1; 2013-382, s. 12.1.)

§ 105A-3. Remedy additional; mandatory State usage; optional local usage; obtaining identifying information; registration.

(a)   Remedy Additional. - The collection remedy under this Chapter is in addition to and not in substitution for any other remedy available by law.

(b)   Mandatory State Usage. - A State agency must submit a debt owed to it for collection under this Chapter unless the State Controller has waived this requirement or the State agency has determined that the validity of the debt is legitimately in dispute, an alternative means of collection is pending and believed to be adequate, or such a collection attempt would result in a loss of federal funds. The State Controller may waive the requirement for a State agency, other than the Department of Health and Human Services or a county acting on behalf of that Department, to submit a debt owed to it for collection under this Chapter if the State Controller finds that collection by this means would not be practical or cost effective. A waiver may apply to all debts owed a State agency or a type of debt owed a State agency.

(b1)   Optional Local Usage. - A local agency may submit a debt owed to it for collection under this Chapter. A local agency that decides to submit a debt owed to it for collection under this Chapter must establish the debt by following the procedure set in G.S. 105A-5 and must submit the debt through one of the following:

(1)   A clearinghouse that is established pursuant to an interlocal agreement adopted under Article 20 of Chapter 160A of the General Statutes and has agreed to submit debts on behalf of any requesting local agency.

(2)   The North Carolina League of Municipalities.

(3)   The North Carolina Association of County Commissioners.

(c) Identifying Information. - All claimant agencies shall whenever possible obtain the full name, social security number or federal identification number, address, and any other identifying information required by the Department from any person for whom the agencies provide any service or transact any business and who the claimant agencies can foresee may become a debtor under this Chapter.

(d) Registration and Reports. - A State agency must register with the Department and with the State Controller. Every State agency must report annually to the State Controller the amount of debts owed to the agency for which the agency did not submit a claim for setoff and the reason for not submitting the claim.

A clearinghouse or an organization that submits debts on behalf of a local agency must register with the Department. Once a clearinghouse registers with the Department under this subsection, no other clearinghouse may register to submit debts for collection under this Chapter. (1979, c. 801, s. 94; 1989 (Reg. Sess., 1990), c. 946, s. 1; 1993, c. 512, s. 4; 1997-443, s. 11A.122; 1997-490, s. 1; 1998-212, s. 12.3A(a), (b); 2010-31, s. 31.8(e).)

§ 105A-4. Minimum debt and refund.

This Chapter applies only to a debt that is at least fifty dollars ($50.00) and to a refund that is at least this same amount. (1979, c. 801, s. 94; 1997-490, s. 1.)

§ 105A-5. Local agency notice, hearing, and decision.

(a) Prerequisite. - A local agency may not submit a debt for collection under this Chapter until it has given the notice required by this section and the claim has been finally determined as provided in this section.

(b) Notice. - A local agency must send written notice to a debtor that the agency intends to submit the debt owed by the debtor for collection by setoff. The notice must explain the basis for the agency's claim to the debt, that the agency intends to apply the debtor's refund against the debt, and that a collection assistance fee of fifteen dollars ($15.00) will be added to the debt if it is submitted for setoff. The notice must also inform the debtor that the debtor has the right to contest the matter by filing a request for a hearing with the local agency, must state the time limits and procedure for requesting the hearing, and must state that failure to request a hearing within the required time will result in setoff of the debt.

(c)   Administrative Review. - A debtor who decides to contest a proposed setoff must file a written request for a hearing with the local agency within 30 days after the date the local agency mails a notice of the proposed action to the debtor. A request for a hearing is considered to be filed when it is delivered for mailing with postage prepaid and properly addressed. The governing body of the local agency or a person designated by the governing body must hold the hearing.

If the debtor disagrees with the decision of the governing body or the person designated by the governing body, the debtor may file a petition for a contested case under Article 3 of Chapter 150B of the General Statutes. The petition must be filed within 30 days after the debtor receives a copy of the local decision. Notwithstanding the provisions of G.S. 105-241.21, a local agency is considered an agency for purposes of contested cases and appeals under this Chapter.

In a hearing under this section, an issue that has previously been litigated in a court proceeding cannot be considered.

(d)   Decision. - A decision made after a hearing under this section must determine whether a debt is owed to the local agency and the amount of the debt.

(e)   Return of Amount Set Off. - If a local agency submits a debt for collection under this Chapter without sending the notice required by subsection (b) of this section, the agency must send the taxpayer the entire amount set off plus the collection assistance fees provided in G.S. 105A-13. Similarly, if a local agency submits a debt for collection under this Chapter after sending the required notice but before final determination of the debt and a decision finds that the local agency is not entitled to any part of the amount set off, the agency must send the taxpayer the entire amount set off plus the collection assistance fees provided in G.S. 105A-13. That portion of the amount returned that reflects the collection assistance fees must be paid from the local agency's funds.

If a local agency submits a debt for collection under this Chapter after sending the required notice and the net proceeds collected that are credited to the local agency for the debt exceed the amount of the debt, the local agency must send the balance to the debtor. No part of the collection assistance fees provided in G.S. 105A-13 may be returned when a notice was sent and a debt is owed but the debt is less than the amount set off.

Interest accrues on the amount of a refund returned to a taxpayer under this subsection in accordance with G.S. 105-241.21. A local agency that returns a refund to a taxpayer under this subsection must pay from the local agency's funds any interest that has accrued since the fifth day after the Department mailed the notice of setoff to the taxpayer. (1979, c. 801, s. 94; 1997-490, s. 1; 2002-156, s. 5(b); 2007-491, s. 44(1)c.)

§ 105A-6. Procedure Department to follow in making setoff.

(a) Notice to Department. - A claimant agency seeking to attempt collection of a debt through setoff must notify the Department in writing and supply information necessary to identify the debtor whose refund is sought to be set off. The claimant agency may include with the notification the date, if any, that the debt is expected to expire. The agency must notify the Department in writing when a debt has been paid or is no longer owed the agency.

(b) Setoff by Department. - The Department, upon receipt of notification, must determine each year whether the debtor to the claimant agency is entitled to a refund of at least fifty dollars ($50.00) from the Department. Upon determination by the Department that a debtor specified by a claimant agency qualifies for such a refund, the Department must set off the debt against the refund to which the debtor would otherwise be entitled and must refund any remaining balance to the debtor. The Department must mail the debtor written notice that the setoff has occurred and must credit the net proceeds collected to the claimant agency. If the claimant agency is a State agency, that agency must credit the amount received to a nonreverting trust account and must follow the procedure set in G.S. 105A-8. (1979, c. 801, s. 94; 1989 (Reg. Sess., 1990), c. 946, s. 2; 1997-490, s. 1.)

§ 105A-7: Repealed by Session Laws 1997-490, s. 1, effective January 1, 2000, and applicable to income tax refunds determined on or after that date.

§ 105A-8. State agency notice, hearing, decision, and refund of setoff.

(a) Notice. - Within 10 days after a State agency receives a refund of a debtor, the agency must send the debtor written notice that the agency has received the debtor's refund. The notice must explain the debt that is the basis for the agency's claim to the debtor's refund and that the agency intends to apply the refund against the debt. The notice must also inform the debtor that the debtor has the right to contest the matter by filing a request for a hearing, must state the time limits and procedure for requesting the hearing, and must state that failure to request a hearing within the required time will result in setoff of the debt. A State agency that does not send a debtor a notice within the time required by this subsection must refund the amount set off plus the collection assistance fee, in accordance with subsection (d) of this section.

(b) Hearing. - A hearing on a contested claim of a State agency, except a constituent institution of The University of North Carolina or the Division of Employment Security, must be conducted in accordance with Article 3 of Chapter 150B of the General Statutes. A hearing on a contested claim of a constituent institution of The University of North Carolina must be conducted in accordance with administrative procedures approved by the Attorney General. A hearing on a contested claim of the Division of Employment Security must be conducted in accordance with rules adopted by that Division. A request for a hearing on a contested claim of any State agency must be filed within 30 days after the State agency mails the debtor notice of the proposed setoff. A request for a hearing is considered to be filed when it is delivered for mailing with postage prepaid and properly addressed. In a hearing under this section, an issue that has previously been litigated in a court proceeding cannot be considered.

(c) Decision. - A decision made after a hearing under this section must determine whether a debt is owed to the State agency and the amount of the debt.

(d) Return of Amount Set Off. - If a State agency fails to send the notice required by subsection (a) of this section within the required time or a decision finds that a State agency is not entitled to any part of an amount set off, the agency must send the taxpayer the entire amount set off plus the collection assistance fee retained by the Department. That portion of the amount returned that reflects the collection assistance fee must be paid from the State agency's funds.

If a debtor owes a debt to a State agency and the net proceeds credited to the State agency for the debt exceed the amount of the debt, the State agency must send the balance to the debtor. No part of the collection assistance fee retained by the Department may be returned when a debt is owed but it is less than the amount set off.

Interest accrues on the amount of a refund returned to a taxpayer under this subsection in accordance with G.S. 105-241.21. A State agency that returns a refund to a taxpayer under this subsection must pay from the State agency's funds any interest that has accrued since the fifth day after the Department mailed the notice of setoff to the taxpayer. (1979, c. 801, s. 94; 1983, c. 419; 1987, c. 827, s. 16; 1989, c. 539, s. 2; 1997-490, s. 1; 2005-435, s. 42; 2007-491, s. 44(1)c; 2011-401, s. 3.10.)

§ 105A-9. Appeals from hearings.

Appeals from hearings allowed under this Chapter, other than those conducted by the Division of Employment Security, shall be in accordance with the provisions of Chapter 150B of the General Statutes, the Administrative Procedure Act, except that the place of initial judicial review shall be the superior court for the county in which the debtor resides. Appeals from hearings allowed under this Chapter that are conducted by the Division of Employment Security shall be in accordance with the provisions of Chapter 96 of the General Statutes. (1979, c. 801, s. 94; 1989, c. 539, s. 3; 1997-490, s. 1; 2011-401, s. 3.11.)

§ 105A-10. Repealed by Session Laws 1997-490, s. 1, effective January 1, 2000, and applicable to income tax refunds determined on or after that date.

§ 105A-11. Repealed by Session Laws 1997-490, s. 1, effective January 1, 2000, and applicable to income tax refunds determined on or after that date.

§ 105A-12. Priorities in claims to setoff.

The Department has priority over all other claimant agencies for collection by setoff whenever it is a competing agency for a refund. State agencies have priority over local agencies for collection by setoff. When there are multiple claims by State agencies other than the Department, the claims have priority based on the date each agency registered with the Department under G.S. 105A-3. When there are multiple claims by two or more organizations submitting debts on behalf of local agencies, the claims have priority based on the date each organization registered with the Department under G.S. 105A-3. When there are multiple claims among local agencies whose debts are submitted by the same organization, the claims have priority based on the date each local agency requested the organization to submit debts on its behalf. (1979, c. 801, s. 94; 1997-490, s. 1.)

§ 105A-13. Collection assistance fees.

(a) State Setoff. - To recover the costs incurred by the Department in collecting debts under this Chapter, a collection assistance fee of five dollars ($5.00) is imposed on each debt collected through setoff. The Department must collect this fee as part of the debt and retain it. The collection assistance fee shall not be added to child support debts or collected as part of child support debts. Instead, the Department shall retain from collections under Division II of Article 4 of Chapter 105 of the General Statutes the cost of collecting child support debts under this Chapter.

(b) Repealed by Session Laws 2001-380, s. 3, effective November 1, 2001.

(c) Local Debts. - To recover the costs incurred by local agencies in submitting debts for collection under this Chapter, a local collection assistance fee of fifteen dollars ($15.00) is imposed on each local agency debt submitted under G.S. 105A-3(b1) and collected through setoff. The Department must collect this fee as part of the debt and remit it to the clearinghouse that submitted the debt. The local collection assistance fee does not apply to child support debts.

(d) Priority. - If the Department is able to collect only part of a debt through setoff, the collection assistance fee provided in subsection (a) of this section has priority over the local collection assistance fee and over the remainder of the debt. The local collection assistance fee has priority over the remainder of the debt. (1979, c. 801, s. 94; 1989 (Reg. Sess., 1990), c. 946, s. 3; 1995, c. 360, s. 4(a); 1997-490, s. 1; 2000-126, s. 6; 2001-380, s. 3; 2002-156, s. 5(c); 2004-21, s. 1.)

§ 105A-14. Accounting to the claimant agency; credit to debtor's obligation.

(a) Simultaneously with the transmittal of the net proceeds collected to a claimant agency, the Department must provide the agency with an accounting of the setoffs for which payment is being made. The accounting must whenever possible include the full names of the debtors, the debtors' social security numbers or federal identification numbers, the gross proceeds collected per setoff, the net proceeds collected per setoff, and the collection assistance fee added to the debt and collected per setoff.

(b) Upon receipt by a claimant agency of net proceeds collected on the claimant agency's behalf by the Department, a final determination of the claim if it is a State agency claim, and an accounting of the proceeds as specified under this section, the claimant agency must credit the debtor's obligation with the net proceeds collected. (1979, c. 801, s. 94; 1997-490, s. 1; 2010-31, s. 31.8(f).)

§ 105A-15. Confidentiality exemption; nondisclosure.

(a) Notwithstanding G.S. 105-259 or any other provision of law prohibiting disclosure by the Department of the contents of taxpayer records or information and notwithstanding any confidentiality statute of any claimant agency, the exchange of any information among the Department, the claimant agency, the organization submitting debts on behalf of a local agency, and the debtor necessary to implement this Chapter is lawful.

(b) The information a claimant agency or an organization submitting debts on behalf of a local agency obtains from the Department in accordance with the exemption allowed by subsection (a) may be used by the agency or organization only in the pursuit of its debt collection duties and practices and may not be disclosed except as provided in G.S. 105-259, 153A-148.1, or 160A-208.1. (1979, c. 801, s. 94; 1997-490, s. 1.)

§ 105A-16. Rules.

The Secretary of Revenue may adopt rules to implement this Chapter. The State Controller may adopt rules to implement this Chapter. (1979, c. 801, s. 94; 1997-490, s. 1.)

Chapter 105B.

Defaulted Student Loan Recovery Act.

Article 1.

Withholding of Personal Earnings.

§ 105B-1. Purpose and Definitions.

(a) It is the purpose of this Article to enable the State Education Assistance Authority to seek an order of withholding of personal earnings against a debtor who owes money to the Authority through default on a student loan as a means of enforcing a judgment which requires the payment of money to the Authority.

(b) As used in this Article:

(1) "Annual federal poverty guidelines" means the annual federal poverty guidelines issued by the United States Department of Health and Human Services in effect at the time in question.

(2) "Authority" means the State Education Assistance Authority as enabled by Article 23 of Chapter 116 of the General Statutes.

(3) "Debtor" means any individual owing money to the Authority through default on a student loan made, guaranteed or owned by the Authority, which obligation has not been adjudicated satisfied by court order, set aside by court order, or discharged in bankruptcy.

(4) "Family" means a parent or parents and minor children or spouses that reside together.

(5) "Family income" means family income as set out in the annual federal poverty guidelines.

(6) "Mistake of fact" means that the debtor:

a. Is not the actual person named in the judgment that is the basis for a withholding action under this section;

b. Has satisfied the obligation represented by the judgment in full and is entitled to have the judgment cancelled; or

c. Does not have monthly disposable earnings or is not employed by the payor as stated by the Authority in its motion to the court.

d. Has family income at or below two hundred percent (200%) of the annual federal poverty guidelines.

(7) "Payor" means the person, firm, association or corporation by whom the debtor is employed.

(8) "Student loan" means a loan or loans made to eligible students or parents of students to aid in obtaining an education beyond the high school level. (1989, c. 475, s. 1.)

§ 105B-2. Remedy additional.

The collection remedy under this Article is in addition to and not in substitution for any other remedy available by law. (1989, c. 475, s. 1.)

§ 105B-3. Procedure.

(a) Notwithstanding any other provision of the law, in any case in which the Authority obtains a judgment against a debtor as defined in this Chapter, a judge of the district court in the county where the debtor resides or is found may enter an order of withholding whereby no more than ten percent (10%) of the debtor's monthly disposable earnings shall be withheld for the repayment of the debt owed to the Authority. For purposes of this section, "disposable earnings" is defined as that part of the compensation paid or payable to the debtor for personal services; whether denominated as wages, salary, commission, bonus, or otherwise (including periodic payments pursuant to a pension or retirement program) which remains after the deduction of any amounts required by law to be withheld.

(b) The Authority may move the court for an order of withholding. The motion shall be verified and shall state the name and address of the employer of the debtor, the debtor's monthly disposable earnings from said employer (which may be based upon information and belief), and the amount sought to be withheld, not to exceed ten percent (10%) of the debtor's monthly disposable earnings. The motion shall be accompanied by a letter to the debtor which includes information that the Authority will withdraw the motion if the debtor executes a sworn statement to the Authority that his family income is at or below two hundred percent (200%) of the annual federal poverty guidelines. The letter shall include the definitions of family and family income, the federal poverty guidelines in effect as of the date of the letter, and the procedure to contest the proposed garnishment. The Authority shall provide a form to the debtor for the purpose of securing his sworn statement about the level of his annual family income. The motion shall be served on both the debtor and his alleged employer either personally or by certified mail, return receipt requested as set forth in G.S. 1A-1, Rules of Civil Procedure.

(c) At any time following the filing with the district court of a motion under this section, the debtor may inspect and copy records relating to the debt or debts at the offices of the Authority.

(d) In lieu of or in conclusion of any legal proceeding instituted under this section, the debtor may enter into a written agreement with the State Education Assistance Authority to establish a schedule for the repayment of the debt or debts by periodic payments made directly to the Authority. Upon acceptance of any such repayment agreement, the Authority shall withdraw the motion for withholding.

(e) Contested Withholding. - The debtor or the payor may contest the withholding only on the basis of mistake of fact. To contest the withholding, the debtor or the payor must, within 30 days from the date of service, request a hearing before the district court by serving a written request upon the court and the Authority which specifies the mistake of fact upon which the hearing request is based. If the asserted mistake of fact can be resolved by agreement between the Authority and the debtor or the payor, whoever has asserted the mistake of fact, no hearing shall occur. Otherwise, a hearing shall be held and a determination made within 30 days of the filing of the request by the debtor or payor. Following the hearing the court may enter an order of withholding not to exceed ten percent (10%) of the debtor's monthly disposable earnings and not to reduce the debtor's annual family income to a point at or below two hundred percent (200%) of the annual federal poverty guidelines. However, the court shall not enter an order of garnishment unless the court makes findings of fact that the family income of the debtor at the time of the hearing exceeds two hundred percent (200%) of the annual federal poverty guidelines. If an order of withholding is entered, a copy of same shall be served on the debtor and the payor either personally or by certified mail, return receipt requested. The order shall set forth sufficient findings of fact to support the action by the court and the amount to be withheld for each pay period. The order shall be subject to review for modification and dissolution upon the filing of a motion in the cause.

(f)   Uncontested Withholding. - If neither the debtor nor the payor contests the withholding as provided in subsection (e) within the 30-day response period, the court may, without further hearing, enter an order of withholding not to exceed ten percent (10%) of the debtor's monthly disposable earnings and not to reduce the debtor's annual family income to a point at or below two hundred percent (200%) of the annual federal poverty guidelines. However, the court shall not enter an order of garnishment unless the court makes findings of fact that the family income of the debtor at the time of the hearing exceeds two hundred percent (200%) of the annual federal poverty guidelines. If an order of withholding is entered, a copy of same shall be served on the debtor and the payor either personally or by certified mail, return receipt requested. The order shall set forth sufficient findings of fact to support the action by the court and the amount to be withheld for each pay period. The order shall be subject to review for modification and dissolution upon the filing of a motion in the cause.

(g)   Upon receipt of an order of withholding, the payor shall transmit without delay the amount ordered to be withheld to the clerk of superior court who shall disburse it to the State Education Assistance Authority. The amount ordered to be withheld shall be increased by a processing fee of two dollars ($2.00) to be retained by the payor, unless waived, for each withholding under the order. (1989, c. 475, s. 1.)

§ 105B-4. Prohibited conduct by payor; civil penalty.

(a)   Notwithstanding any other provision of law, when a court finds, pursuant to a motion in the cause filed by the Authority joining the payor as a third party defendant, with 30 days notice to answer the motion, that a payor has willfully refused to comply with the provisions of this section, such payor shall be ordered to commence withholding and shall be held liable to the Authority for any amount which such payor should have withheld, except that such payor shall not be required to vary his normal pay or disbursement cycles in order to comply with these provisions.

(b) A payor shall not discharge from employment, refuse to employ, or otherwise take disciplinary action against any debtor because of the withholding. When a court finds that a payor has taken any of these actions, the payor shall be liable for a civil penalty. For a first offense, the civil penalty shall be one hundred dollars ($100.00). For second and third offenses, the civil penalty shall be five hundred dollars ($500.00) and one thousand dollars ($1,000), respectively. Any payor who violates any provision of this paragraph shall be liable in a civil action for reasonable damages suffered by a debtor as a result of the violation, and a debtor discharged or demoted in violation of this paragraph shall be entitled to be reinstated to his former position. The statute of limitations for actions under this subsection shall be one year pursuant to G.S. 1-54.

The clear proceeds of civil penalties provided for in this section shall be remitted to the Civil Penalty and Forfeiture Fund in accordance with G.S. 115C-457.2.

(c) Any payor who withholds the sum provided in any notice or order to the payor shall not be liable for any penalties under this section. (1989, ch. 475, s. 1; 1998-215, s. 116, s. 1.)

§ 105B-5. Termination of withholding.

A requirement that income be withheld under this section shall promptly terminate as to prospective payments when the payor receives notice from the court that the withholding order has expired or become invalid. (1989, c. 475, s. 1.)

Chapter 106.

Agriculture.

Article 1.

Department of Agriculture and Consumer Services.

Part 1. Board Of Agriculture.

§ 106-1: Repealed by Session Laws 1995, c. 509, s. 52.

§ 106-2. Department of Agriculture and Consumer Services established; Board of Agriculture, membership, terms of office, etc.

(a) Department and Board Established. - The Department of Agriculture and Consumer Services is created and established and shall be under the control of the Commissioner of Agriculture, with the consent and advice of a board to be established and named "The Board of Agriculture."

(b) Membership; Qualifications. - The Board of Agriculture shall consist of the Commissioner of Agriculture, who shall be an ex officio member and chairman thereof and shall preside at all meetings, and of 11 other members from the State, so distributed as to reasonably represent the different sections and agriculture of the State. The Commissioner of Agriculture and the members of the Board of Agriculture shall be practicing farmers engaged in their profession. The members of the Board shall be appointed by the Governor by and with the consent of the Senate. In the appointment of the members of the Board the Governor shall also take into consideration the different agricultural interests of the State, and shall appoint members with the following qualifications:

(1) One member who shall be a practicing tobacco farmer to represent the tobacco farming interest.

(2) One member who shall be a practicing cotton grower to represent the cotton interest.

(3) One member who shall be a practicing fruit or vegetable farmer to represent the fruit and vegetable farming interest.

(4) One member who shall be a practicing dairy farmer to represent the dairy and cattle interest of the State.

(5) One member who shall be a practicing poultryman to represent the poultry interest of the State.

(6) One member who shall be a practicing peanut grower to represent the peanut interests of the State.

(7)   One member who shall be experienced in marketing to represent the marketing of products of the State.

(8)   One member who shall be actively involved in forestry to represent the forestry interests of the State.

(9)   One member who shall be actively involved in the nursery business to represent the nursery industry of the State.

(10)   One member who shall be a practicing general farmer to represent the general farming interest.

(11)   One member who shall be a practicing pork farmer to represent the swine interest of the State.

(c)   Terms. - The term of office of members of the Board shall be six years and until their successors are duly appointed and qualified.

(d)   Vacancies. - Vacancies in the Board shall be filled by the Governor for the unexpired term. (Code, s. 2184; 1901, c. 479, ss. 2, 4; Rev., s. 3931; 1907, c. 497, s. 1; C.S., s. 4667; 1931, c. 360, s. 1; 1937, c. 174; 1995, c. 509, s. 53; 1997-261, ss. 15, 16; 2011-145, s. 13.22A(dd); 2013-99, s. 1; 2013-342, s. 1.)

§ 106-3: Repealed by Session Laws 1995, c. 509, s. 54.

§ 106-4. Meetings of Board.

The Board of Agriculture, herein established, hereafter called "the Board," shall meet for the transaction of business in the City of Raleigh at least twice a year, and oftener, if called by the Commissioner of Agriculture. (1901, c. 479, s. 3; Rev., s. 3935; C.S., s. 4669; 1921, c. 24; 1929, c. 252; 1931, c. 360, s. 2.)

§ 106-5: Repealed by Session Laws 1997-74, s. 1.

§ 106-6: Repealed by Session Laws 1995, c. 509, s. 54.

§ 106-6.1. Fees.

(a) A board or commission within the Department of Agriculture and Consumer Services may establish fees or charges for the services it provides. The Board of Agriculture, subject to the provisions of Chapter 146 of the General Statutes, may establish a rate schedule for the use of facilities operated by the Department of Agriculture and Consumer Services.

(b) Repealed by Session Laws 2011-145, s. 11.2, effective July 1, 2011. (1981, c. 495, s. 10; 1987, c. 827, s. 25; 1997-261, s. 109; 1999-413, s. 5; 2009-451, s. 11.3; 2011-145, s. 11.2.)

§ 106-6.2. Create special revenue funds for certain agricultural centers.

(a) The Eastern North Carolina Agricultural Center Fund is created within the Department of Agriculture and Consumer Services as a special revenue fund. This Fund shall consist of receipts from the sale of naming rights to any facility located at the Eastern North Carolina Agricultural Center at Williamston, investments earnings on these monies, and any gifts, devises, or grants from any source for the benefit of the Eastern North Carolina Agricultural Center. All interest that accrues to this Fund shall be credited to this Fund. Any balance remaining in this Fund at the end of any fiscal year shall not revert. The Department may use this Fund only to promote, improve, repair, maintain, or operate the Eastern North Carolina Agricultural Center.

(b) The Southeastern North Carolina Agricultural Center Fund is created within the Department of Agriculture and Consumer Services as a special revenue fund. This Fund shall consist of receipts from the sale of naming rights to any facility located at the Southeastern North Carolina Agricultural Center at Lumberton, investments earnings on these monies, and any gifts, devises, or grants from any source for the benefit of the Southeastern North Carolina Agricultural Center. All interest that accrues to this Fund shall be credited to this Fund. Any balance remaining in this Fund at the end of any fiscal year shall not revert. The Department may use this Fund only to promote, improve, repair, maintain, or operate the Southeastern North Carolina Agricultural Center. (1998-212, s. 13.2; 2011-284, s. 72.)

§ 106-6.3. Create special revenue fund for research stations.

The Research Stations Fund is established as a special revenue fund within the Department of Agriculture and Consumer Services, Division of Research Stations. This Fund shall consist of receipts from the sale of commodities produced on the Department's research stations and any gifts, bequests, or grants for the benefit of this Fund. No General Fund appropriations shall be credited to this Fund. Any balance remaining in this Fund at the end of any fiscal year shall not revert. The Department may use this Fund only to develop, improve, repair, maintain, operate, or otherwise invest in research stations operated by the Department's Research Station Division. (2012-142, s. 11.4.)

§§ 106-7 through 106-8: Repealed by Session Laws 1995, c. 509, s. 54.

§ 106-9: Repealed by Session Laws 1997-74, s. 2.

§ 106-9.1: Repealed by Session Laws 1995, c. 509, s. 54.

Part 1A. Collection and Refund of Fees and Taxes.

§ 106-9.2. Records and reports required of persons paying fees or taxes to Commissioner or Department; examination of records; determination of amount due by Commissioner in case of noncompliance.

(a) Every person paying fees or taxes to the Commissioner of Agriculture or to the Department of Agriculture and Consumer Services under the provisions of this Chapter shall keep such records as the Commissioner may prescribe to indicate accurately the fees or taxes due to the Commissioner or Department, and such records shall be preserved for a period of three years, and shall at all times during the business hours of the day be subject to inspection by the Commissioner or his deputies or such other agents as may be duly authorized by the Commissioner. Any person failing to comply with or violating any of the provisions of this section shall be guilty of a Class 1 misdemeanor.

(b) It shall be the duty of the Commissioner of Agriculture, by competent auditors, to have the books and records of every person paying fees or taxes to the Commissioner or Department examined at least once each year to determine if such persons are keeping complete records as provided by this section, and to determine if correct reports have been made to the Commissioner or Department covering the total amount of fees or taxes due by such persons.

(c) If any person shall fail, neglect or refuse to keep such records or to make such reports or pay fees or taxes due as required, and within the time provided in this Chapter, the Commissioner shall immediately inform himself as best he may as to the matters and things required to be set forth in such records and reports, and from such information as he may be able to obtain, determine and fix the amount of fees or taxes due the State from such delinquent person for the period covering the delinquency. The Commissioner shall proceed immediately to collect the fees or taxes due the State, including any penalties and interest thereon, in the manner provided in this Article. (1963, c. 458; 1993, c. 539, s. 736; 1994, Ex. Sess., c. 24, s. 14(c); 1997-261, s. 109.)

§ 106-9.3. Procedure for assessment of fees and taxes.

(a) If the Commissioner of Agriculture discovers from the examination of any report filed by a taxpayer or otherwise that any fee or tax or additional fee or tax is due from any taxpayer, he shall give notice to the taxpayer in writing of the kind and amount of fee or tax which is due and of his intent to assess the same, which notice shall contain advice to the effect that unless application for a rehearing is made within the time specified in subsection (c), the proposed assessment will become conclusive and final.

If the Commissioner is unable to obtain from the taxpayer adequate and reliable information upon which to base such assessment, the assessment may be made upon the basis of the best information available and, subject to the provisions hereinafter made, such assessment shall be deemed correct.

(b) The notice required to be given in subsection (a) may be delivered to the taxpayer by an agent of the Commissioner or may be sent by mail to the last known address of the taxpayer and such notice will be deemed to have been received in due course of the mail unless the taxpayer shall make an affidavit to the contrary within 90 days after such notice is mailed, in which event the taxpayer shall be heard by the Commissioner in all respects as if he had made timely application.

(c) Any taxpayer who objects to a proposed assessment of fee or tax or additional fee or tax shall be entitled to a hearing before the Commissioner of Agriculture, provided application therefor is made in writing within 30 days after the mailing or delivery of the notice required by subsection (a). If application for a hearing is made in due time, the Commissioner of Agriculture shall set a time and place for the hearing and after considering the taxpayer's objections shall give written notice of his decision to the taxpayer. The amount of fee or tax or additional fee or tax due from the taxpayer as finally determined by the Commissioner shall thereupon be assessed and upon assessment shall become immediately due and collectible.

Provided, the taxpayer may request the Commissioner at any time within 30 days of notice of such proposed assessment for a written statement, or transcript, of the information and the evidence upon which the proposed assessment is based, and the Commissioner of Agriculture shall furnish such statement, or transcript, to the taxpayer. Provided, further, after request by the taxpayer for such written statement, or transcript, the taxpayer shall have 30 days after the receipt of the same from the Commissioner of Agriculture to apply in writing for such hearing, explaining in detail his objections to such proposed assessment. If no request for such hearing is so made, such proposed assessment shall be final and conclusive.

(d) If no timely application for a hearing is made within 30 days after notice of a proposed assessment of fee or tax or additional fee or tax is given pursuant to subsection (a), such proposed fee or tax or additional fee or tax assessment shall become final without further notice and shall be immediately due and collectible.

(e) Where a proper report has been filed by a taxpayer and in the absence of fraud, the Commissioner of Agriculture shall assess any fee or tax or additional fee or tax due from the taxpayer within three years after the date upon which such report is filed or within three years after the date upon which such report was required by law to be filed, whichever is the later. If no report has been filed, and in the absence of fraud, any fee or tax or additional fee or tax due from a taxpayer may be assessed at any time within five years after the date upon which such report was required by law to be filed. In the event a false and fraudulent report has been filed or there has been an attempt in any manner to fraudulently defeat or evade a fee or tax, any fee or tax or additional fee or tax due from the taxpayer may be assessed at any time.

(f) Except as hereinafter provided in subsection (g), the Commissioner of Agriculture shall have no authority to assess any fee or tax or additional fee or tax under this section until the notice required by subsection (a) shall have been given and the period within which an application for a hearing may be filed has expired, or if a timely application for a hearing if filed, until written notice of the Commissioner's decision has been given to the taxpayer, provided, however that if the notice required by subsection (a) shall be mailed or delivered within the limitation prescribed in subsection (e), such limitation shall be deemed to have been complied with and the proceeding may be carried forward to its conclusion.

(g) Notwithstanding any other provision of this section, the Commissioner of Agriculture shall have authority at any time within the applicable period of limitations to proceed at once to assess any fee or tax or additional fee or tax which he finds is due from a taxpayer if, in his opinion, the collection of such fee or tax is in jeopardy and immediate assessment is necessary in order to protect the interest of the State, provided, however, that if an assessment is made pursuant to the authority set forth in this subsection before the notice required by subsection (a) is given, such assessment shall not be valid unless the notice required by subsection (a) shall be given within 30 days after the date of such assessment.

(h) All assessments of fees or taxes or additional fees or taxes (exclusive of penalties assessed thereon) shall bear interest at the rate of one half of one percent (0.5%) per month or fraction thereof from the time said fees or taxes or additional fees or taxes were due to have been paid until paid. (1963, c. 458.)

§ 106-9.4. Collection of delinquent fees and taxes.

(a) If any fee or tax imposed by this Chapter, or any other fee or tax levied by the State and payable to the Commissioner of Agriculture or the Department of Agriculture and Consumer Services, or any portion of such fee or tax, be not paid within 30 days after the same becomes due and payable, and after the same has been assessed, the Commissioner of Agriculture shall issue an order under his hand and official seal, directed to the sheriff of any county of the State commanding him to levy upon and sell the real and personal property of the taxpayer found within his county for the payment of the amount thereof, with the added penalties, additional taxes, interest, and cost of executing the same, and to return to the Commissioner of Agriculture the money collected by virtue thereof within a time to be therein specified, not less than 60 days from the date of the order. The said sheriff shall, thereupon, proceed upon the same in all respects with like effect and in the same manner prescribed by law in respect to executions issued against property upon judgments of a court of record, and shall be entitled to the same fees for his services in executing the order, to be collected in the same manner.

(b)   Bank deposits, rents, salaries, wages, and all other choses in action or property incapable of manual levy or delivery, hereinafter called the intangible, belonging, owing, or to become due to any taxpayer subject to any of the provisions of this Chapter, or which has been transferred by such taxpayer under circumstances which would permit it to be levied upon if it were tangible, shall be subject to attachment or garnishment as herein provided, and the person owing said intangible, matured or unmatured, or having same in his possession or control, hereinafter called the garnishee, shall become liable for all sums due by the taxpayer under this Chapter to the extent of the amount of the intangible belonging, owing, or to become due to the taxpayer subject to the setoff of any matured or unmatured indebtedness of the taxpayer to the garnishee. To effect such attachment or garnishment the Commissioner of Agriculture shall serve or cause to be served upon the taxpayer and the garnishee a notice as hereinafter provided, which notice may be served by any deputy or employee of the Commissioner of Agriculture or by any officer having authority to serve summonses. Said notice shall show:

(1)   The name of the taxpayer and his address, if known;

(2)   The nature and amount of the fee or tax, and the interest and penalties thereon, and the year or years for which the same were levied or assessed, and

(3)   Shall be accompanied by a copy of this subsection, and thereupon the procedure shall be as follows:

If the garnishee has no defense to offer or no setoff against the taxpayer, he shall, within 10 days after service of said notice, answer the same by sending to the Commissioner of Agriculture by registered mail a statement to that effect, and if the amount due or belonging to the taxpayer is then due or subject to his demand, it shall be remitted to the Commissioner with said statement, but if said amount is to mature in the future, the statement shall set forth that fact and the same shall be paid to the Commissioner upon maturity, and any payment by the garnishee hereunder shall be a complete extinguishment of any liability therefor on his part to the taxpayer. If the garnishee has any defense or setoff, he shall state the same in writing under oath, and, within 10 days after service of said notice, shall send two copies of said statement to the Commissioner by registered mail; if the Commissioner admits such defense or setoff, he shall so advise the garnishee in writing within 10 days after receipt of such statement and the attachment or garnishment shall thereupon be discharged to the amount required by such defense or setoff, and any amount attached or garnished hereunder which is not affected by such defense or setoff shall be remitted to the Commissioner as above provided in cases where the garnishee has no defense or setoff, and with like effect. If the Commissioner shall not admit the defense or setoff, he shall set forth in writing his objections thereto and shall send a copy thereof to the garnishee within 10 days after receipt of the garnishee's statement, or within such further time as may be agreed on by the garnishee, and at the same time he shall file a copy of said notice, a copy of the garnishee's statement, and a copy of his objections thereto in the superior court of the county where the garnishee resides or does business where the issues made shall be tried as in civil actions.

If judgment is entered in favor of the Commissioner of Agriculture by default or after hearing, the garnishee shall become liable for the fee or taxes, interest and penalties due by the taxpayer to the extent of the amount over and above any defense or setoff of the garnishee belonging, owing, or to become due to the taxpayer, but payments shall not be required from amounts which are to become due to the taxpayer until the maturity thereof, nor shall more than ten percent (10%) of any taxpayer's salary or wages be required to be paid hereunder in any one month. The garnishee may satisfy said judgment upon paying said amount, and if he fails to do so, execution may issue as provided by law. From any judgment or order entered upon such hearing either the Commissioner of Agriculture or the garnishee may appeal as provided by law. If, before or after judgment, adequate security is filed for the payment of said taxes, interest, penalties, and costs, the attachment or garnishment may be released or execution stayed pending appeal, but the final judgment shall be paid or enforced as above provided. The taxpayer's sole remedies to question his liability for said fees or taxes, interest, and penalties shall be those provided in this Article, as now or hereinafter amended or supplemented. If any third person claims any intangible attached or garnished hereunder and his lawful right thereto, or to any part thereof, is shown to the Commissioner, he shall discharge the attachment or garnishment to the extent necessary to protect such right, and if such right is asserted after the filing of said copies as aforesaid, it may be established by interpleader as now or hereafter provided by the General Statutes in cases of attachment and garnishment. In case such third party has no notice of proceedings hereunder, he shall have the right to file his petition under oath with the Commissioner at any time within 12 months after said intangible is paid to him and if the Commissioner finds that such party is lawfully entitled thereto or to any part thereof, he shall pay the same to such party as provided for refunds by G.S. 105-407 and if such payment is denied, said party may appeal from the determination of the Commissioner to the Superior Court of Wake County or to the superior court of the county wherein he resides or does business. The intangibles of a taxpayer shall be paid or collected hereunder only to the extent necessary to satisfy said fees or taxes, interest, penalties, and costs. Except as hereinafter set forth, the remedy provided in this section shall not be resorted to unless a warrant for collection or execution against the taxpayer has been returned unsatisfied: Provided, however, if the Commissioner is of opinion that the only effective remedy is that herein provided, it shall not be necessary that a warrant for collection or execution shall be first returned unsatisfied, and in no case shall it be a defense to the remedy herein provided that a warrant for collection or execution has not been first returned unsatisfied: Provided, however, that no salary or wage at the rate of less than two hundred dollars ($200.00) per month, whether paid weekly or monthly, shall be attached or garnished under the provisions of this section.

(c) In addition to the remedy herein provided, the Commissioner of Agriculture is authorized and empowered to make a certificate setting forth the essential particulars relating to the said fee or tax, including the amount thereof, the date when the same was due and payable, the person, firm, or corporation chargeable therewith, and the nature of the fee or tax, and under his hand and seal transmit the same to the clerk of the superior court of any county in which the delinquent taxpayer resides or has property; whereupon, it shall be the duty of the clerk of the superior court of the county to docket the said certificate and index the same on the cross index of judgments, and execution may issue thereon with the same force and effect as an execution upon any other judgment of the superior court; said tax shall become a lien on realty only from the date of the docketing of such certificate in the office of the clerk of the superior court and in personalty only from the date of the levy on such personalty and upon execution thereon no homestead or personal property exemption shall be allowed.

(d) The remedies herein given are cumulative and in addition to all other remedies provided by law for the collection of said fees and taxes. (1963, c. 458; 1997-261, s. 109.)

§ 106-9.5. Refund of overpayment.

If the Commissioner of Agriculture discovers from the examination of any report, or otherwise, that any taxpayer has overpaid the correct amount of any fee or tax (including penalties, interest and costs, if any), such overpayment shall be refunded to the taxpayer within 60 days after it is ascertained together with interest thereon at the rate of six percent (6%) per annum: Provided, that interest on any such refund shall be computed from a date 90 days after date tax was originally paid by the taxpayer. Provided, further, that demand for such refund is made by the taxpayer within three years from the date of such overpayment or the due date of the report, whichever is later. (1963, c. 458.)

§ 106-9.6. Suits to prevent collection prohibited; payment under protest and recovery of fee or tax so paid.

No court of this State shall entertain a suit of any kind brought for the purpose of preventing the collection of any fee or tax imposed in this Chapter. Whenever a person shall have a valid defense to the enforcement of the collection of a fee or tax assessed or charged against him or his property, such person shall pay such fee or tax to the proper officer, and notify such officer in writing that he pays the same under protest. Such payment shall be without prejudice to any defense or rights he may have in the premises, and he may, at any time within 30 days after such payment, demand the same in writing from the Commissioner of Agriculture; and if the same shall not be refunded within 90 days thereafter, may sue such official in the courts of the State for the amount so demanded. Such suit must be brought in the Superior Court of Wake County, or in the county in which the taxpayer resides. (1963, c. 458.)

Part 2. Commissioner of Agriculture.

§ 106-10. Election; term; vacancy.

The Commissioner of Agriculture shall be elected at the general election for other State officers, shall be voted for on the same ballot with such officers, and his term of office shall be four years, and until his successor is elected and qualified. Any vacancy in the office of such Commissioner shall be filled by the Governor, the appointee to hold until the next regular election to the office and the qualification of his successor. (1901, c. 479, s. 4; Rev., s. 3938; C.S., s. 4675.)

§ 106-11. Salary of Commissioner of Agriculture.

The salary of the Commissioner of Agriculture shall be set by the General Assembly in the Current Operations Appropriations Act. In addition to the salary set by the General Assembly in the Current Operations Appropriations Act, longevity pay shall be paid on the same basis as is provided to employees of the State who are subject to the North Carolina Human Resources Act. (1901, c. 479, s. 4; 1905, c. 529; Rev., s. 2749; 1907, c. 887, s. 1; 1913, c. 58; C. S., s. 3872; 1921, c. 25, s. 1; 1933, c. 282, s. 5; 1935, c. 293; 1937, c. 415; 1939, c. 338; 1943, c. 499, s. 1; 1947, c. 1041; 1949, c. 1278; 1953, c. 1, s. 2; 1957, c. 1; 1963, c. 1178, s. 4; 1967, c. 1130; c. 1237, s. 4; 1969, c. 1214, s. 4; 1971, c. 912, s. 4; 1973, c. 778, s. 4; 1975, 2nd Sess., c. 983, s. 19; 1977, c. 802, s. 42.10; 1983, c. 761, s. 208; 1983 (Reg. Sess., 1984), c. 1034, s. 164; 1987, c. 738, s. 32(b); 2013-382, s. 9.1(c).)

§§ 106-12 through 106-13: Repealed by Session Laws 1997-74, ss. 3, 4.

§ 106-14. To establish regulations for transportation of livestock.

The Commissioner of Agriculture, by and with the consent and advice of the Board of Agriculture, shall promulgate and enforce such rules and regulations as may be necessary for the proper transporting of livestock by motor vehicle, and may require a permit for such vehicles if it becomes necessary in order to prevent the spread of animal diseases. This section shall not apply to any county having a local law providing for the vaccination of hogs against cholera. (1937, c. 427, ss. 1, 2.)

Part 3. Powers and Duties of Department and Board.

§§ 106-15 through 106-19: Repealed by Session Laws 1997-74, s. 5.

§ 106-20: Repealed by Session Laws 1987, c. 244, s. 1(a).

§ 106-21: Repealed by Session Laws 1997-74, s. 7.

§ 106-21.1. Feed Advisory Service; fee.

The Department of Agriculture and Consumer Services shall operate a Feed Advisory Service for the analysis of animal feeds in order to provide a feeding management service to all animal producers in North Carolina. A fee of ten dollars ($10.00) shall accompany each feed sample sent to the Department for testing. A fee of seventy-five dollars ($75.00) shall accompany each feed sample which is to be tested for the presence of fumonisin. (1979, c. 1026; 1989, c. 544, s. 9; 1991, c. 649, s. 1; 1997-261, s. 21.)

§ 106-21.2. Food Bank information and referral service.

The Department of Agriculture and Consumer Services may maintain an information and referral service for persons and organizations that have notified the department of their desire to donate food to a nonprofit organization or a nonprofit corporation. (1979, 2nd Sess., c. 1188, s. 2; 1997-261, s. 22.)

§ 106-22. Joint duties of Commissioner and Board.

The Commissioner of Agriculture, by and with the consent and advice of the Board of Agriculture shall:

(1) General. - Investigate and promote such subjects relating to the improvement of agriculture, the beneficial use of commercial fertilizers and composts, and for the inducement of immigration and capital as he may think proper; but he is especially charged:

(2) Commercial Fertilizers. - With such supervision of the trade in commercial fertilizers as will best protect the interests of the farmers, and shall report to district attorneys and to the General Assembly information as to the existence or formation of trusts or combinations in fertilizers or fertilizing materials which are or may be offered for sale in this State, whereby the

interests of the farmers may be injuriously affected, and shall publish such information in the Bulletin of the Department;

(3)   Cattle and Cattle Diseases. - With investigations adapted to promote the improvement of milk and beef cattle, and especially investigations relating to the diseases of cattle and other domestic animals, and shall publish and distribute from time to time information relative to any contagious diseases of stock, and suggest remedies therefor, and shall have power in such cases to quarantine the infected animals and to regulate the transportation of stock in this State, or from one section of it to another, and may cooperate with the United States Department of Agriculture in establishing and maintaining cattle districts or quarantine lines, to prevent the infection of cattle from splenic or Spanish fever. Any person willfully violating such regulations shall be liable in a civil action to any person injured, and for any and all damages resulting from such conduct, and shall also be guilty of a Class 1 misdemeanor;

(4)   Honey and Bee Industry. - With investigations adapted to promote the improvement of the honey and bee industry in this State, and especially investigations relating to the diseases of bees, and shall publish and distribute from time to time information relative to such diseases, and such remedies therefor, and shall have power in such cases to quarantine the infected bees and to control or eradicate such infections and to regulate the transportation or importation into North Carolina from any other state or country of bees, honey, hives, or any apiary equipment, or from one section of the State to another, and may cooperate with the United States Department of Agriculture in establishing and maintaining quarantine lines or districts. The Commissioner of Agriculture, by and with the consent and advice of the Board of Agriculture, shall have power to make rules and regulations to carry out the provisions of this section; and in event of failure to comply with any such rules and regulations, the Commissioner of Agriculture or his duly authorized agent is authorized to confiscate and destroy any infected bees and equipment and any bees and/or used apiary equipment moved in violation of these regulations;

(5)   Insect Pests. - With investigations relative to the ravages of insects and with the dissemination of such information as may be deemed essential for their abatement, and making regulations for destruction of such insects. The willful violation of any of such regulations by any person shall be a Class 1 misdemeanor;

(6)   New Agricultural Industries. - With investigations and experiments directed to the introduction and fostering of new agricultural industries, adapted

to the various climates and soils of the State, especially the culture of truck and market gardens, the grape and other fruits;

(7) Drainage and Irrigation; Fertilizer Sources. - With the investigations of the subject of drainage and irrigation and publication of information as to the best methods of both, and what surfaces, soils, and locations may be most benefited by such improvements; also with the collection and publication of information in regard to localities, character, accessibility, cost, and modes of utilization of native mineral and domestic sources of fertilizers, including formulae for composting adapted to the different crops, soils, and materials;

(8) Farm Fences. - With the collection of statistics relating to the subject of farm fences, with suggestions for diminishing their cost, and the conditions under which they may be dispensed with altogether;

(9) Sales of Fertilizers, Seeds, and Food Products. - With the enforcement and supervision of the laws which are or may be enacted in this State for the sale of commercial fertilizers, seeds and food products, with the authority to make regulations concerning the same;

(10) Inducement of Capital and Immigration. - With the inducement of capital and immigration by the dissemination of information relative to the advantages of soil and climate and to the natural resources and industrial opportunities offered in this State, by the keeping of a land registry and by the publication of descriptions of agricultural, mineral, forest, and trucking lands which may be offered the Department for sale; which publication shall be in tabulated form, setting forth the county, township, number of acres, names and addresses of owners, and such other information as may be needful in placing inquiring homeseekers in communication with landowners; and he shall publish a list of such inquiries in the Bulletin for the benefit of those who may have land for sale;

(11) Diversified Farming. - With such investigations as will best promote the improvement and extension of diversified farming, including the rotation of crops, the raising of home supplies, vegetables, fruits, stock, grasses, etc.;

(12) Farmers' Institutes. - With the holding of farmers' institutes in the several counties of the State, as frequently as may be deemed advisable, in order to instruct the people in improved methods in farming, in the beneficial use of fertilizers and composts, and to ascertain the wants and necessities of the various farming communities; and may collect the papers and addresses made at these institutes and publish the same in pamphlet form annually for

distribution among the farmers of the State. He may secure such assistants as may be necessary or beneficial in holding such institutes;

(13)   Publication of Bulletin. - The Commissioner shall publish bulletins which shall contain a list of the fertilizers and fertilizing materials registered for sale each year, the guaranteed constituents of each brand, reports of analyses of fertilizers, the dates of meeting and reports of farmers' institutes and similar societies, description of farm buildings suited to our climate and needs, reports of interesting experiments of farmers, and such other matters as may be deemed advisable. The Department may determine the number of bulletins which shall be issued each year;

(14)   Reports to Legislature. - He shall transmit to the General Assembly at each session a report of the operations of the Department with suggestions of such legislation as may be deemed needful;

(15)   Repealed by Session Laws 1993, c. 561, s. 116.

(16)   State Agricultural Policies. - Establish State government policies relating to agriculture.

(17)   Agronomic Testing. - Provide agronomic testing services and charge reasonable fees for plant analysis, nematode testing, in-State soil testing during peak season, out-of-state soil testing, and expedited soil testing. The Board shall charge at least four dollars ($4.00) for plant analysis, at least two dollars ($2.00) for nematode testing, at least four dollars ($4.00) for in-State soil testing during peak season, at least five dollars ($5.00) for out-of-state soil testing, and at least two hundred dollars ($200.00) for expedited soil testing. As used in this subdivision, "peak season" includes at a minimum the four-month period beginning no later than December 1 of any year and extending until at least March 31 of the following year. The Board may modify the meaning of peak season by starting a peak season earlier in any year or ending it later the following year or both.

(18)   Forests. - Have charge of forest maintenance, forest fire protection, reforestation, and the protection of the forests.

(19)   State forests. - Have charge of all State forests and measures for forest fire prevention.

(20) Property for State forests. - Acquire real and personal property as desirable and necessary for the performance of the duties and functions of the Department under subdivision (19) of this section and pay for the property out of any funds appropriated for the Department or available unappropriated revenues of the Department, when such acquisition is approved by the Governor and Council of State. The title to any real estate acquired under this subdivision shall be in the name of the State of North Carolina for the use and benefit of the Department.

(21) State recreational forests. - Have charge of all State recreational forests.

(22) Property for State recreational forests. - Acquire real and personal property as desirable and necessary for the performance of the duties and functions of the Department under subdivision (21) of this section and pay for the property out of any funds appropriated for the Department or available unappropriated revenues of the Department, when such acquisition is approved by the Governor and Council of State. The title to any real estate acquired under this subdivision shall be in the name of the State of North Carolina for the use and benefit of the Department.

(23) Administration of North Carolina Century Farms Program. - Administer the North Carolina Century Farms Program, which recognizes farms in the State that have been continuously owned by the same family for at least 100 years. (1901, c. 479, s. 4; Rev., ss. 3294, 3724, 3944; 1917, c. 16; C.S., s. 4688; 1939, c. 173; 1973, c. 47, s. 2; 1979, c. 344, s. 1; 1981, c. 495, s. 9; 1989, c. 544, s. 4; 1993, c. 539, ss. 737, 738; c. 561, s. 116(d); 1994, Ex. Sess., c. 24, s. 14(c); 2011-145, ss. 13.25(i), (l), 31.7; 2011-201, s. 1; 2011-391, s. 33(a); 2013-360, s. 13.1(a).)

§ 106-22.1. State farms.

State-owned farmland, including timberland, allocated to the Department of Agriculture and Consumer Services for the State Farm Program, shall be managed by the Department for research, teaching, and demonstration in agriculture, forestry, and aquaculture. Research projects on the State farms shall be approved by the Department. The Department may sell surplus commodities produced on the farms. (1989, c. 500, s. 107(c); 1997-261, s. 23.)

§ 106-22.2:   Recodified as § 143B-344.23 by Session Laws 1998-212, s. 21(a).

§ 106-22.3. Organic Production Program.

(a)   The Board of Agriculture may establish rules, standards, guidelines, and policies for the establishment and implementation of a voluntary program for the certification of organically produced agricultural products.

(b)   The Commissioner of Agriculture may enter into agreements with the United States Department of Agriculture and may apply for approval, accreditation, certification, or similar authority as may be necessary to comply with the requirements of the Organic Foods Production Act of 1990, Public Law 101-624. (1993, c. 147.)

§ 106-22.4. Llamas as livestock.

Any rules adopted by the Board of Agriculture that affect llamas shall not refer to llamas as exotic or wild animals. It is the intent of the General Assembly that llamas be treated as domesticated livestock in order to promote the development and improvement of the llama industry in the State. This section does not prohibit the Board of Agriculture from classifying llamas for animal health purposes in accordance with generally accepted standards of veterinary medicine. For purposes of the section, "llama" means a South American camelid that is an animal of the genus llama. Llama includes llamas, alpacas, and guanacos. Llama does not include vicunas. (1997-84, s. 3.)

§ 106-22.5. Agricultural tourism signs.

(a)   The Department of Agriculture and Consumer Services shall provide directional signs on major highways at or in reasonable proximity to the nearest interchange or within one mile leading to an agricultural facility that promotes tourism by providing tours and on-site sales or samples of North Carolina agricultural products to area tourists.

(b) An agricultural facility must be open for business at least four days a week, 10 months of the year in order to qualify for the directional signs provided for in this section. The Department shall assess the facility the actual reasonable costs of the sign and its installation. (1999-356, s. 1.)

§ 106-22.6. Exercise of enforcement powers.

When any board, commission, or official within the North Carolina Department of Agriculture and Consumer Services has the authority to assess civil penalties, such authority shall not be construed to require the issuance of a monetary penalty when the board, commission, or official determines that nonmonetary sanctions, education, or training are sufficient to address the underlying violation. (2013-265, s. 5.)

Part 4. Cooperation of Federal and State Governments in Agricultural Work.

§ 106-23. Legislative assent to Adams Act for experiment station.

Legislative assent be and the same is hereby given to the purpose of an act of Congress approved March 16, 1906, entitled "An Act to provide for an increased annual appropriation for agricultural experiment stations, and regulating the expenditure thereof," known as the Adams Act, and the money appropriated by this act be and the same is hereby accepted on the part of the State for the use of the agricultural experiment station, and the whole amount shall be used for the benefit of the said agricultural experiment station, in accordance with the act of Congress making appropriations for agricultural experiment stations and governing the expenditure thereof. (1907, c. 793; C.S., s. 4689.)

Part 5. Cooperation Between Department and United States Department of Agriculture, and County Commissioners.

§ 106-24. Collection and publication of information relating to agriculture; cooperation.

(a) The Department of Agriculture and Consumer Services shall collect, compile, systematize, tabulate, and publish statistical information relating to agriculture. The Department is authorized to use sample surveys to collect primary data relating to agriculture. The Department is authorized to cooperate with the United States Department of Agriculture and the several boards of county commissioners of the State, to accomplish the purpose of this Part.

(b) The Department of Agriculture and Consumer Services shall biennially collect information on water use by persons who withdraw 10,000 gallons per day or more of water from the surface or groundwater sources of the State for activities directly related or incidental to the production of crops, fruits, vegetables, ornamental and flowering plants, dairy products, livestock, poultry, and other agricultural products. The information shall be collected by survey conducted pursuant to subsection (a) of this section and in accordance with Title 7 United States Code Section 2276 (Confidential Information Protection and Statistical Efficiency Act). The Department shall develop the survey form in consultation with the Department of Environment and Natural Resources. The Department shall report the results of the water use survey to the Environmental Review Commission no later than July 1 of each year in which the survey was collected and shall provide a copy of the report to the Department of Environment and Natural Resources. The report shall include recommendations about modifications to the survey, including changes in the gallons per day threshold for water use data collection. The report shall provide agricultural water use data by county. If the county is located in more than one river basin, the report shall separate the county data to show agricultural water use by river basin within the county. If publication of county or watershed data would result in disclosure of an individual operation's water use, the data will be combined with data from another county or watershed. (1921, c. 201, s. 1; C.S., s. 4689(a); 1941, c. 343; 1975, c. 611, s. 1; 1979, c. 228, s. 1; 1997-261, s. 25; 2008-143, s. 2(a); 2013-265, s. 6.)

§ 106-24.1. Confidentiality of information collected and published.

All information published by the Department of Agriculture and Consumer Services pursuant to this Part shall be classified so as to prevent the identification of information received from individual farm operators. All information received pursuant to this Part from individual farm operators shall be held confidential by the Department and its employees. All information collected by the Department from individual farm operators for the purposes of its animal health programs, including, but not limited to, certificates of veterinary inspection, animal medical records, laboratory reports, or other records that may be used to identify a person or private business entity subject to regulation by the Department shall not be disclosed without the permission of the owner unless the State Veterinarian determines that disclosure is necessary to prevent the spread of an animal disease or to protect the public health, or the disclosure is necessary in the implementation of these animal health programs. (1979, c. 228, s. 3; 1993, c. 5, s. 1; 1997-261, s. 26; 2002-179, s. 8; 2013-265, s. 7.)

§§ 106-25 through 106-26.2. Repealed by Session Laws 1979, c. 288, s. 2.

§§ 106-26.3 through 106-26.6. Reserved for future codification purposes.

Article 1A.

State Farm Operations Commission.

§§ 106-26.7 through 106-26.12. Repealed by Session Laws 1977, c. 1122, s. 10.

Article 1B.

State Farm Operations Commission.

§§ 106-26.13 through 106-26.21: Repealed by Session Laws 1989, c. 500, s. 107(a).

Article 2.

North Carolina Fertilizer Law of 1947.

§§ 106-27 through 106-50: Superseded by G.S. 106-50.1 through 106-50.22.

§§ 106-50.1 through 106-50.22. Repealed by Session Laws 1977, c. 303, s. 24.

§§ 106-50.23 through 106-50.27. Reserved for future codification purposes.

Article 2A.

North Carolina Soil Additives Act of 1977.

§ 106-50.28. Short title.

This Article shall be known as the North Carolina Soil Additives Act of 1977. (1977, c. 233, s. 1.)

§ 106-50.29. Administration of Article.

This Article shall be administered by the Commissioner of Agriculture of the State of North Carolina. (1977, c. 233, s. 2.)

§ 106-50.30. Definitions.

Words used in this Article shall be defined as follows:

(1)   "Adulterated" means any soil additive:

a.   Which contains any deleterious substance in sufficient quantity to be injurious to desirable terrestrial or aquatic organisms when applied in accordance with the directions for use shown on the label; or

b.   Whose composition differs from that offered in support of registration or shown on the label; or

c.   Which contains noxious weed seed.

(2)   "Bulk" means in nonpackaged form.

(3)   "Commissioner" means the Commissioner of Agriculture of the State of North Carolina or his designated agent.

(4)   "Distribute" means to import, consign, offer for sale, sell, barter, exchange, or to otherwise supply soil additives to any person in this State.

(5)   "Distributor" means any person who imports, consigns, sells, offers for sale, barters, exchanges, or otherwise supplies soil additives in this State.

(6)   "Label" means the display of written, printed, or graphic matter upon the immediate container of, or accompanying soil additives.

(7)   "Labeling" means all written, printed, or graphic matter accompanying any soil additive and all advertisements, brochures, posters, television, radio or oral claims used in promoting its sale.

(8)   "Percent" or "percentage" means the parts per hundred by weight.

(9)   "Person" means individuals, partnerships, associations, corporations or other legal entity.

(10)   "Product name" means the designation under which a soil additive is offered for distribution.

(11)   "Registrant" means any person who registers a soil additive under the provisions of this Article.

(12)   "Sale" means any transfer of title or possession, or both, exchange or barter of tangible personal property, conditioned or otherwise for a consideration paid or to be paid, and this shall include any of said transactions whereby title or ownership is to pass and shall further mean and include any bailment, loan, lease, rental, or license to use or consume tangible personal property for a consideration paid in which possession of said property passes to the bailor, borrower, lessee, or licensee.

(13)   "Sell" means the alienation, exchange, transfer or contract for such transfer of property for a fixed price in money or its equivalent.

(14)   "Soil additive" means any substance intended for changing the characteristics of soil or other growth medium for purposes of:

a.   Increasing the biological population, or

b.   Increasing penetrability of water or air, or

c. Increasing water holding capacity, or

d. Increasing root development, or

e. Alleviating or decreasing soil compaction, or

f. Otherwise altering the soil or other medium in such manner that the physical and biological properties are materially enhanced.

g. The term "soil additive" does not include any substance for which nutritional claims are made, such as, but not limited to, commercial fertilizers, liming materials, or unmanipulated vegetable or animal manures. It also specifically does not include rhizobial inoculants, pine bark, peat moss, other unfortified mulches, or pesticides. (1977, c. 233, s. 3.)

§ 106-50.31. Registration of additives.

Every soil additive distributed in North Carolina shall be registered with the Commissioner by the person whose name appears on the label on forms furnished by the Commissioner. The applicant shall furnish such information as the Commissioner may require. In determining the acceptability of any product for registration, the Commissioner may require proof of claims made for the soil additive. If no specific claims are made, the Commissioner may require proof of usefulness and value of the soil additive. As evidence of proof, the Commissioner may rely on experimental data furnished by the applicant and may require that such data be developed by a recognized research or experimental institution. The Commissioner may further require that such data be developed from tests conducted under conditions identical to or closely related to those present in North Carolina. The Commissioner may reject any data not developed under such conditions and may rely on the advice of the Director of the North Carolina Agricultural Experiment Station in evaluating data for registration.

The registration fee shall be one hundred dollars ($100.00) per year for each product. Registration shall expire on December 31, annually, unless an application for renewal has been received prior to the expiration date.

The application for registration shall include the following:

(1)   The name and address of the registrant;

(2)   Product name;

(3)   Guaranteed analysis;

a.   Active ingredients (name of each ingredient and percent)

b.   Inert ingredients (name of each ingredient and percent)

(4)   Directions for use;

(5)   Purpose of product.

The application shall be accompanied by the label for the product and all advertisements including brochures, posters, or other information promoting the product. The registrant is responsible for all guaranteed analysis and claims appearing on the label. (1977, c. 233, s. 4; 1989, c. 544, s. 8.)

§ 106-50.32. Labeling of containers.

Every soil additive container shall be labeled on the face or display side in readable and conspicuous form showing:

(1)   The product name;

(2)   The guaranteed analysis;

(3)   A statement of claim or purpose;

(4)   Adequate directions for use;

(5)   Net weight or volume;

(6)   Name and address of registrant. (1977, c. 233, s. 5.)

§ 106-50.33. When additive considered misbranded.

A soil additive shall be considered misbranded if:
(1)   Its label or labeling is false or misleading in any particular;

(2)   It is distributed under the name of another soil additive;

(3)   It is represented as a soil additive or is represented to contain a soil additive unless such soil additive conforms to the soil additive definition in this Article. (1977, c. 233, s. 6.)

§ 106-50.34. Records and reports of registrants.

Each registrant shall keep accurate records of his sales, and shall file a semiannual report covering the periods January 1 through June 30, and July 1 through December 31. Such reports shall be due within 30 days from the close of each period. If the report is not filed within the 30-day period or is false in any respect, the Commissioner may revoke the registration. For the purpose of auditing reports, each registrant shall make his records available for audit from time to time as the Commissioner may deem necessary. (1977, c. 233, s. 7.)

§ 106-50.35. Violations of Article.

It shall be a violation of this Article for any person:

(1)   To distribute an unregistered soil additive;

(2)   To distribute an unlabeled soil additive;

(3)   To distribute a misbranded soil additive;

(4)   To distribute an "adulterated" soil additive;

(5)   To fail to comply with a "stop sale, use or removal" order; or

(6)   To fail to submit semiannual reports. (1977, c. 233, s. 8.)

§ 106-50.36. Inspection and sampling of additives.

The Commissioner is authorized to enter upon any public or private property with permission or with a proper court order during normal business hours for the purpose of inspecting or sampling any soil additive to determine if such additive is being distributed in compliance with the provisions of this Article. In the examination of such samples, the Commissioner may rely on such tests as he may establish as necessary for the enforcement of this Article. (1977, c. 233, s. 9.)

§ 106-50.37. Stop sale, etc., orders.

The Commissioner may issue and enforce a written or printed stop sale, use, or removal order to the owner or custodian of any lot of soil additive, and hold at a designated place, any such lot of soil additive which the Commissioner determines does not comply with the provisions of this Article. When such soil additive has been made to comply with the provisions of this Article, it shall then be released in writing by the Commissioner. (1977, c. 233, s. 10.)

§ 106-50.38. Injunctions.

The Commissioner may bring an action to enjoin the violation or threatened violation of any provision of this Article or regulations adopted hereunder, in the Superior Court of Wake County, or in the superior court of the county in which such violation occurs or is about to occur. (1977, c. 233, s. 11.)

§ 106-50.39. Refusal or revocation of registration.

The Commissioner shall refuse to register any soil additive which fails to comply with the provisions of this Article, and may revoke, after opportunity for a hearing, any registration, upon sufficient evidence that the registrant or any of his designated agents has used misleading, fraudulent, or deceptive practices in the distribution of any soil additive. (1977, c. 233, s. 12.)

§ 106-50.40. Rules and regulations.

The Board of Agriculture is authorized to promulgate and adopt, pursuant to Chapter 150B of the General Statutes of North Carolina, such rules and regulations as may be necessary to enforce the provisions of this Article. Such regulations may relate to, but shall not be limited to:

(1) Methods of inspection and sampling;

(2) Examination and analysis of samples;

(3) Designation of ingredients;

(4) Identity of product;

(5) Monetary penalties for samples not meeting guarantees;

(6) Acceptable ingredients for registration;

(7) Labeling format. (1977, c. 233, s. 13; 1987, c. 827, s. 1.)

§ 106-50.41. Penalties.

Any person violating the provisions of this Article or the regulations adopted thereunder, shall be guilty of a Class 2 misdemeanor. In addition, if any person continues to violate or further violates any provision of this Article after written notice from the Commissioner each day during which the violation continued or is repeated constitutes a separate violation subject to the foregoing penalties. (1977, c. 233, s. 14; 1993, c. 539, s. 739; 1994, Ex. Sess., c. 24, s. 14(c).)

Article 3.

Fertilizer Laboratories.

§ 106-51: Repealed by Session Laws 1987, c. 244, s. 1(b).

Article 4.
Insecticides and Fungicides.

§§ 106-52 through 106-65: Repealed by Session Laws 1971, c. 832, s. 4.

Article 4A.

Insecticide, Fungicide and Rodenticide Act of 1947.

§§ 106-65.1 through 106-65.12: Repealed by Session Laws 1971, c. 832, s. 4.

Article 4B.

Aircraft Application of Pesticides.

§§ 106-65.13 through 106-65.21: Repealed by Session Laws 1971, c. 832, s. 4.

Article 4C.

Structural Pest Control Act.

§ 106-65.22. Title.

This Article shall be known by the title of "Structural Pest Control Act of North Carolina of 1955." It is declared to be the policy of this State that the regulation of persons, corporations and firms engaged in the business of structural pest control in this State, as defined in G.S. 106-65.25, is in the public interest in order to ensure a high quality of workmanship and in order to prevent deception, fraud and unfair trade practices in the conduct of said business. The General Assembly finds that quality of structural pest control work is not easily determined by the general public due to the inaccessibility of the areas treated and the complexity of the methods of treatment. (1955, c. 1017; 1977, c. 231, s. 1.)

§ 106-65.23. Structural Pest Control and Pesticides Division of Department of Agriculture and Consumer Services recreated; Director; powers and duties of Commissioner; Structural Pest Control Committee created; appointment; terms; powers and duties; quorum.

(a) There is recreated, within the North Carolina Department of Agriculture and Consumer Services, a Division to be known as the Structural Pest Control and Pesticides Division. The Commissioner of Agriculture may appoint a Director of the Division, chosen from a list of nominees submitted to him or her by the Structural Pest Control Committee created in this section, whose duties and authority shall be determined by the Commissioner in consultation with the Committee. The Director shall be responsible for and answerable to the Commissioner of Agriculture and the Structural Pest Control Committee as to the operation and conduct of the Structural Pest Control and Pesticides Division. The Director shall act as secretary to the Structural Pest Control Committee.

(b) The Commissioner shall have the following powers and duties under this Article:

(1) To administer and enforce the provisions of this Article and the rules adopted thereunder by the Structural Pest Control Committee. In order to carry out these powers and duties, the Commissioner may delegate to the Director of the Structural Pest Control and Pesticides Division the powers and duties assigned to him or her under this Article.

(2) To assign the administrative and enforcement duties assigned to him or her in this Article.

(3) To direct, in consultation with the Structural Pest Control Committee, the work of the personnel employed by the Structural Pest Control Committee and the work of the personnel of the Department assigned to perform the administrative and enforcement functions of this Article.

(4) To develop, for the Structural Pest Control Committee's consideration for adoption, proposed rules, policies, new programs, and revisions of existing programs under this Article.

(5) To monitor existing enforcement programs and to provide evaluations of these programs to the Structural Pest Control Committee.

(6) To attend all meetings of the Structural Pest Control Committee, but without the power to vote unless the Commissioner attends as the designee on the Committee from the Department of Agriculture and Consumer Services.

(7) To keep an accurate and complete record of all meetings of the Structural Pest Control Committee and to have legal custody of all books, papers, documents, and other records of the Committee.

(8) To perform such other duties as may be assigned to him or her by the Structural Pest Control Committee.

(c) There is hereby created a Structural Pest Control Committee to be composed of the following members. The Commissioner shall appoint one member of the Committee who is not in the structural pest control business for a four-year term. The Commissioner of Agriculture shall designate an employee of the Department of Agriculture and Consumer Services to serve on the Committee at the pleasure of the Commissioner. The dean of the School of Agriculture of North Carolina State University at Raleigh shall appoint one member of the Committee who shall serve for one term of two years and who shall be a member of the entomology faculty of the University. The vacancy occurring on the Committee by the expired term of the member from the entomology faculty of the University shall be filled by the dean of the School of Agriculture of North Carolina State University at Raleigh who shall designate any person of the dean's choice from the entomology faculty of the University to serve on the Committee at the pleasure of the dean. The Secretary of Health and Human Services shall appoint one member of the Committee who shall be an epidemiologist and who shall serve at the pleasure of the Secretary. The Governor shall appoint two members of the Committee who are actively engaged in the pest control industry, who are licensed in at least two phases of structural pest control as provided under G.S. 106-65.25(a), and who are residents of the State of North Carolina but not affiliates of the same company.

The Governor's initial appointees from the pest control industry shall be appointed as follows: one for a two-year term and one for a three-year term. The Governor shall appoint one member of the Committee who is a public member and who is unaffiliated with the structural pest control industry, the pesticide industry, the Department of Agriculture and Consumer Services, the Department of Health and Human Services and the School of Agriculture at North Carolina

State University at Raleigh. The initial public member shall be appointed for a term of two years, commencing July 1, 1991. After the initial appointments by the Governor, all ensuing appointments by the Governor shall be for terms of four years. Any vacancy occurring on the Committee by reason of death, resignation, or otherwise shall be filled by the Governor or the Commissioner of Agriculture, as the case may be, for the unexpired term of the member whose seat is vacant.

One member of the Committee shall be appointed by the General Assembly upon the recommendation of the Speaker of the House of Representatives in accordance with G.S. 120-121, and one member of the Committee shall be appointed by the General Assembly upon the recommendation of the President Pro Tempore of the Senate in accordance with G.S. 120-121. The member appointed by the General Assembly upon the recommendation of the Speaker of the House of Representatives shall be actively engaged in the pest control industry, licensed in at least two phases of structural pest control as provided under G.S. 106-65.25(a), and a resident of the State of North Carolina but not an affiliate of the same company as either of the two members from the industry appointed by the Governor. Appointments made by the General Assembly shall be for terms of four years. Vacancies in such appointments shall be filled in accordance with G.S. 120-122.

(d)   The Structural Pest Control Committee shall have the following powers and duties:

(1)   To adopt rules and make policies as provided in this Article.

(2)   To issue, deny, suspend, revoke, modify, or restrict licenses, certified applicator cards, and registered technician cards under the provisions of this Article. In all matters affecting licensure, the decision of the Committee shall constitute the final agency decision.

(3)   Repealed by Session Laws 2013-265, s. 8, effective July 17, 2013.

(e)   Each member of the Committee who is not an employee of the State shall receive as compensation for services per diem and necessary travel expenses and registration fees in accordance with the provisions as outlined for members of occupational licensing boards and currently provided for in G.S. 93B-5. Such per diem and necessary travel expenses and registration fees shall apply to the same effect that G.S. 93B-5 might hereafter be amended.

Five members of the Committee shall constitute a quorum but no action at any meeting of the Committee shall be taken without four votes in accord. The chairman shall be entitled to vote at all times.

The Committee shall meet at such times and such places in North Carolina as the chairman shall direct; provided, however, that four members of the Committee may call a special meeting of the Committee on five days' notice to the other members thereof.

Except as otherwise provided herein, all members of the Committee shall be appointed or designated, as the case may be, prior to and shall commence their respective terms on July 1, 1967.

At the first meeting of the Committee they shall elect a chairman who shall serve as such at the pleasure of the Committee. (1955, c. 1017; 1057, c. 1243, s. 1; 1967, c. 1184, s. 1; 1969, c. 541, s. 7; 1973, c. 556, s. 1; 1975, c. 570, ss. 1, 2; 1977, c. 231, s. 2; 1987, c. 827, s. 26; 1989, c. 238; c. 727, s. 219(30); 1997-261, s. 27; 1997-443, s. 11A.40; 1998-224, s. 19(a); 1999-381, s. 1; 2000-175, s. 1; 2013-265, s. 8.)

§ 106-65.24. Definitions.

As used in this Article:

(1) "Animal" means all vertebrate and invertebrate species, including but not limited to man and other mammals, birds, fish, and shellfish.

(1a) "Applicant for a certified applicator's identification card" means any person making application to use restricted use pesticides in any phase of structural pest control.

(2) "Applicant for a license" means any person in charge of any individual, firm, partnership, corporation, association, or any other organization or any combination thereof, making application for a license to engage in structural pest control, control of structural pests or household pests, or fumigation operations, or any person qualified under the terms of this Article.

(3) "Attractants" means substances, under whatever name known, which may be toxic to insects and other pests but are used primarily to induce insects and other pests to eat poisoned baits or to enter traps.

(3a) Repealed by Session Laws 1989, c. 725.

(3b) "Branch Office" means any office under the management of a licensee that is not a home office.

(4) "Certified applicator" means any individual who is certified under G.S. 106-65.25 as authorized to use or supervise the use of any pesticide which is classified for restricted use.

(5) "Commissioner" means the Commissioner of Agriculture of the State of North Carolina.

(6) "Committee" means the Structural Pest Control Committee.

(6a) "Deviation" means failure of the licensee or certified applicator or registered technician card holder to follow any rule adopted by the Committee under provisions of this Article.

(7) "Device" means any instrument or contrivance (other than a firearm) which is intended for trapping, destroying, repelling, or mitigating any pest or any other form of plant or animal life (other than man and other than bacteria, virus, or other microorganism on or in living man or other living animals); but not including equipment used for the application of pesticides when sold separately therefrom.

(8) Repealed by Session Laws 1975, c. 570, s. 4.

(8a) "Director" means the Director of the Structural Pest Control Division of the Department of Agriculture and Consumer Services.

(9) "Employee" means any person employed by a licensee with the exceptions of clerical, janitorial, or office maintenance employees, or those employees performing work completely disassociated with the control of insect pests, rodents or the control of wood-destroying organisms.

(9a) "Enforcement agency" means the Structural Pest Control and Pesticides Division of the Department of Agriculture and Consumer Services.

(10) "Fumigants" means any substance which by itself or in combination with any other substance emits or liberates a gas or gases, fumes or vapors and

which gas or gases, fumes or vapors when liberated and when used will destroy vermin, rodents, insects, and other pests; but may be lethal, poisonous, noxious, or dangerous to human life.

(11) "Fungi" means wood-decaying fungi.

(11a) "Home office" means the office identified to the enforcement agency by a licensee as his or her principal place of business.

(12) "Insect" means any of the numerous small invertebrate animals generally having the body more or less obviously segmented, for the most part belonging to the class Insecta, comprising six-legged, usually winged forms, as for example, beetles, bugs, bees, flies, and to other allied classes of arthropods whose members are wingless and usually have more than six legs, as for example, spiders, mites, ticks, centipedes, and sowbugs.

(13) "Insecticides" means substances, not fumigants, under whatever name known, used for the destruction or control of insects and similar pests.

(14) "Label" means the written, printed, or graphic matter on, or attached to, the pesticide or device or any of its containers or wrappers.

(14a) The term "labeling" means all labels and other written, printed, or graphic matter:

a. Upon the pesticide (or device) or any of its containers or wrappers;

b. Accompanying the pesticide (or device) at any time;

c. To which reference is made on the label or in literature accompanying the pesticide (or device) except when accurate nonmisleading reference is made to current official publications of the United States Department of Agriculture or Interior, the United States Public Health Service, state experiment stations, state agricultural colleges, or other similar federal institutions or official agencies of this State or other states authorized by the law to conduct research in the field of pesticides.

(15) "Licensee" means any person qualified for and holding a license for any phase of structural pest control pursuant to this Article.

(16) "Person" means any individual, partnership, association, corporation, or any organized group of persons whether incorporated or not.

(17) "Pest" means any living organism, including but not limited to, insects, rodents, birds, and fungi, which the Commissioner declares to be a pest.
(18) "Pesticide" means any substance or mixture of substances intended for preventing, destroying, repelling, or mitigating any pest.

(19) "Registered pesticide" means a pesticide which has been registered by federal and/or State agency responsible for registering pesticides.

(19a) "Registered technician" means any individual who is required to be registered with the Structural Pest Control and Pesticides Division under G.S. 106-65.31.

(20) "Repellents" means substances, not fumigants, under whatever name known, which may be toxic to insects and related pests, but are generally employed because of capacity for preventing the entrance or attack of pests.

(21) "Restricted use pesticide" means a pesticide which has been designated as such by the federal and/or State agency responsible for registering pesticides.

(22) "Rodenticides" means substances, not fumigants, under whatever name known, whether poisonous or otherwise, used for the destruction or control of rodents.

(23) "Structural pest control" means the control of wood-destroying organisms or household pests (including, but not limited to, animals such as moths, cockroaches, ants, beetles, flies, mosquitoes, ticks, wasps, bees, fleas, mites, silverfish, millipedes, centipedes, sowbugs, crickets, termites, wood borers, etc.), including the identification of infestations or infections, the making of inspections, the use of pesticides, including insecticides, repellents, attractants, rodenticides, fungicides, and fumigants, as well as all other substances, mechanical devices or structural modifications under whatever name known, for the purpose of preventing, controlling and eradicating insects, vermin, rodents and other pests in household structures, commercial buildings, and other structures (including household structures, commercial buildings and other structures in all stages of construction), and outside areas, as well as all phases of fumigation, including treatment of products by vacuum fumigation, and the fumigation of railroad cars, trucks, ships, and airplanes, or any one or any combination thereof.

(24)   "Under the direct supervision of a certified applicator" means, unless otherwise prescribed by its labeling, a pesticide shall be considered to be applied under the direct supervision of a certified applicator if it is applied by a competent person acting under the instructions and control of a certified applicator who is available if and when needed, even though such certified applicator is not physically present at the time and place the pesticide is applied. (1955, c. 1017; 1957, c. 1243, s. 2; 1967, c. 1184, ss. 2, 3; 1973, c. 556, s. 2; 1975, c. 570, ss. 3, 4; 1977, c. 231, ss. 3-5; 1989, c. 725, s. 1; 1997-261, ss. 28, 29; 1999-381, s. 2; 2013-265, s. 9.)

§ 106-65.25. Phases of structural pest control; prohibited acts; license required; exceptions.

(a)   The Committee shall classify license phases to be issued under this Article. Separate phases or subphases shall be specified for:

(1)   Control of household pests by any method other than fumigation ("P" phase);

(2)   Control of wood-destroying organisms by any method other than fumigation ("W" phase); and

(3)   Fumigation ("F" phase).

(b)   It shall be unlawful for any person to:

(1)   Advertise as, offer to engage in, or engage in or supervise work as a manager, owner, or owner-operator in any phase of structural pest control or otherwise act in the capacity of a structural pest control licensee unless the person is licensed pursuant to this Article or has engaged the services of a licensee as a full-time regular employee who is responsible for the structural pest control performed by the company. A license is required for each phase of structural pest control.

(2)   Hold more than one license for each phase of structural pest control.

(3)   Use a restricted use pesticide in any phase of structural pest control, whether it be on the person's own property or on the property of another, unless the person:

a. Qualifies as a certified applicator for that phase of structural pest control; or

b. Is under the direct supervision of a certified applicator who possesses a valid certified applicator's identification card for that phase of structural pest control.

(4) Use or supervise the use of restricted use pesticides in demonstrating or supervising a demonstration to the public of the proper use and techniques of the application of pesticides or conducting field research with pesticides unless:

a. The person possesses a valid certified applicator's identification card;

b. The person is conducting laboratory research involving restricted use pesticides; or

c. The person is a doctor of medicine or a doctor of veterinary medicine applying restricted use pesticides as drugs or medication during the course of his or her normal professional practice.

This subdivision applies to all persons, including cooperative extension specialists demonstrating pesticide products, individuals demonstrating methods used in public programs, and local, State, federal, commercial, and other persons conducting field research on or using restricted use pesticides.

(c) It shall be unlawful for any licensee to do any of the following:

(1) Establish, be in charge of, or manage any branch office in excess of the number of branch offices that may be established, supervised, or managed by a licensee as set forth in rules adopted by the Committee.

(2) Fail to supervise the structural pest control performed out of the licensee's home office or any branch office under the licensee's management.

(3) Allow his or her license to be used by any person or company for which he or she is not a full-time regular employee actively and personally engaged in the supervision of the structural pest control performed under the license.

(4) Use any pesticide, material, or device prohibited by the Committee or use any approved pesticide, material, or device in a manner prohibited by the Committee.

(5) Use or supervise the use of restricted use pesticides in a phase of structural pest control for which the person is not licensed or qualified as a certified applicator unless the person's use is under the supervision of a licensee or certified applicator certified in that phase of structural pest control.

(c1) The Committee shall adopt rules that permit a licensee to establish branch offices in addition to a home office. In no event shall the rules adopted restrict the number of branch offices a licensee can establish, supervise, or manage to fewer than two branch offices. The rules shall include provisions to ensure that the licensee can adequately supervise all structural pest control performed from the offices and under his or her license.

(d) A license is not required for any person (or the person's full-time regular employees) doing structural pest control on the person's own property. No fee may be charged for structural pest control performed by any such person.

(e), (f) Repealed by Session Laws 1999-381, s. 3.

(g) Any person issued a license for any one or any combination of the phases of structural pest control shall be deemed to be a "certified applicator" to use or supervise the use of restricted use pesticides so long as the pesticides are being used only in the phase of structural pest control for which the person is licensed.

(h) Licenses and certified applicator's identification cards may only be issued to individuals. License certificates and certified applicator's identification cards shall be issued in the name of the individual, shall bear the name and address of the individual's business or employer's business and shall indicate the phase or phases for which the individual is qualified and such other information as the Committee may specify. (1955, c. 1017; 1957, c. 1243, s. 3; 1967, c. 1184, s. 4; 1973, c. 556, s. 3; 1975, c. 570, s. 5; 1989, c. 725, s. 2; 1999-381, s. 3.)

§ 106-65.26. Qualifications for certified applicator and licensee; applicants for certified applicator's identification card and license.

(a) An applicant for a certified applicator's identification card or license must present satisfactory evidence to the Committee concerning his qualifications for such card or license.

(b) Certified Applicator. - Each applicant for a certified applicator's identification card must demonstrate that he possesses a practical knowledge of the pest problems and pest control practices associated with the phase or phases of structural pest control for which he is seeking certification.

(c) Licensee. - The basic qualifications for a license shall be:

(1) Qualify as a certified applicator for the phase or phases of structural pest control for which he is making application; and

(2) Two years as an employee or owner-operator in the field of structural pest control, control of wood-destroying organisms or fumigation, for which license is applied; or

(3) One or more years' training in specialized pest control, control of wood-destroying organisms or fumigation under university or college supervision may be substituted for practical experience. Each year of such training may be substituted for one year of practical experience; provided, however, if applicant has had less than 12 months' practical experience, the Committee is authorized to determine whether said applicant has had sufficient experience to take the examination; or

(4) A degree from a recognized college or university with training in entomology, sanitary or public health engineering, or related subjects; provided, however, if applicant has had less than 12 months' practical experience, the Committee is authorized to determine whether said applicant has had sufficient experience to take the examination.

(d) All applicants for license must have practical experience and knowledge of practical and scientific facts underlying the practice of structural pest control, control of wood-destroying organisms, or fumigation. No applicant is entitled to take an examination for the issuance of a license pursuant to this Article who has within five years of the date of application been convicted, entered a plea of guilty or of nolo contendere, or forfeited bond in any State or federal court for a violation of G.S. 106-65.25(b), any felony, or any crime involving moral turpitude.

(e) The Department of Justice may provide a criminal record check to the Committee for a person who has applied for a new or renewal license through the Committee. The Committee shall provide to the Department of Justice, along with the request, the fingerprints of the applicant, any additional information required by the Department of Justice, and a form signed by the applicant consenting to the check of the criminal record and to the use of the fingerprints and other identifying information required by the State or national repositories. The applicant's fingerprints shall be forwarded to the State Bureau of Investigation for a search of the State's criminal history record file, and the State Bureau of Investigation shall forward a set of the fingerprints to the Federal Bureau of Investigation for a national criminal history check. The Committee shall keep all information pursuant to this subsection privileged, in accordance with applicable State law and federal guidelines, and the information shall be confidential and shall not be a public record under Chapter 132 of the General Statutes.

The Department of Justice may charge each applicant a fee for conducting the checks of criminal history records authorized by this subsection. (1955, c. 1017; 1967, c. 1184, s. 5; 1973, c. 556, s. 4; 1975, c. 570, s. 6; 1999-381, s. 4; 2002-147, s. 13.)

§ 106-65.27. Examinations of applicants; fee; license not transferable.

(a) Certified Applicator. - All applicants for a certified applicator's identification card shall demonstrate practical knowledge of the principles and practices of pest control and safe use of pesticides. Competency shall be determined on the basis of written examinations to be provided and administered by the Committee and, as appropriate, performance testing. Testing shall be based upon examples of problems and situations appropriate to the particular phase or subphase of structural pest control for which application is made and shall include, where relevant, the following areas of competency:

(1) Label and labeling comprehension.

(2) Safety factors associated with pesticides - toxicity, precautions, first aid, proper handling, etc.

(3) Influence of and on the environment.

(4) Pests - identification, biology, and habits.

(5) Pesticides - types, formulations, compatibility, hazards, etc.

(6) Equipment - types and uses.

(7) Application techniques.

(8) Laws and regulations.

An applicant for a certified applicator's identification card shall submit an examination fee of twenty-five dollars ($25.00) for each phase or subphase of structural pest control in which the applicant chooses to be examined. An examination for more than one phase or subphase may be taken at the same time at any regularly scheduled examination. Frequency of such examinations shall be at the discretion of the Committee, provided that a minimum of two examinations be given annually. The examination will cover each phase or subphase of structural pest control for which application is being made.

(b) License. - Each applicant for an original license must demonstrate upon written examination, to be provided and administered by the Committee, his competency as a structural pest control operator for the phase or subphase in which he is applying for a license. Frequency of such examinations shall be at the discretion of the Committee, provided that a minimum of two examinations shall be given annually. The examination will cover each phase or subphase of structural pest control for which application is being made. All applicants for a license shall register with the Division on a prescribed form. A license examination fee of fifty dollars ($50.00) shall be charged for each phase or subphase of structural pest control in which the applicant chooses to be examined. An examination for more than one phase or subphase of structural pest control may be taken at the same time.

(c) A license, certified applicator's identification card or registered technician's identification card is not transferable from one person to another. A licensee or certified applicator may change the name of his business or employer's business on his license certificate or certified applicator's identification card upon application to the Division.

(c1) When there is a transfer of ownership, management, operation of a structural pest control business or in the event of the death or disability of a licensee there shall be not more than a total of 90 days during any 12-month period in which said business shall operate without a licensee assigned to it; provided that, in the event of the death or disability of a licensee, the Committee shall have the authority to grant up to an additional 90 days within the 12-month period in which a business may operate without a licensee assigned to it. The owner, partnership, corporation, or other entity operating said business shall, within 10 days of such transfer or disability or within 30 days of death, designate in writing to the Division a certified applicator who shall be responsible for and in charge of the structural pest control operations of said business during the 90-day period. If the owner, partnership, corporation, or other entity operating the business fails to designate a certified applicator who shall be responsible for the operation of the business during the 90-day period, the business shall cease all structural pest control activities upon expiration of the applicable notification period and shall not resume operations until a certified applicator is so designated.

During the 90-day period the use of any restricted use pesticide shall be by or under the direct supervision of the certified applicator designated in writing to the Division. The designated certified applicator shall be responsible for correcting all deviations on all existing contracts and for all work performed under his supervision.

The new licensee shall be responsible for correcting all deviations on all existing contracts and for all work performed under his supervision.

(d) The Committee shall by regulation provide for:

(1) Establishing categories of certified applicators, along with such appropriate subcategories as are necessary, to meet the requirements of this Article;

(2) All licensees licensed prior to October 21, 1976, to become qualified as certified applicators; and

(3) Requalifying certified applicators thereafter as required by the federal government at intervals no more frequent than that specified by federal law and federal regulations. (1955, c. 1017; 1967, c. 1184, s. 6; 1973, c. 556, ss. 5, 6; 1975, c. 570, s. 7; 1977, c. 231, s. 6; 1989, c. 725, s. 3; 1999-381, s. 5; 2010-31, s. 11.2(a).)

§ 106-65.28. Revocation or suspension of license or identification card.

(a) Any license or certified applicator's identification card or registered technician's identification card may be denied, revoked or suspended by a majority vote of the Committee for any one or more of the following causes:

(1) Misrepresentation for the purpose of defrauding; deceit or fraud; the making of a false statement with knowledge of its falsity for the purpose of inducing others to act thereon to their damage; or the use of methods or materials which are not reasonably suitable for the purpose contracted.

(2) Failure of the licensee or certified applicator to give the Committee, the Commissioner, or their authorized representatives, upon request, true information regarding methods and materials used, or work performed.

(3) Failure of the licensee or certified applicator to make registrations herein required or failure to pay the registration fees.

(4) Any misrepresentation in the application for a license or certified applicator's identification card or registered technician's identification card.

(5) Willful violation of any rule or regulation adopted pursuant to this Article.

(6) Aiding or abetting a licensed or unlicensed person or a certified applicator or a noncertified person to evade the provisions of this Article, combining or conspiring with such a licensed or unlicensed person or a certified applicator or noncertified person to evade the provisions of this Article, or allowing one's license, certified applicator's identification card or registered technician's identification card, to be used by any person other than the individual to whom it has been issued.

(7) Impersonating any State, county or city inspector or official.

(8) Storing or disposing of containers or pesticides by means other than those prescribed on the label or adopted regulations.

(9) Using any pesticide in a manner inconsistent with its labeling.

(10) Payment, or the offer to pay, by any licensee to any party to a real estate transaction of any commission, bonus, rebate, or other thing of value as

compensation or inducement for the referral to such licensee of structural pest control work arising out of such transaction.

(11)   Falsification of records required to be kept by this Article or the rules and regulations of the Committee.

(12)   Failure of a licensee or certified applicator to pay the original or renewal license or identification card fee when due and continuing to operate as a licensee or a certified applicator.

(13)   Conviction of a felony or conviction of a violation of G.S. 106-65.28 within five years preceding the date of application for a license or a certified applicator's identification card or conviction of any said crimes while such license or card is in effect.

(14)   Applying any substance that:

a.   Has the active ingredients contained in a pesticide that is registered pursuant to G.S. 143-442, but

b.   Is not registered as a pesticide pursuant to G.S. 143-442.

(15)   Combining any substance whose application is prohibited under subdivision (14) of this subsection with any other substance to apply as a pesticide or to apply for any other reason, whether the combination occurs before, during, or after the application.

(b)   Suspension of any license or certified applicator's identification card or registered technician's identification card under the provisions of this Article shall not be for less than 10 days nor more than two years, in the discretion of the Committee.

(c)   If a license or certified applicator's identification card or registered technician's identification card is suspended or revoked under the provisions hereof, the licensee shall within five days of such suspension or revocation, surrender all licenses and identification cards issued thereunder to the Commissioner or his authorized representative.

(d)   Any licensee whose license or certified applicator or operator whose identification card is revoked under the provisions of this Article shall not be eligible to apply for a new license or certified applicator's identification card or registered technician's identification card hereunder until two years have elapsed from the date of the order revoking said license or certified applicator's identification card or registered technician's identification card or if an appeal is taken from said order of revocation, two years from the date of the order or final judgment sustaining said revocation.

(e) The lapsing of a State structural pest control license or certified applicator's identification card or registered technician's identification card by operation of law or the voluntary surrender of said license or said card shall not deprive the Committee of jurisdiction to proceed with any investigation or disciplinary proceedings against such licensee or card holder or to render a decision suspending or revoking such license or card.

(f) The Committee may deny an application for a license, a certified applicator's identification card or a registered technician's identification card of any person whose license, certified applicator's identification card or equivalent thereto has been suspended or revoked in another state within two years prior to the application.

(g) Any pesticide, material, or device for which such information is requested by the Committee pursuant to G.S. 106-65.29(9a) and denied by the registrant or manufacturer shall not be used in any structural pest control performed for compensation and may only be used by an individual performing structural pest control on the individual's own property. (1955, c. 1017; 1967, c. 1184, s. 7; 1973, c. 556, ss. 7, 8; 1975, c. 19, s. 30; c. 570, ss. 8-13; 1977, c. 231, ss. 7-9; 1987, c. 827, s. 27; 1989, c. 725, s. 4; 1995, c. 478, s. 2; 1999-381, s. 6.)

§ 106-65.29. Rules and regulations.

In order to ensure that persons licensed and certified under this Article are capable of performing a high quality of workmanship, the Committee may adopt rules with respect to:

(1) The amount and kind of training required of an applicant for a license and certified applicator's card to engage in any one or more of the three phases of structural pest control, and the amount and kind of training required of an applicant for a registered technician's identification card.

(2) The type, frequency and passing score of any examination given an applicant for a license and certified applicator's card under this Article.

(3) The amount, kind and frequency of continuing education required of a licensee and certified applicator.

(4) The methods and materials to be used in performing any work authorized by the issuance of a license and certified applicator's card under this Article.

(5) The business records to be made and maintained by licensees and certified applicators under this Article necessary for the Committee to determine whether the licensee and certified applicator is performing a high quality of workmanship.

(6) The credentials and identification required of licensees and certified applicators, their employees and equipment, including service vehicles, when engaged in any work defined under this Article.

(7) Safety methods and procedures for structural pest control work.

(8) Fees for reinspection following a finding of a deviation, as defined by the Committee.

(9) Fees for training materials provided by the Committee or the Division. Such fees may be placed in a revolving fund to be used for training and continuing education purposes and shall not revert to the General Fund.

(9a) Efficacy data and other technical information to be submitted by registrants and manufacturers of pesticides and other materials or devices for review and approval, in order for the Committee and the enforcement agency to ensure the efficacy of pesticides and other materials or devices used in structural pest control in this State. This subdivision does not require either the Committee or the enforcement agency to disclose any information that is confidential information within the meaning of G.S. 132-1.2.

(10) The policies and programs set forth in this Article. (1955, c. 1017; 1967, c. 1184, s. 8; 1975, c. 570, s. 14; 1977, c. 231, s. 9; 1981, c. 495, s. 3; 1987, c. 368, s. 2; c. 827, s. 28; 1989, c. 725, s. 5; 1999-381, s. 7.)

§ 106-65.30. Inspectors; inspections and reports of violations; designation of resident agent.

(a)   For the enforcement of the provisions of this Article the Commissioner is authorized to appoint one or more qualified inspectors and such other employees as are necessary in order to carry out and enforce the provisions of this Article. The inspectors shall be known as "structural pest control inspectors." The Commissioner may enforce compliance with the provisions of this Article by making or causing to be made periodical and unannounced inspections of work done by licensees and certified applicators under this Article who engage in or supervise any one or more phases of structural pest control as defined in G.S. 106-65.25. The Commissioner shall cause the prompt and diligent investigation of all reports of violations of the provisions of this Article and all rules and regulations adopted pursuant to the provisions hereof; provided, however, no inspection shall be made by a representative of the Commissioner of any property without first securing the permission of the owner or occupant thereof.

(b)   Prior to the issuance or renewal of a license or certified applicator's identification card, every nonresident owner of a business performing any phase of structural pest control work shall designate in writing to the Commissioner or his authorized agent a resident agent upon whom service of notice or process may be made to enforce the provisions of this Article and rules and regulations adopted pursuant to the provisions hereof or any civil or criminal liabilities arising hereunder.

(c)   The Commissioner shall have authority to appoint personnel of the Structural Pest Control and Pesticides Division as special inspectors and said special inspectors are hereby vested with the authority to arrest with a warrant, or to arrest without a warrant when a violation of this Article is being committed in their presence or they have reasonable grounds to believe that a violation of this Article is being committed in their presence. Said special inspectors shall take offenders before the several courts of this State for prosecution or other proceedings. The provisions of this section do not apply to any person holding a valid structural pest control license, or a certified applicator's identification card, or a registered technician's identification card as issued under the provisions of this Article. Special inspectors shall not be entitled to the benefits of the Law Enforcement Officers' Benefit and Retirement Fund or the benefits of the Law Enforcement Officers' and Others Death Benefit Act as provided for in Articles 12 and 12A of Chapter 143 of the General Statutes, respectively. (1955, c.

1017; 1967, c. 1184, s. 9; 1973, c. 556, s. 9; 1975, c. 570, s. 15; 1977, c. 231, s. 10; 1989, c. 725, s. 6; 1999-381, s. 8; 2013-265, s. 10.)

§ 106-65.31. Annual certified applicator card and license fee; registration of servicemen, salesmen, solicitors, and estimators; identification cards.

(a) Certified Applicator's Identification Card. - The fee for issuance or renewal of a certified applicator's identification card shall be fifty dollars ($50.00). Within 75 days after the employment of a certified applicator, the licensee shall apply to the Division for the issuance of a certified applicator's identification card. A certified applicator's identification card shall expire on June 30 of each year and shall be renewed annually. All certified applicators who fail or neglect to renew their card on or before June 30 but make application before January 1 of the following year may have their card renewed without having to be reexamined unless the applicant is scheduled for periodic reexamination under regulations adopted pursuant to G.S. 106-65.27(d)(3). All applicants submitting applications for the renewal of their cards after June 30 shall not use or supervise the use of restricted use pesticides until a new card has been issued.

Any certified applicator whose employment is terminated with a licensee or agent prior to the end of any license year may at any time prior to the end of the license year be reissued a certified applicator's identification card for the remainder of the license year as an employee of another licensee or agency or as an individual for a fee of five dollars ($5.00). The licensee shall notify the Division of the termination or change in status of any certified applicator.

Any certified applicator whose identification card is lost or destroyed or changed in any way may be reissued a new card for the remainder of the license year for a fee of five dollars ($5.00).

(b) License. - The fee for the issuance or renewal of a license for any one phase of structural pest control shall be two hundred dollars ($200.00). Each additional phase shall be seventy-five dollars ($75.00). The fee for each subphase shall be fifteen dollars ($15.00). Licenses shall expire on June 30 of each year and shall be renewed annually. All licensees who fail or neglect to renew their license on or before June 30, but who make application before January 1 of the following year, may have their license renewed without having to be reexamined, unless the applicant is scheduled for periodic reexamination under regulations adopted pursuant to G.S. 106-65.27(d)(3). No structural pest control work may be performed until the icense has been renewed or until a new license has been issued.

Any licensee whose employment is terminated by his employer or any licensee who is transferred to another company or location other than the company or location shown on his license certificate may at any time, have his license reissued for the remainder of the license year for a fee of ten dollars ($10.00).

Any licensee whose license is lost or destroyed may secure a duplicate license for a fee of ten dollars ($10.00).

(b1)   Registration. - Within 75 days after the hiring of an employee who is either an estimator, salesman, serviceman, or solicitor, the licensee shall apply to the Division for the issuance of an identification card for such employee. The application must be accompanied by a fee of forty dollars ($40.00) for each card. The card shall be issued in the name of the employee and shall bear the name of the employing licensee, the employer's license number and phases, the name and address of the employer's business, and such other information as the Committee may specify. The identification card shall be carried by the employee on his person at all times while performing any phase of structural pest control work. The card must be d splayed upon demand by the Commissioner, the Committee, the Division, or any representative thereof, or the person for whom any phase of structural pest control work is being performed. A registered technician's identification card must be renewed annually on or before June 30 by payment of a renewal fee of forty dollars ($40.00). If a card is lost or destroyed the licensee may secure a duplicate for a fee of five dollars ($5.00).The licensee shall notify the Division of the termination or change in status of any registered technician. All identification cards expire when a license expires.

When a license is reissued, the licensee shall be responsible for registering and securing identification cards for all existing employees who engage in structural pest control within 10 days of the reissuance of the license.

A certified applicator who is not an employee of a licensed individual shall register the names of all employees under his supervision who are engaged in the performance of structural pest control with the Division and shall purchase a registered technician's identification card for each such employee.

(b2)   No person shall act as an estimator, serviceman, salesman, solicitor, or agent for any licensee under this Article nor shall any such person be issued an identification card by the Committee who has within three years of the date of application for an identification card been convicted of, plead guilty or nolo contendere, or forfeited bond in any State or federal court for a felony or any violation of the North Carolina Structural Pest Control Act or any regulation promulgated by the Committee. This provision shall not apply to any person whose citizenship has been restored as provided by law.

(b3)   No person or business shall advertise as a contractor for structural pest control services nor actually contract for such services unless that person or business advertises or contracts in the name of the company shown on the license certificate of the licensee or identification card of the certified applicator who will perform the services.

(c)   Notwithstanding any other provision of this law, the Committee may adopt rules to provide for the issuance of licenses, certified applicator's cards, and registered technician's identification cards with staggered expiration dates and may prorate renewal fees on a monthly basis to implement such rules. (1955, c. 1017; 1957, c. 1243, s. 4; 1967, c. 1184, s. 10; 1973, c. 47, s. 2; c. 556, s. 10; 1975, c. 570, s. 16; 1981, c. 495, s. 2; 1987, c. 368, s. 3; 1989, c. 544, s. 16; c. 725, s. 7; 1991, c. 636, s. 7; 1999-381, s. 9; 2010-31, s. 11.2(b); 2011-145, s. 31.8(b).)

§ 106-65.32. Administrative Procedure Act applicable.

A denial, suspension, or revocation of a license, certified applicator card, or identification card under this Article shall be made in accordance with Chapter 150B of the General Statutes. (1955, c. 1017; 1957, c. 1243, s. 5; 1967, c. 1184, s. 11; 1973, c. 556, s. 11; 1975, c. 570, s. 17; 1987, c. 827, s. 29.)

§ 106-65.33. Violation of Article, falsification of records, or misuse of registered pesticide a misdemeanor.

(a)   Any person who shall be adjudged to have violated any provision of this Article or who falsifies any records required to be kept by this Article or by the rules and regulations pursuant to this Article or who uses a registered pesticide in a manner inconsistent with its labeling shall be guilty of a Class 2 misdemeanor. In addition, if any person continues to violate or further violates any provision of this Article after written notice from the Committee, the court may determine that each day during which the violation continued or is repeated constitutes a separate violation subject to the foregoing penalties.

(b) Nothing in this Article shall be construed to require the Committee or the Commissioner to initiate, or attempt to initiate, any criminal or administrative proceedings under this Article for a minor violation of this Article whenever the Committee or Commissioner determines that the public interest will be adequately served in the circumstances by a suitable written notice or warning. (1955, c. 1017; 1957, c. 1243, s. 6; 1967, c. 1184, s. 12; 1977, c. 231, s. 11; 1993, c. 539, s. 740; 1994, Ex. Sess., c. 24, s. 14(c); 1999-381, s. 10.)

§ 106-65.34. Repealed by Session Laws 1967, c. 1184, s. 13.

§ 106-65.35. Repealed by Session Laws 1973, c. 556, s. 12.

§ 106-65.36. Reciprocity; intergovernmental cooperation.

The Committee may cooperate or enter into formal agreements with any other agency of this State or its subdivisions or with any agency of any other state or of the federal government for the purpose of enforcing any of the provisions of this Article. (1973, c. 556, s. 13.)

§ 106-65.37. Financial responsibility.

(a) The Committee may require by regulation from a licensee or certified applicator or an applicant for a license or certified applicator's identification card under this Article evidence of his financial ability to properly indemnify persons suffering from the use or application of pesticides in the form of liability insurance or other means acceptable to the Committee. The amount of this insurance or financial ability shall be determined by the Committee.

(b) Any regulation adopted by the Committee pursuant to G.S. 106-65.29 to implement this section may provide for such conditions, limitations and requirements concerning the financial responsibility required by this section as the Committee deems necessary including but not limited to notice or reduction or cancellation of coverage and deductible provisions. Such regulations may classify financial responsibility requirements according to the separate license classifications and subclassifications as may be prescribed by the Committee. (1975, c. 570, s. 18.)

§ 106-65.38. Disposition of fees and charges.

Except as otherwise provided in G.S. 106-65.41, all fees and charges received by the Division under this Article shall be deposited in the Department of Agriculture and Consumer Services General Fund Budget for the purpose of administration and enforcement of this Article, with proper approved accounting procedures accounting for all expenditures and receipts. (1977, c. 231, s. 12; 1997-261, s. 109; 1998-215, s. 5(b).)

§ 106-65.39. Judicial enforcement.

The commissioner may apply to either the superior or district court for an injunction to prevent and restrain violations of this Article and the rules and regulations adopted under this Article, provided however, that the district court shall have original jurisdiction to hear and determine alleged misdemeanor violations of the Article and the rules and regulations of the committee. (1977, c. 231, s. 13; 1981, c. 836.)

§ 106-65.40. City privilege license tax prohibited.

A city, as defined in G.S. 160A-1(2), may not levy a privilege license tax on persons engaged in a business licensed under this Article. (1983, c. 193.)

§ 106-65.41. Civil penalties.

A civil penalty of not more than two thousand dollars ($2,000) may be assessed by the Committee against any person for any one or more of the causes set forth in G.S. 106-65.28(a)(1) through (12) and G.S. 106-65.28(a)(14) and (15), or who violates or directly causes a violation of any provision of this Article or any rule adopted pursuant to this Article. In determining the amount of any penalty, the Committee shall consider the degree and extent of harm caused by the violation. No civil penalty may be assessed under this section unless the person has been given an opportunity for a hearing pursuant to Chapter 150B of the General Statutes. Assessments may be collected, following judicial review, if any, of the Committee's final decision imposing the assessment, in any lawful manner for the collection of a debt.

The clear proceeds of civil penalties assessed pursuant to this section shall be remitted to the Civil Penalty and Forfeiture Fund in accordance with G.S. 115C-457.2. (1987, c. 368, s. 1; 1989, c. 725, s. 8; 1998-215, s. 5(a); 1999-381, s. 11.)

Article 4D.

North Carolina Biological Organism Act.

§ 106-65.42. Short title.

This Article shall be known as the "North Carolina Biological Organism Act." (1973, c. 713, s. 2.)

§ 106-65.43. Purpose.

The purpose of this Article is to regulate the production, sale, use and distribution of biological organisms that may have an adverse effect on the environment. (1973, c. 713, s. 1.)

§ 106-65.44. Definitions.

For the purposes of this Article, unless the context clearly requires otherwise:

(1) The term "biological organism" means any plant, lower animal, virus or disease causal agent intended for release into the environment; or, an organism which affects the environment by its presence or absence.

(2) The term "Board" means North Carolina Board of Agriculture.

(3) The term "Commissioner" means the Commissioner of Agriculture of North Carolina or his designated agent or agents.

(4) The term "Division of Entomology" means the Division of the Department of Agriculture and Consumer Services. (1973, c. 713, s. 3; 1997-261, s. 30.)

§ 106-65.45. Authority of the Board to adopt regulations.

The Board of Agriculture is hereby authorized to adopt regulations to implement and carry out the purposes of this Article so as to protect the environment from detrimental importation, rearing, sale, and/or release of insects, parasites, predators and other biological organisms in North Carolina, and to protect organisms that are beneficial to man and/or his environment. No viable biological organism shall be brought into North Carolina, reared, collected, propagated or offered for sale or released except under such conditions as are prescribed by regulations adopted under the provisions of this Article. (1973, c. 713, s. 4.)

§ 106-65.46. Commissioner of Agriculture to enforce Article; further authority of Board.

It shall be the duty of the Commissioner to exercise the powers and duties imposed upon him by this Article and such regulations as shall be adopted under these provisions for the purpose of protecting the environment from adverse effects of biological organisms released into the environment of North Carolina and to protect beneficial biological organisms in the State. The Board is hereby authorized to cause importation, collection, release, destruction and propagation of beneficial organisms when such action is deemed to be in the best interest of North Carolina and its environment. The Board is authorized to promote and/or regulate businesses, persons or agencies engaged in the importation, collection, rearing, sales, release, or use of biological organisms. The Board is authorized to establish standards of positive identification, purity of culture or colony, freedom from disease and hyperparasites of biological organisms and to establish standards of competence and responsibility for the private practitioner engaged in the propagation, use, distribution, release or sale of biological organisms.

The Commissioner is hereby authorized to cause or cooperate in management or mitigation programs to be conducted against such plant, environmental, or nuisance pests as can be controlled in an economically, ecologically, and biologically sound manner. The Board is authorized to cause use of pesticides, parasites, predators, pheromones, genetic material, and other control techniques which are consistent with the pesticide, environmental and other laws applicable in the State of North Carolina.

The Commissioner shall have authority to designate such employees of the North Carolina Department of Agriculture and Consumer Services and/or to enter into cooperative agreements with other governmental agencies as may be needed to carry out the duties and exercise the powers provided by this Article. Persons collaborating with the Division of Entomology may also be designated by the Commissioner as agents for the purpose of this Article. (1973, c. 713, s. 5; 1997-261, s. 109.)

§ 106-65.47. Authority under other statutes not abrogated; memoranda of understanding.

The provisions of this Article shall in no way abrogate the authority as defined in other Articles of the General Statutes of the State of North Carolina as previously enacted. The Commissioner is hereby authorized to enter into memoranda of understanding with other State and federal agencies and individuals concerning biological organisms or pest mitigation programs when such action is desirable to ensure cooperation and prevent conflicts of interest. (1973, c. 713, s. 6.)

§ 106-65.48. Criminal penalties; violation of law or regulations.

If anyone shall interfere with or attempt to interfere with the Commissioner or any of his agents, while engaged in the performance of his duties under this Article, or shall violate any provision of this Article or any regulation of the Board of Agriculture adopted pursuant to this Article, he shall be guilty of a Class 3 misdemeanor. Each day's violation shall constitute a separate offense. (1973, c. 713, s. 7; 1993, c. 539, s. 741; 1994, Ex. Sess., c. 24, s. 14(c).)

§ 106-65.49. Article not applicable in certain cases.

The provisions of this Article and/or regulations promulgated hereunder shall not apply to:

(1) Any virus, serum, toxin, antitoxin, vaccine, blood, blood component or derivative, allergenic product, or other product propagated or manufactured and prepared at an establishment holding an unsuspended and unrevoked license issued pursuant to section 351 of the Public Health Service Act (42 U.S.C. section 262) and regulations promulgated thereunder;

(2) Any finished virus, serum, toxin, antitoxin, vaccine, blood, blood component or derivative, allergenic product or other biological product shipped prior to licensing for development or investigational purposes in compliance with the requirements of the Federal Food, Drug and Cosmetic Act (21 U.S.C. section 301 et seq.) or the Animal Virus, Serum, and Toxin Law of March 4, 1913 (37 Stat. 832; 21 U.S.C. section 151 et seq.), and rules and regulations promulgated thereunder; and

(3) Any etiological agent shipped in accordance with regulations promulgated under section 361 of the Public Health Service Act (42 U.S.C. section 264). (1973, c. 1091.)

§§ 106-65.50 through 106-65.54. Reserved for future codification purposes.

Article 4E.

Pest Control Compact.

§§ 106-65.55 through 106-65.61: Repealed by Session Laws 2013-265, s. 12, effective July 17, 2013.

§§ 106-65.62 through 106-65.66. Reserved for future codification purposes.

Article 4F.

Uniform Boll Weevil Eradication Act.

§ 106-65.67. Short title.

This Article may be cited as the Uniform Boll Weevil Eradication Act. (1975, c. 958, s. 1.)

§ 106-65.68. Declaration of policy.

The Anthonomus grandis Boheman, known as the boll weevil, is hereby declared to be a public nuisance, a pest, and a menace to the cotton industry. The purpose of this Article is to secure the eradication of the boll weevil. (1975, c. 958, s. 2.)

§ 106-65.69. Definitions.

As used in this Article, the following words shall have the meaning stated below, unless the context requires otherwise:

(1)   Boll Weevil. - Anthonomus grandis Boheman, the boll weevil, in any stage of development.

(2)   Certificate. - A document issued or authorized by the Commissioner indicating that a regulated article is not contaminated with boll weevils.

(3)   Commissioner. - The Commissioner of Agriculture of this State or any officer or employee of the Department of Agriculture and Consumer Services or designated cooperator to whom authority to act in his stead has been or hereafter may be delegated.

(4)   Cotton. - Any cotton plant or cotton plant product upon which the boll weevil is dependent for completion of any portion of its life cycle.

(5) Host. - Any plant or plant product upon which the boll weevil is dependent for completion of any portion of its life cycle.
(6) Infested. - Actually infested with a boll weevil or so exposed to infestation that it would be reasonable to believe that an infestation exists.

(7) Permit. - A document issued or authorized by the Commissioner to provide for the movement of regulated articles to restricted destinations for limited handling, utilization, or processing.

(8) Person. - Any individual, corporation, company, society, or association, or other business entity.

(9) Regulated Article. - Any article of any character carrying or capable of carrying the boll weevil, including, but not limited to cotton plants, seed cotton, other hosts, gin trash, and mechanical cotton pickers, as designated by regulations of the Commissioner. (1975, c. 958, s. 3; 1997-261, s. 31.)

§ 106-65.70. Cooperative programs authorized.

The Commissioner is hereby authorized and directed to carry out programs to destroy and eliminate boll weevils in this State. The Commissioner is authorized to cooperate with any agency of the federal government or any state contiguous to this State, any other agency in this State, or any person engaged in growing, processing, marketing, or handling cotton, or any group of such persons, in this State, in programs to effectuate the purposes of this Article, and may enter into written agreements to effectuate such purposes. Such agreements may provide for cost sharing, and for division of duties and responsibilities under this Article and may include other provisions generally to effectuate the purposes of this Article. (1975, c. 958, s. 4.)

§ 106-65.71. Entry of premises; eradication activities; inspections.

The Commissioner, or his authorized representative, shall have authority, as provided in this section, to enter cotton fields and other premises in order to carry out such activities, including but not limited to treatment with pesticides, monitoring, and destruction of growing cotton and/or other host plants, as may be necessary to carry out the provisions of this Article. The Commissioner, or his authorized representative, shall have authority to make inspection of any fields or premises in this State and any property located therein or thereon for the purpose of determining whether such property is infested with the boll weevil. Such inspection and other activities may be conducted at any hour with the permission of the owner or person in charge. If permission is denied the Commissioner or his authorized representative, such inspection and other activities may be conducted without a warrant with respect to any outdoor premises, if conducted in a reasonable manner between the hours of sunrise and sunset. Such inspections and other activities may be conducted in a reasonable manner, with a warrant, with respect to any premises. Any judge of this State may, within his territorial jurisdiction, and upon proper cause to believe that any cotton or other regulated article is in or upon any premises in this State, issue warrants for the purpose of conducting administrative inspections and other activities authorized by this Article. (1975, c. 958, s. 5.)

§ 106-65.72. Reports.

Every person growing cotton in this State shall furnish to the Commissioner, or his authorized representative, on forms supplied by the Commissioner, such information as the Commissioner may require, concerning the size and location of all commercial cotton fields and of noncommercial patches of cotton grown as ornamentals or for other purposes. (1975, c. 958, s. 6.)

§ 106-65.73. Quarantine.

The Commissioner is authorized to promulgate regulations, quarantining this State, or any portion thereof, and governing the storage or other handling in the quarantined areas of regulated articles and the movement of regulated articles into or from such areas, when he shall determine that such action is necessary, or reasonably appears necessary, to prevent or retard the spread of the boll weevil. The Commissioner is also authorized to promulgate regulations governing the movement of regulated articles from other states or portions thereof into this State when such state is known to be infested with the boll weevil. Before quarantining any area, the Commissioner shall hold a public hearing under such rules as he shall determine, at which hearing any interested party may appear and be heard either in person or by attorney: Provided, however, the Commissioner may promulgate regulations, imposing a temporary quarantine for a period not to exceed 60 days, during which time a public hearing, as herein provided, shall be held if it appears that a quarantine for more than 60 days will be necessary to prevent or retard the spread of the boll weevil. It shall be unlawful for any person to store or handle any regulated article in a quarantined area, or to move into or from a quarantined area any regulated article, except under such conditions as may be prescribed by the regulations promulgated by the Commissioner. (1975, c. 958, s. 7; 1977, c. 507, s. 1.)

§ 106-65.74. Authority to designate elimination zones; authority to prohibit planting of cotton and to require participation in eradication program.

The Commissioner, subject to the provisions of section 13 of this act [Session Laws 1975, chapter 958, section 13] is authorized to designate by regulation one or more areas of this State as "elimination zones" where boll weevil eradication programs will be undertaken. The Commissioner is authorized to promulgate reasonable regulations rearding areas where cotton cannot be planted within an elimination zone when he has reason to believe it will jeopardize the success of the program or present a hazard to public health or safety. The Commissioner is authorized to issue regulations prohibiting the planting of noncommercial cotton in such elimination zones, and requiring that all growers of commercial cotton in the elimination zones participate in a program of boll weevil eradication including cost sharing as prescribed in the regulations. Notice of such prohibition and requirement shall be given by publication for one day each week for three successive weeks in a newspaper having general circulation in the affected area. The Commissioner is authorized to set by regulation a reasonable schedule of penalty fees to be assessed when growers in designated "elimination zones" do not meet the requirements of (G.S. 106-65.73) and participation in cost sharing as prescribed by regulation. Such penalty fees shall not exceed a charge of twenty-five dollars ($25.00) per acre. When a grower fails to meet the requirements of regulations promulgated by the Commissioner, the Commissioner shall have authority in elimination zones to destroy cotton not in compliance with such regulations. (1975, c. 958, s. 8; 1977, c. 507, ss. 2, 3.)

§ 106-65.75. Authority for destruction or treatment of cotton in elimination zones; when compensation payable.

The Commissioner or his authorized representative shall have authority to destroy, or in his discretion, to treat with pesticides volunteer or other noncommercial cotton and to establish procedures for the purchase and destruction of commercial cotton in elimination zones when the Commissioner deems such action necessary to effectuate the purposes of this Article. No payment shall be made by the Commissioner to the owner or lessee for the destruction or injury of any cotton which was planted in an elimination zone after publication of notice as provided in G.S. 106-65.74, or which was otherwise handled in violation of this Article or the regulations adopted pursuant thereto. However, the Commissioner shall pay for losses resulting from the destruction of cotton which was planted in such zones prior to promulgation of such notice. (1975, c. 958, s. 9; 1977, c. 507, ss. 4, 5.)

§ 106-65.76. Authority to regulate pasturage, entry, and honeybee colonies in elimination zones and other areas.

The Commissioner is authorized to promulgate regulations restricting the pasturage of livestock, entry by persons, and location of honeybee colonies in any premises in an elimination zone which have been or are to be treated with pesticides or otherwise treated to cause the eradication of the boll weevil, or in any other area that may be affected by such treatments. (1975, c. 958, s. 10.)

§ 106-65.77. Rules and regulations.

The Commissioner shall have authority to adopt such other rules and regulations as he deems necessary to further effectuate the purposes of this Article. All rules and regulations issued under this Article shall be adopted and published in accordance with any additional requirements prescribed in this Article. (1975, c. 958, s. 11.)

§ 106-65.78. Penalties.

(a) Any person who shall violate any of the provisions of this Article or the regulations promulgated hereunder, or who shall alter, forge or counterfeit, or use without authority, any certificate or permit or other document provided for in this Article or in the regulations promulgated hereunder, shall be guilty of a Class 1 misdemeanor.

(b) Any person who shall, except in compliance with the regulations of the Commissioner, move any regulated article into this State from any other state which the Commissioner found in such regulations is infested by the boll weevil, shall be guilty of a Class 1 misdemeanor. (1975, c. 958, s. 12; 1993, c. 539, s. 742; 1994, Ex. Sess., c. 24, s. 14(c).)

§§ 106-65.79 through 106-65.83. Reserved for future codification purposes.

Article 4G.

Official Cotton Growers' Organization.

§ 106-65.84. Findings and purpose.

The General Assembly of North Carolina finds that due to the interstate nature of boll weevil infestation, it is necessary to secure the cooperation of cotton growers, other State governments and agencies of the federal government, in order to carry out a program of boll weevil suppression and eradication. The purpose of this Article is to provide for the certification of a cotton growers' organization to cooperate with State and federal agencies in the administration of cost-sharing programs for the eradication and suppression of the boll weevil (Anthonomus grandis Boheman) and other cotton pests. (1983, c. 136, s. 1.)

§ 106-65.85. Definitions.

As used in this Article:

(1) "Board" means the North Carolina Board of Agriculture.

(2) "Commissioner" means the Commissioner of Agriculture of the State of North Carolina.

(3) "Cotton grower" means any person who is engaged in and has an economic risk in the business of producing or causing to be produced, for market, cotton.

(4) "Department" means the North Carolina Department of Agriculture and Consumer Services. (1983, c. 136, s. 2; 1997-261, s. 109.)

§ 106-65.86. Certification by Board; requirements.

(a) The Board may certify a cotton growers' organization for the purpose of entering into agreements with the State of North Carolina, other states, the federal government and other parties as may be necessary to carry out the purposes of this Article.

(b) In order to be eligible for certification by the Board, the cotton growers' organization must demonstrate to the satisfaction of the Board that:

(1) It is a nonprofit organization and could qualify as a tax-exempt organization under section 501(a) of the Internal Revenue Code of 1954 (26 USC 501(a));

(2) Membership in the organization shall be open to all cotton growers in this State;

(3) The organization shall have only one class of members with each member entitled to only one vote;

(4) The organization's board of directors shall be composed of:

a. Two cotton growers from this State being appointed by the Commissioner, with the consent of the Board; and

b. One representative of State government from this State, appointed by the Commissioner, with the consent of the Board.

(5) All books and records of account and minutes of proceedings of the organization shall be available for inspection or audit by the Commissioner or his representative at any reasonable time; and

(6)   Employees or agents of the growers' organization who handle funds of the organization shall be adequately bonded. (1983, c. 136, s. 3.)

§ 106-65.87. Certification; revocation.

(a)   Upon determination by the Board that the organization meets the requirements of the preceding section, the Board shall certify the organization as the official cotton growers' organization. Such certification shall be for the purposes of this Article only, and shall not affect other organizations or associations of cotton growers established for other purposes.

(b)   The Board shall certify only one such organization; provided, that the Board may revoke the certification of the organization if at any time the organization shall fail to meet the requirements of this Article. (1983, c. 136, s. 4.)

§ 106-65.88. Referendum; assessments.

(a)   At the request of the certified organization, the Board shall authorize a referendum among cotton growers upon the question of whether an assessment shall be levied upon cotton growers in the State to offset, in whole or in part, the cost of boll weevil or other cotton pest eradication and suppression programs authorized by this Article or by any other law of this State.

(b)   The assessment levied under this Article shall be based upon the number of acres of cotton planted. The amount of the assessment, the period of time for which it shall be levied, and the geographical area to be covered by the assessment shall be determined by the Board.

(c)   All affected cotton growers shall be entitled to vote in any such referendum and the Board shall determine any questions of eligibility to vote.

(d)   If at least two-thirds of those voting vote in favor of the assessment, then the assessment shall be collected by the Department from the affected cotton growers.

(e)   The assessments collected by the Department under this Article shall be promptly remitted to the certified organization under such terms and conditions as the Commissioner shall deem necessary to ensure that such assessments are used in a sound program of eradication or suppression of the boll weevil or other cotton pests.

(f)   The certified organization shall provide to the Department an annual audit of its accounts performed by a certified public accountant.

(g)   For the purposes of the State Budget Act, Chapter 143C of the General Statutes, the assessments collected by the Department under this Article shall not be "State funds". (1983, c. 136, s. 5; 2006-203, s. 25.)

§ 106-65.89. Agreements.

The Board may authorize the Department to enter into agreements with the certified organization, other state governments, the federal government and individual cotton growers as may be necessary to carry out the purposes of this Article. (1983, c. 136, s. 6.)

§ 106-65.90. Failure to pay assessments.

(a)   A cotton grower who fails to pay, when due and upon reasonable notice, any assessment levied under this Article, shall be subject to a penalty of not more than twenty-five dollars ($25.00) per acre, as established in the Board's regulations.

(b)   A cotton grower who fails to pay all assessments, including penalties, within 30 days of notice of penalty, shall destroy any cotton plants growing on his acreage which is subject to the assessment. Any such cotton plants which are not destroyed shall be deemed to be a public nuisance. The Commissioner may apply to a court of competent jurisdiction to abate and prevent such nuisance. Upon judgment and order of the court, such nuisance shall be condemned and destroyed in the manner directed by the court. The grower shall be liable for all court costs and fees, and other proper expenses incurred in the enforcement of this section.

(c)   In addition to any other remedies for the collection of assessments, including penalties, the Department of Agriculture and Consumer Services has a lien upon cotton subject to such assessments. Provided, that any buyer of cotton shall take free of such lien if he has not received written notice of the lien from the Department or if he has paid for such cotton by a check in which the Department is named as joint payee. In any action to enforce the lien, the burden shall be upon the Department to prove that the buyer of cotton received written notice of the lien. A buyer of cotton other than a person buying cotton from the grower takes free of the lien created herein. (1983, c. 136, s. 7; 1987, c. 293; 1997-261, s. 109.)

§ 106-65.91. Regulations.

The Board of Agriculture may adopt such regulations as are necessary to carry out the purposes of this Article. (1983, c. 136, s. 8.)

§ 106-65.92: Reserved for future codification purposes.

§ 106-65.93: Reserved for future codification purposes.

§ 106-65.94: Reserved for future codification purposes.

Article 4H.

Bedding.

§ 106-65.95. Definitions.

The following definitions shall apply throughout this Article:

(1)   "Bedding" means any mattress, upholstered spring, sleeping bag, pad, comforter, cushion, pillow, decorative pillow, and any other padded or stuffed item designed to be or commonly used for reclining or sleeping. This definition includes dual purpose furniture such as studio couches and sofa beds. The term "mattress" does not include water bed liners, bladders or cylinders unless they contain padding or stuffing. The term "mattress" also does not include quilts and comforters made principally by hand sewing or stitching in a home or community workshop.

(2) "Itinerant vendor" means a person who sells bedding from a movable conveyance.

(3) "Manufacture" means the making of bedding out of new materials.

(4) "New material" means any material or article that has not been used for any other purpose and by-products of industry that have not been in human use.

(5) "Previously used material" means any material of which previous use has been made, but manufacturing processes shall not be considered previous use.

(6) "Renovate" means the reworking or remaking of used bedding or the making of bedding from previously used materials, except for the renovator's own personal use or the use of the renovator's immediate family.

(7) "Sanitize" means treatment of secondhand bedding or previously used materials to be used in renovating for the destruction of pathogenic microorganisms and arthropods and the removal of dirt and filth.

(8) "Secondhand bedding" means any bedding of which prior use has been made.

(9) "Sell" or "sold" means sell, have to sell, give away in connection with a sale, delivery or consignment; or possess with intent to sell, deliver or consign in sale. (1937, c. 298, s. 1; 1957, c. 1357, s. 1; 1959, c. 619; 1965, c. 579, s. 1; 1983, c. 891, s. 2; 1987, c. 456, s. 1; 1991, c. 223, s. 1; 1993 (Reg. Sess., 1994), c. 647, s. 5; 2011-145, s. 13.3(v), (w).)

§ 106-65.96. Sanitizing.

(a) No person shall sell any renovated bedding or secondhand bedding unless it is sanitized in accordance with rules adopted by the Board of Agriculture.

(b) A sanitizing apparatus or process shall not be used for sanitizing bedding or material required to be sanitized under this Article until the apparatus is approved by the Department of Agriculture and Consumer Services.

(c) A person who sanitizes bedding shall attach to the bedding a yellow tag containing information required by the rules of the Board of Agriculture.

(d) A person who sanitizes material or bedding for another person shall keep a complete record of the kind of material and bedding which has been sanitized. The record shall be subject to inspection by the Department of Agriculture and Consumer Services.

(e) A person who receives used bedding for renovation or storage shall attach to the bedding a tag on which is legibly written the date of receipt and the name and address of the owner. (1937, c. 298, s. 2; 1957, c. 1357, s. 1; 1973, c. 476, s. 128; 1983, c. 891, s. 2; 1987, c. 456, s. 2; 2011-145, s. 13.3(v), (x).)

§ 106-65.97. Manufacture regulated.

All materials used in the manufacture of bedding in this State or used in manufactured bedding to be sold in this State shall be free of toxic materials and shall be made from new materials. (1937, c. 298, s. 3; 1951, c. 929, s. 2; 1957, c. 1357, s. 1; 1959, c. 619; 1965, c. 579, s. 2; 1971, c. 371, ss. 1, 2; 1973, c. 476, s. 128; 1983, c. 891, s. 2; 2011-145, s. 13.3(v).)

§ 106-65.98. Storage of used materials.

No establishment shall store any unsanitized previously used materials in the same room with bedding or materials that are new or have been sanitized unless the new or sanitized bedding or materials are completely segregated from the unsanitized materials in a manner approved by the rules of the Board of Agriculture. (1937, c. 298, s. 3; 1951, c. 929, s. 2; 1957, c. 1357, s. 1; 1959, c. 619; 1965, c. 579, s. 2; 1971, c. 371, ss. 1, 2; 1973, c. 476, s. 128; 1983, c. 891, s. 2; 2011-145, s. 13.3(v), (y).)

§ 106-65.99. Tagging requirements.

(a) A tag of durable material approved by the Board of Agriculture shall be sewed securely to all bedding. The tag shall be at least two inches by three inches in size.

(b) The following shall be plainly stamped or printed upon the tag with ink in English:

(1) The name and kind of material or materials used to fill the bedding which are listed in the order of their predominance;

(2) A registration number obtained from the Department of Agriculture and Consumer Services; and

(3) In letters at least one-eighth inch high the words "made of new material", if the bedding contains no previously used material; or the words "made of previously used materials", if the bedding contains any previously used material; or the word "secondhand" on any bedding which has been used but not remade.

(4) Repealed by Session Laws 1987, c. 456, s. 4.

(c) A white tag shall be used for manufactured bedding and a yellow tag for renovated or sanitized bedding.

(d) The tag must be sewed to the outside covering before the filling material has been inserted. No trade name, advertisement nor any other wording shall appear on the tag. (1937, c. 298, ss. 2, 3; 1951, c. 929, s. 2; 1957, c. 1357, s. 1; 1959, c. 619; 1965, c. 579, s. 2; 1971, c. 371, ss. 1, 2; 1973, c. 476 s. 128; 1983, c. 891, s. 2; 1987, c. 456, ss. 3, 4; 2011-145, s. 13.3(v), (z).)

§ 106-65.100. Altering tags prohibited.

No person, other than one purchasing bedding for personal use or a representative of the Department of Agriculture and Consumer Services shall remove, deface or alter the tag required by this Article. (1937, c. 298, s. 4; 1957, c. 1357, s. 1; 1973, c. 476, s. 128; 1983, c. 891, s. 2; 2011-145, s. 13.3(v), (aa).)

§ 106-65.101. Selling regulated.

(a) No person shall sell any bedding in this State (whether manufactured within or without this State) which has not been manufactured, tagged, and labeled in the manner required by this Article and which does not otherwise comply with the provisions of this Article.

(b) This Article shall not apply to bedding sold by the owner and previous user from the owner's home directly to a purchaser for the purchaser's own personal use unless the bedding has been exposed to an infectious or communicable disease.

(c) Possession of any bedding in any store, warehouse, itinerant vendor's conveyance or place of business, other than a private home, hotel or other place where these articles are ordinarily used, shall constitute prima facie evidence that the item is possessed with intent to sell. No secondhand bedding shall be possessed with intent to sell for a period exceeding 60 days unless it has been sanitized. (1957, c. 1357, s. 1; 1973, c. 476, s. 128; 1983, c. 891, s. 2; 1987, c. 456, s. 5; 2011-145, s. 13.3(v), (bb).)

§ 106-65.102. Registration numbers.

All persons manufacturing or sanitizing bedding in this State or manufacturing bedding to be sold in this State shall apply for a registration number on a form prescribed by the Commissioner of Agriculture. Upon receipt of the completed application and applicable fees, the Department of Agriculture and Consumer Services shall issue to the applicant a certificate of registration showing the person's name and address, registration number and other pertinent information required by the rules of the Board of Agriculture. (1937, c. 298, s. 7; 1951, c. 929, s. 1; 1957, c. 1357, s. 1; 1959, c. 619; 1971, c. 371, s. 3; 1973, c. 476, s. 128; 1983, c. 891, s. 2; 1987, c. 456, s. 6; 2011-145, s. 13.3(v), (cc).)

§ 106-65.103. Payment of fees; licenses.

(a) The Department of Agriculture and Consumer Services shall administer and enforce this Article. A person who has done business in this State throughout the preceding calendar year shall obtain a license by paying a fee to the Department of Agriculture and Consumer Services in an amount determined by the total number of bedding units manufactured, sold, or sanitized in this State by the applicant during the calendar year immediately preceding, at the rate of five and two tenths cents (5.2¢) per bedding unit. However, if this amount is less than fifty dollars ($50.00), a minimum fee of fifty dollars ($50.00) shall be paid to the Department of Agriculture and Consumer Services.

(b)   A person who has not done business in this State throughout the preceding calendar year shall obtain a license by paying an initial fee to the Department of Agriculture and Consumer Services in the amount of seven hundred twenty dollars ($720.00) for the first year in which business is done in this State, prorated in accordance with the quarter of the calendar year in which the person begins doing business. After submission of proof of business volume in accordance with subsection (h) of this section for the part of the preceding calendar year in which the person did business in this State, the Department of Agriculture and Consumer Services shall determine the amount of fee for which the person is responsible for that time period by using a rate of five and two tenths cents (5.2¢) for each bedding unit. However, if this amount is less than fifty dollars ($50.00), then the amount of the fee for which the person is responsible shall be fifty dollars ($50.00). If the person's initial payment is more than the amount of the fee for which the person is responsible, the Department of Agriculture and Consumer Services shall make a refund or adjustment to the cost of the fee due for the next year in the amount of the difference. If the initial payment is less than the amount of the fee for which the person is responsible, the person shall pay the difference to the Department of Agriculture and Consumer Services.

(c)   Payments, refunds, and adjustments shall be made in accordance with rules adopted by the Board of Agriculture.

(d)   Upon payment of the fees charged pursuant to subsections (c) and (d), or the first installment thereof as provided by rules adopted by the Board of Agriculture, the Department of Agriculture and Consumer Services shall issue a license to the person. Licenses shall be kept conspicuously posted in the place of business of the licensee at all times. The Commissioner of Agriculture may suspend a license for a maximum of six months for two or more serious violations of this Article or of the rules of the Board of Agriculture within any 12-month period.

(e)   A maximum fee of seven hundred fifty dollars ($750.00) shall be charged for units of bedding manufactured in this State but not sold in this State.

(f) For the sole purpose of computing fees for which a person is responsible, the following definitions shall apply: One mattress is defined as one bedding unit; one upholstered spring is defined as one bedding unit; one pad is defined as one bedding unit; one sleeping bag is defined as one bedding unit; five comforters, pillows or decorative pillows are defined as one bedding unit; and any other item is defined as one bedding unit.

(g) An application for license must be submitted on a form prescribed by the Commissioner of Agriculture. No license may be issued to a person unless the person complies with the rules of the Board of Agriculture governing the granting of licenses.

(h) The Board of Agriculture shall adopt rules for the proper enforcement of this section. The rules shall include provisions governing the type and amount of proof which must be submitted by the applicant to the Department of Agriculture and Consumer Services in order to establish the number of bedding units that were, during the preceding calendar year:

(1) Manufactured and sold in this State;

(2) Manufactured outside of this State and sold in this State; and

(3) Manufactured in this State but not sold in this State.

(i) The Board of Agriculture may provide in its rules for additional proof of the number of bedding units sold during the preceding calendar year when it has reason to believe that the proof submitted by the manufacturer is incomplete, misleading or incorrect. (1937, c. 298, s. 5; 1949, c. 636; 1957, c. 1357, s. 1; 1965, c. 579, s. 3; 1967, c. 771; 1971, c. 371, ss. 4-7; 1973, s. 476, s. 128; 1983, c. 891, s. 2; 1987, c. 456, s. 7; 2011-145, s. 13.3(v), (dd).)

§ 106-65.104. Bedding Law Account.

The Bedding Law Account is established as a nonreverting account within the Department of Agriculture and Consumer Services. All fees collected under this Article shall be credited to the Account and applied to the following costs:

(1) Salaries and expenses of inspectors and other employees who enforce this Article.

(2) Expenses directly connected with the enforcement of this Article, including attorney's fees, which are expressly authorized to be incurred by the Commissioner of Agriculture without authority from any other source when in the opinion of the Commissioner of Agriculture it is advisable to employ an attorney to prosecute any persons. (1937, c. 298, s. 5; 1949, c. 636; 1957, c. 1357, s. 1; 1965, c. 579, s. 3; 1967, c. 771; 1971, c. 371, ss. 4-7; 1973, c. 476, s. 128; 1983, c. 891, s. 2; c. 913, s. 23; 1991 (Reg. Sess., 1992), c. 1039, s. 20.2; 2011-145, s. 13.3(v), (ee).)

§ 106-65.105. Enforcement by the Department of Agriculture and Consumer Services.

(a) The Department of Agriculture and Consumer Services shall enforce the provisions of this Article and the rules adopted by the Board of Agriculture.

(b) The Commissioner of Agriculture may prohibit sale and place an "off sale" tag on any bedding which is not made, sanitized, or tagged as required by this Article and the rules of the Board of Agriculture. The bedding shall not be sold or otherwise removed until the violation is remedied and the Commissioner of Agriculture has reinspected it and removed the "off sale" tag.

(c) A person supplying material to a bedding manufacturer shall furnish an itemized invoice of all furnished material. Each material entering into willowed or other mixtures shall be shown on the invoice. The bedding manufacturer shall keep the invoice on file for one year subject to inspection by the Department of Agriculture and Consumer Services.

(d) When the Commissioner of Agriculture has reason to believe that bedding is not tagged or filled as required by this Article, the Commissioner of Agriculture shall have authority to open a seam of the bedding to examine the filling, and, if unable after this examination to determine if the filling is of the kind stated on the tag, shall have the authority to examine purchase or other records necessary to determine definitely the kind of material used in the bedding. The Commissioner of Agriculture shall have authority to seize and hold for evidence any records and any bedding or bedding material which in the opinion of the Commissioner of Agriculture is made, possessed or offered for sale in violation of this Article or the rules of the Board of Agriculture. The Commissioner of

Agriculture shall have authority to take a sample of any bedding or bedding material for the purpose of examination or for evidence.

(e) The Commissioner of Agriculture shall have the right of entry upon the premises of any place where entry is necessary to enforce the provisions of this Article or the rules adopted by the Board of Agriculture. If consent for entry is not obtained, an administrative search and inspection warrant shall be obtained pursuant to G.S. 15-27.2. (1937, c. 298, s. 6; 1957, c. 1357, s. 1; 1971, c. 371, s. 8; 1973, c. 476, s. 128; 1983, c. 891, s. 2; 1987, c. 456, s. 8; 2011-145, s. 13.3(v), (ff); 2013-155, s. 25.)

§ 106-65.106. Exemptions for blind persons and State institutions.

(a) In cases where bedding is manufactured, sanitized or renovated in a plant or place of business which has qualified as a nonprofit agency for the blind or severely handicapped under P.L. 92-28, as amended, the responsible person shall satisfy the provisions of this Article and the rules of the Board of Agriculture. However, the responsible persons at these plants or places of business shall not be required to pay fees in accordance with G.S. 106-65.103.

(b) State institutions engaged in the manufacture, renovation or sanitizing of bedding for their own use or that of another State institution are exempted from all provisions of this Article. (1937, c. 298, s. 11; 1957, c. 1357, s. 1; 1971, c. 371, s. 9; 1983, c. 891, s. 2; 1987, c. 456, s. 9; 2011-145, s. 13.3(v), (gg).)

§ 106-65.107. Rules.

The Board shall adopt rules required by this Article in order to protect the public health. (1983, c. 891, s. 2; 2011-145, s. 13.3(v), (hh).)

Article 5.

Seed Cotton and Peanuts.

§§ 106-66 through 106-67: Repealed by Session Laws 1987, c. 244, s. 1(c).

Article 5A.

Marketing of Farmers Stock Peanuts.
§§ 106-67.1 through 106-67.8: Repealed by Session Laws 1983, c. 248, s. 1.

Article 6.

Cottonseed Meal.

§§ 106-68 through 106-78: Repealed by Session Laws 1987, c. 244, s. 1(d).

Article 7.

Pulverized Limestone and Marl.

§§ 106-79 through 106-80: Repealed by Session Laws 1987, c. 244, s. 1(e).

Article 8.

Sale, etc., of Agricultural Liming Material, etc.

§§ 106-81 through 106-92: Repealed by Session Laws 1981, c. 284.

Article 8A.

Sale of Agricultural Liming Materials and Landplaster.

§ 106-92.1. Title of Article.

This Article shall be known as the North Carolina Agricultural Liming Materials and Landplaster Act. (1979, c. 590.)

§ 106-92.2. Purpose of Article.

The purpose of this Article shall be to assure the manufacturer, distributor, and consumer of the correct quality and quantity of all agricultural liming materials and landplaster sold in this State. (1979, c. 590.)

§ 106-92.3. Definitions of terms.

For the purpose of this Article:

(1)   "Agricultural liming materials" means oxides, hydroxides, silicates or carbonates of calcium and/or magnesium compounds capable of neutralizing soil acidity.

(1a)   "Agricultural liming material and fertilizer mixture" means any agricultural liming material combined with a single fertilizer element or single plant nutrient.

(2)   "Brand" means the term, designation, trademark, product name or other specific designation truly descriptive of the product under which individual agricultural liming material is offered for sale.

(3)   "Bulk" means in nonpackaged form.

(4)   "Burnt lime" means a material, made from limestone which consists essentially of calcium oxide or combination of calcium oxide with magnesium oxide.

(5)   "Calcitic limestone" means limestone which contains less than six percent (6%) magnesium from magnesium carbonate.

(6)   "Calcium carbonate equivalent" means the acid neutralizing capacity of an agricultural liming material expressed as weight percentage of calcium carbonate.

(7) "Dolomitic limestone" means limestone having a minimum of six percent (6%) magnesium from magnesium carbonate.

(8) "Fineness" means the percentage by weight of the material which will pass U.S. Standard sieves of specified sizes.

(9) "Hydrated lime" means a material, made from burnt lime, which consists essentially of calcium hydroxide or a combination of calcium hydroxide with magnesium oxide and/or magnesium hydroxide.

(10) "Industrial by-product liming material" means any industrial waste or by-product containing calcium or calcium and magnesium in forms that will neutralize soil acidity.

(11) "Label" means any written or printed matter on or attached to the package or on the delivery ticket which accompanies bulk shipments.

(12) "Landplaster" means a material containing calcium sulfate.

(13) "Limestone" means a material consisting essentially of calcium carbonate or a combination of calcium carbonate with magnesium carbonate capable of neutralizing soil acidity.

(14) "Marl" means a granular or loosely consolidated earth-like material composed largely of sea shell fragments and calcium carbonate.

(15) "Percent" or "percentage" which means by weight.

(16) "Person" means individual, partnership, association, firm or corporation.

(17) "Sale" means any transfer of title or possession, or both, exchange or barter of tangible personal property, conditional or otherwise for a consideration paid or to be paid, and this shall include any of said transactions whereby title or ownership is to pass and shall further mean and include any bailment, loan, lease, rental or license to use or consume tangible personal property for a consideration paid in which possession of said property passes to bailee, borrower, lessee, or licensee.

(18) "Sell" means the alienation, exchange, transfer or contract for such transfer of property for a fixed price in money or its equivalent.

(19) "Suspension lime" means a product made by mixing agricultural liming materials with water and a suspending agent.

(20) "Ton" means a net weight of 2,000 pounds avoirdupois.

(21) "Weight" means the weight of undried material as offered for sale. (1979, c. 590; 1981, c. 449, s. 2.)

§ 106-92.4. Enforcing official.

This Article shall be administered by the Commissioner of Agriculture of the State of North Carolina, or his authorized agent, hereinafter referred to as the "Commissioner." (1979, c. 590.)

§ 106-92.5. Labeling.

(a) Agricultural liming materials sold, offered for sale or distributed in the State shall have affixed to each package in a conspicuous manner on the outside thereof, a plainly printed, stamped or otherwise marked label, tag or statement, or in the case of bulk sales, a delivery slip, setting forth at least the following information:

(1) The name and principal office address of the manufacturer or distributor.

(2) The brand or trade name truly descriptive of the material.

(3) The identification of the product as to the type of the agricultural liming material.

(4) The net weight of the agricultural liming material.

(5) The minimum percentages of calcium and magnesium.

(6) Calcium carbonate equivalent as determined by methods prescribed by the Association of Official Analytical Chemists. Minimum calcium carbonate equivalent shall be prescribed by regulation.

(7) The minimum percent by weight passing through U. S. Standard sieves as prescribed by regulations.

(b) Landplaster sold, offered for sale or distributed in this State shall have affixed to each package in a conspicuous manner on the outside thereof, a plainly printed, stamped or otherwise marked label, tag or statement, or in the case of bulk sales, a delivery slip, setting forth at least the following information:

(1) The name and address of the manufacturer or distributor guaranteeing the registration.

(2) The brand or trade name of the material.

(3) The net weight.

(4) The guaranteed analysis showing the minimum percentage of calcium sulfate. (1979, c. 590.)

§ 106-92.6. Prohibited acts.

(a) Agricultural liming material or landplaster shall not be sold or offered for sale or distributed in this State unless it complies with provisions of this law or regulations.

(b) Agricultural liming material or landplaster shall not be sold or offered for sale in this State which contains toxic materials in quantities injurious to plants or animals.

(c) It is unlawful to make any false or misleading statement or representation with regard to any agricultural liming material or landplaster product offered for sale, sold, or distributed in this State, or to use any misleading or deceptive trademark or brand name in connection therewith. The Commissioner may refuse, suspend, revoke, or terminate the registration of any such product for any violation of this section. (1979, c. 590; 1993, c. 144, s. 2.)

§ 106-92.7. Registration of brands.

(a) Each separately identified product shall be registered before being sold, offered for sale, or distributed in this State. Registration fee shall be twenty-five dollars ($25.00) for each separately identified product in packages of 10 pounds or less. For each other separately identified product registration fee shall be five dollars ($5.00). The application for registration shall be submitted to the Commissioner on forms furnished by the Commissioner and shall be accompanied by the appropriate registration fee. Upon approval by the Commissioner, a copy of the registration shall be furnished to the applicant. All registrations expire on June 30 of each year.

(b) A distributor shall not be required to register any brand of agricultural liming material or landplaster which is already registered under this Article by another person, providing the label does not differ in any respect.

(c) In determining the acceptability of any product for registration, the Commissioner may require proof of claims made for the product. If no specific claims are made, the Commissioner may require proof of usefulness and value of the product. As evidence of proof, the Commissioner may rely on experimental data furnished by the applicant and may require that the data be developed by a recognized research or experimental institution. The Commissioner may further require that the data be developed from tests conducted under conditions identical to or closely related to those present in North Carolina. The Commissioner may reject any data not developed under those conditions and may rely on advice from sources such as the Cooperative Extension Service of North Carolina State University. (1979, c. 590; 1993, s. 144, s. 1.)

§ 106-92.8. Tonnage fees: reporting system.

For the purpose of defraying expenses connected with the registration, inspection and analysis of the materials coming under this Article, each manufacturer or registrant shall pay to the Department of Agriculture and Consumer Services tonnage fees in addition to registration fees as follows: for agricultural liming material, fifty cents (50¢) per ton; for landplaster, fifty cents (50¢) per ton; excepting that these fees shall not apply to materials which are sold to fertilizer manufacturers for the sole purpose for use in the manufacture of fertilizer or to materials when sold in packages of 10 pounds or less.

Any manufacturer, importer, jobber, firm, corporation or person who distributes materials coming under this Article in this State shall make application for a permit to report the materials sold and pay the tonnage fees as set forth in this section.

The Commissioner of Agriculture shall grant such permits on the following conditions: The applicant's agreement that he will keep such records as may be necessary to indicate accurately the tonnage of liming materials, etc., sold in the State and his agreement for the Commissioner or this authorized representative to examine such records to verify the tonnage statement. The registrant shall report quarterly and pay the applicable tonnage fees quarterly, on or before the tenth day of October, January, April, and July of each year. The report and payment shall cover the tonnage of liming materials, etc., sold during the preceding quarter. The report shall be on forms furnished by the Commissioner. If the report is not filed and the tonnage fees paid by the last day of the month in which it is due, or if the report be false, the amount due shall bear a penalty of ten percent (10%) which shall be added to the tonnage fees due. If the report is not filed and the tonnage fees paid within 60 days of the date due, or if the report or tonnage be false, the Commissioner may revoke the permit and cancel the registration. (1979, c. 590; 1997-261, s. 109; 2011-145, s. 31.9.)

§ 106-92.9. Report of tonnage.

(a)   Within 30 days following the expiration of registration each registrant shall submit on a form furnished or approved by the Commissioner an annual statement, setting forth by counties, the number of net tons of each agricultural liming material and landplaster sold by him for use in the State during the previous 12 month period.

(b)   The Commissioner shall publish and distribute annually, to each agricultural liming material and landplaster registrant and other interested persons a composite report showing the tons of agricultural liming material and landplaster sold in each county of the State. This report shall in no way divulge the operation of any registrant. (1979, c. 590.)

§ 106-92.10. Inspection, sampling, analysis.

(a) It shall be the duty of the Commissioner to sample, inspect, make analysis of, and test agricultural liming materials and landplaster distributed within this State as he may deem necessary to determine if such materials are in compliance with the provisions of this Article. The Commissioner is authorized to enter upon any public or private premises or carriers during regular business hours in order to have access to agricultural liming material and landplaster subject to the provisions of this Article, and regulations pertaining thereto, and to the records relating to their distribution.

(b) The methods of analysis and sampling shall be those approved by the State Chemist, and shall be guided by the Association of Official Analytical Chemists procedures.

(c) The results of official analysis of agricultural liming materials and portions of official samples may be distributed to the registrant by the Commissioner at least annually if requested. (1979, c. 590.)

§ 106-92.11. Deficiencies: refunds to consumer.

Should any of the agricultural liming and landplaster materials defined in this Article be found to be deficient in the components claimed by the manufacturer or registrant thereof, said manufacturer or registrant, upon official notification to [of] such deficiency by the Commissioner of Agriculture, shall, within 90 days, make refunds to the consumers of the deficient materials as follows:

In case of "agricultural liming material" if the deficiency is five percent (5%) of the guarantee or more, there shall be refunded an amount equal to three times the value of such deficiency and in case of "landplaster," for deficiencies in excess of one percent (1%) of the guarantee, there shall be refunded an amount equal to three times the value of the deficiency. Values shall be based on the selling price of said materials. When said consumers cannot be found within the above specified time, refunds shall be forwarded to the Commissioner of Agriculture, where said refund shall be held for payment to the proper consumer upon order of the Commissioner. If the consumer to whom the refund is due cannot be found within a period of one year, the clear proceeds of such refund shall be remitted to the Civil Penalty and Forfeiture Fund in accordance with G.S. 115C-457.2. (1979, c. 590; 1997-261, s. 109; 1998-215, s. 6.)

§ 106-92.12. "Stop sale" orders.

The Commissioner may issue and enforce a written or printed "stop sale, use, or removal" order to the owner or custodian of any lot of agricultural liming material or landplaster at a designated place when the Commissioner finds said material is being offered or exposed for sale in violation of any of the provisions of this Article until the law has been complied with and said violation has been otherwise legally disposed of by written authority. The Commissioner shall release the agricultural liming materials or landplaster so withdrawn, when the requirements of the provisions of this Article have been complied with and all costs and expense incurred in connection with the withdrawal have been paid.

If a manufacturer or registrant fails to make a refund as required by G.S. 106-92.11, the Commissioner may stop the sale of any agricultural liming materials or landplaster registered by the manufacturer or registrant and offered for sale in this State. (1979, c. 590; 1993, c. 144, s. 3.)

§ 106-92.13. Appeals from assessments and orders of Commissioner.

Nothing in this Article shall prevent any person from appealing to a court of competent jurisdiction from any assessment of penalty or other final order or ruling of the Commissioner or Board of Agriculture. (1979, c. 590.)

§ 106-92.14. Penalties for violations of this Article.

Any person convicted of violating any provision of this Article or the rules and regulations promulgated thereunder shall be guilty of a Class 3 misdemeanor and fined not less than two hundred dollars ($200.00) nor more than one thousand dollars ($1,000) in the discretion of the court. Nothing in this Article shall be construed as requiring the Commissioner or his authorized agent to report for prosecution or for the institution of seizure proceedings as a result of minor violations of the Article when he believes that the public interest will best be served by a suitable written warning. (1979, c. 590; 1993, c. 539, s. 743; 1994, Ex. Sess., c. 24, s. 14(c).)

§ 106-92.15. Declaration of policy.

The General Assembly hereby finds and declares that it is in the public interest that the State regulate the activities of those persons engaged in the business of preparing, or manufacturing agricultural liming material and landplaster in order to insure the manufacturer, distributor, and consumer of the correct quantity and quality of all said materials sold or offered for sale in this State. It shall therefore be the policy of this State to regulate the activities of those persons engaged in the business of preparing or manufacturing agricultural liming material and landplaster. (1979, c. 590.)

§ 106-92.16. Authority of Board of Agriculture to make rules and regulations.

Because legislation with regard to agricultural liming material and landplaster sold or offered for sale in this State must be adopted (adapted) to complex conditions and standards involving numerous details with which the General Assembly cannot deal directly and in order to effectuate the purposes and policies of the Article, and in order to insure the manufacturer, distributor, and consumer of the correct quality and quantity of all agricultural liming material and landplaster sold or offered for sale in this State, the Board of Agriculture shall have the authority to make rules and regulations with respect to:

(1) Defining a standard agricultural liming material in terms of neutralizing equivalents.

(2) Fineness of agricultural liming material.

(3) Form and order of labeling.

(4) Monetary penalties for deficiencies from guarantee.

(5) Monetary penalties for materials that do not meet screen guarantee. (1979, c. 590.)

§ 106-92.17. Lime and fertilizer mixtures.

The provisions of this Article shall apply to mixtures of agricultural liming material and fertilizer, except as follows:

(1) Such mixtures shall meet the labeling requirements of G.S. 106-92.5(a) in addition to providing information including, but not limited to, a guaranteed analysis of the fertilizer element or plant nutrient;

(2) The tonnage fee for such mixtures under G.S. 106-92.8 shall be twenty-five cents (25¢) per ton; and,

(3) The Board of Agriculture shall establish the allowable deficiency percentage and refund rate for such mixtures under G.S. 106-92.11. (1981, c. 449, s. 1.)

Article 9.

Commercial Feedingstuffs.

§§ 106-93 through 106-110. Repealed by Session Laws 1973, c. 771, s. 19.

Article 10.

Mixed Feed Oats.

§ 106-111: Repealed by Session Laws 1987, c. 244, s. 1(f).

Article 11.

Stock and Poultry Tonics.

§§ 106-112 through 106-119. Repealed by Session Laws 1975, c. 39.

Article 12.

Food, Drugs and Cosmetics.

§ 106-120. Title of Article.

This Article may be cited as the North Carolina Food, Drug and Cosmetic Act. (1939, c. 320, s. 1.)

§ 106-121. Definitions and general consideration.

For the purpose of this Article:

(1) The term "advertisement" means all representations disseminated in any manner or by any means, other than by labeling, for the purposes of inducing, or which are likely to induce, directly or indirectly, the purchase of food, drugs, devices or cosmetics.

(1a) The term "color" includes black, white, and intermediate grays.

(1b) The term "color additive" means a material which:

a. Is a dye, pigment, or other substance made by a process of synthesis or similar artifice, or extracted, isolated, or otherwise derived, with or without intermediate or final change of identity, from a vegetable, animal, mineral, or other source; or

b. When added or applied to a food, drug, or cosmetic, or to the human body or any part thereof, is capable (alone or through reaction with other substance) of imparting color thereto;

Provided, that such term does not apply to any pesticide chemical, soil or plant nutrient, or other agricultural chemical solely because of its effect in aiding, retarding, or otherwise affecting, directly or indirectly, the growth or other natural physiological process of produce of the soil and thereby affecting its color, whether before or after harvest.

(2) The term "Commissioner" means the Commissioner of Agriculture; the term "Department" means the Department of Agriculture and Consumer Services, and the term "Board" means the Board of Agriculture.

(2a) The term "consumer commodity" except as otherwise specifically provided by this subdivision means any food, drug, device, or cosmetic as those terms are defined by this Article. Such term does not include:

a. Any tobacco or tobacco product; or

b. Any commodity subject to packaging or labeling requirements imposed under the North Carolina Pesticide Law of 1971, Article 52, Chapter 143, of the General Statutes of North Carolina, or the provisions of the eighth paragraph under the heading "Bureau of Animal Industry" of the act of March 4, 1913 (37 Stat. 832-833; 21 U.S.C. 151-157) commonly known as the Virus-Serum Toxin Act; or

c. Any drug subject to the provisions of G.S. 106-134(13) or 106-134.1 of this Article or section 503(b)(1) or 506 of the federal act; or

d. Any beverage subject to or complying with packaging or labeling requirements imposed under the Federal Alcohol Administration Act (27 U.S.C., et seq.); or

e. Any commodity subject to the provisions of the North Carolina Seed Law, Article 31, Chapter 106 of the General Statutes of North Carolina.

(3) The term "contaminated with filth" applies to any food, drug, device or cosmetic not securely protected from dust, dirt, and as far as may be necessary by all reasonable means, from all foreign or injurious contaminations.

(4) The term "cosmetic" means

a. Articles intended to be rubbed, poured, sprinkled, or sprayed on, introduced into, or otherwise applied to the human body or any part thereof for cleansing, beautifying, promoting attractiveness, or altering the appearance, and

b. Articles intended for use as a component of any such articles, except that such terms shall not include soap.

(4a) The term "counterfeit drug" means a drug which, or the container or labeling of which, without authorization, bears the trademark, trade name or other identifying mark, imprint, or device, or any likeness thereof, of a drug manufacturer, processor, packer or distributor other than the person or persons who in fact manufactured, processed, packed or distributed such drug and which thereby falsely purports or is represented to be the product of, or to have been packed or distributed by, such other drug manufacturer, processor, packer or distributor.

(5) The term "device," except when used in subdivision (15) of this section and in G.S. 106-122, subdivision (10), 106-130, subdivision (6), 106-134, subdivision (3) and 106-137, subdivision (3) means instruments, apparatus and contrivances, including their components, parts and accessories, intended

a. For use in the diagnosis, cure, mitigation, treatment, or prevention of disease in man or other animals; or

b. To affect the structure or any function of the body of man or other animals.

(6) The term "drug" means

a. Articles recognized in the official United States Pharmacopoeia, official Homeopathic Pharmacopoeia of the United States, or official National Formulary, or any supplement to any of them; and

b. Articles intended for use in the diagnosis, cure, mitigation, treatment or prevention of disease in man or other animals; and

c. Articles (other than food) intended to affect the structure or any function of the body of man or other animals; and

d. Articles intended for use as a component of any article specified in paragraphs a, b or c; but does not include devices or their components, parts, or accessories.

(7) The term "federal act" means the Federal Food, Drug and Cosmetic Act (Title 21 U.S.C. 301 et seq.; 52 Stat. 1040 et seq.).

(8) The term "food" means

a. Articles used for food or drink for man or other animals,

b. Chewing gum, and

c. Articles used for components of any such article.

(8a) The term "food additive" means any substance, the intended use of which results or may be reasonably expected to result, directly or indirectly, in its becoming a component or otherwise affecting the characteristics of any food (including any substance intended for use in producing, manufacturing, packing, processing, preparing, treating, packaging, transporting or holding food; and including any source of radiation intended for any such use) if such substance is not generally recognized, among experts qualified by scientific training and experience to evaluate its safety, as having been adequately shown through scientific procedures (or, in the case of a substance used in a food prior to January 1, 1958, through either scientific procedures or experience based on common use in food) to be safe under the conditions of its intended use; except that such term does not include:

a. A pesticide chemical in or on a raw agricultural commodity; or

b. A pesticide chemical to the extent that it is intended for use or is used in the production, storage, or transportation of any raw agricultural commodity; or

c. A color additive; or

d. Any substance used in accordance with a sanction or approval granted prior to the enactment of the Food Additives Amendment of 1958, pursuant to the federal act; the Poultry Products Inspection Act (21 U.S.C. 451 et seq.) or the Meat Inspection Act of March 4, 1907 (34 Stat. 1260), as amended and extended (21 U.S.C. 71 et seq.).

(9) The term "immediate container" does not include package liners.

(10) The term "label" means a display of written, printed or graphic matter upon the immediate container of any article; and a requirement made by or under authority of this Article that any word, statement, or other information appearing on the label shall not be considered to be complied with unless such word, statement, or other information also appears on the outside container or wrapper, if any there be, of the retail package of such article, or is easily legible through the outside container or wrapper.

(11) The term "labeling" means all labels and other written, printed, or graphic matter

a. Upon an article or any of its containers or wrappers, or

b.	Accompanying such article.

(11a)	Repealed by Session Laws 1989, c. 226, s. 1.

(12)	The term "new drug" means

a.	Any drug the composition of which is such that such drug is not generally recognized, among experts qualified by scientific training and experience to evaluate the safety and effectiveness of drugs, as safe and effective for use under the conditions prescribed, recommended, or suggested in the labeling thereof; or

b.	Any drug the composition of which is such that such drug, as a result of investigations to determine its safety and effectiveness for use under such conditions, has become so recognized, but which has not, otherwise than in such investigation, been used to a material extent or for a material time under such conditions.

(12a)	Repealed by Session Laws 1989, c. 226, s. 1.

(13)	The term "official compendium" means the official United States Pharmacopoeia, official Homeopathic Pharmacopoeia of the United States, official National Formulary, or any supplement to any of them.

(13a)	The term "package" means any container or wrapping in which any consumer commodity is enclosed for use in the delivery or display of that consumer commodity to retail purchasers, but does not include:

a.	Shipping containers or wrappings used solely for the transportation of any consumer commodity in bulk or in quantity to manufacturers, packers, or processors, or to wholesale or retail distributors thereof; or

b.	Shipping containers or outer wrappings used by retailers to ship or deliver any commodity to retail customers if such containers and wrappings bear no printed matter pertaining to any particular commodity.

(14)	The term "person" includes individual, partnership, corporation, and association.

(14a) The term "pesticide chemical" means any substance which, alone, in chemical combination, or in formulation with one or more other substances is a "pesticide" within the meaning of the North Carolina Pesticide Law of 1971, Article 52, Chapter 143, of the General Statutes of North Carolina, or the Federal Insecticide, Fungicide and Rodenticide Act (7 U.S.C. 135 et seq.), and which is used in the production, storage, or transportation of raw agricultural commodities.

(14b) The term "practitioner" means a physician, dentist, veterinarian or other person licensed, registered or otherwise permitted to distribute, dispense, conduct research with respect to or to administer a drug so long as such activity is within the normal course of professional practice or research.

(14c) The term "principal display panel" means that part of a label that is most likely to be displayed, presented, shown, or examined under normal and customary conditions of display for retail sale.

(14d) The term "raw agricultural commodity" means any food in its raw or natural state, including all fruits that are washed, colored, or otherwise treated in their unpeeled natural form prior to marketing.

(14e), (14f) Repealed by Session Laws 1989, c. 226, s. 1.

(15) If an article is alleged to be misbranded because the labeling is misleading, or if an advertisement is alleged to be false because it is misleading, then in determining whether the labeling or advertisement is misleading, there shall be taken into account (among other things) not only representations made or suggested by statement, word, design, device, sound, or any combination thereof, but also the extent to which labeling or advertisement fails to reveal facts material in the light of such representations or material with respect to consequences which may result from the use of the article to which the labeling or advertisement relates under the conditions of use prescribed in the labeling or advertisement thereof or under such conditions of use as are customary or usual.

(16) The representation of a drug, in its labeling or advertisement, as an antiseptic shall be considered to be a representation that it is a germicide, except in the case of a drug purporting to be, or represented as, an antiseptic for inhibitory use as a wet dressing, ointment, dusting powder, or such other use as involves prolonged contact with the body.

(17) The provisions of this Article regarding the selling of food, drugs, devices, or cosmetics, shall be considered to include the manufacture, production, processing, packing, exposure, offer, possession, and holding of any such article for sale; and the sale, dispensing, and giving of any such article; and the supplying or applying of any such article in the conduct of any food, drug or cosmetic establishment. (1939, c. 320, s. 2; 1975, c. 614, ss. 1, 2; 1987, c. 737, s. 1; 1989, c. 226, s. 1; 1997-261, s. 32.)

§ 106-122. Certain acts prohibited.

The following acts and the causing thereof within the State of North Carolina are hereby prohibited:

(1) The manufacture, sale, or delivery, holding or offering for sale of any food, drug, device, or cosmetic that is adulterated or misbranded.

(2) The adulteration or misbranding of any food, drug, device, or cosmetic.

(3) The receipt in commerce of any food, drug, device, or cosmetic that is adulterated or misbranded, and the delivery or proffered delivery thereof for pay or otherwise.

(4) The sale, delivery for sale, holding for sale, or offering for sale of any article in violation of G.S. 106-131 or 106-135.

(5) The dissemination of any false advertisement.

(6) The refusal to permit entry or inspection, or to permit the taking of a sample, or to permit access to or copying of any record as authorized by G.S. 106-140.

(7) The giving of a guaranty or undertaking which guaranty or undertaking is false, except by a person who relied on a guaranty or undertaking to the same effect signed by, and containing the name and address of the person residing in the State of North Carolina from whom he received in good faith the food, drug, device or cosmetic.

(8) The removal or disposal of a detained or embargoed article in violation of G.S. 106-125.

(9) The alteration, mutilation, destruction, obliteration, or removal of the whole or any part of the labeling of, or the doing of any other act with respect to, a food, drug, device or cosmetic, if such act is done while such article is held for sale and results in such article being misbranded or adulterated.

(10) Forging, counterfeiting, simulating, or falsely representing, or without proper authority using any mark, stamp, tag, label or other identification device authorized or required by regulations promulgated under the provisions of this Article.

(11) The using, on the labeling of any drug or in any advertisement relating to such drug, of any representation or suggestion that an application with respect to such drug is effective under G.S. 106-135, or that such drug complies with the provisions of such section.

(12) The sale at retail of any food for which a definition and standard of identity for enrichment with vitamins, minerals or other nutrients has been promulgated by the Board, unless such food conforms to such definition and standard, or has been specifically exempted from same by the Board.

(13) The distribution in commerce of a consumer commodity, as defined in this Article, if such commodity is contained in a package, or if there is affixed to that commodity a label, which does not conform to the provisions of this Article and regulations promulgated under authority of this Article; provided, however, that this prohibition shall not apply to persons engaged in business as wholesale or retail distributors of consumer commodities except to the extent that such persons:

a. Are engaged in the packaging or labeling of such commodities; or

b. Prescribe or specify by any means the manner in which such commodities are packaged or labeled.

(14) The using by any person to his own advantage, or revealing, other than to the Commissioner or authorized officers or employees of the Department, or to the courts when relevant in any judicial proceeding under this Article, any information acquired under authority of this Article concerning any method or process which as a trade secret is entitled to protection.

(15) In the case of a prescription drug distributed or offered for sale in this State, the failure of the manufacturer, packer, or distributor thereof to maintain for transmittal, or to transmit, to any practitioner licensed by applicable law to administer such drug within the normal course of professional practice, who makes written request for information as to such drug, true and correct copies of all printed matter which is required to be included in any package in which that drug is distributed or sold, or such other printed matter as is approved under the federal act. Nothing in this paragraph shall be construed to exempt any person from any labeling requirement imposed by or under other provisions of this Article.

(16) a. Placing or causing to be placed upon any drug or device or container thereof, with intent to defraud, the trade name or other identifying mark, or imprint of another or any likeness of any of the foregoing; or

b. Selling, dispensing, disposing of or causing to be sold, dispensed or disposed of, or concealing or keeping in possession, control or custody, with intent to sell, dispense or dispose of, any drug, device or any container thereof, with knowledge that the trade name or other identifying mark or imprint of another or any likeness of any of the foregoing has been placed thereon in a manner prohibited by subsection (a) of this section; or

c. Making, selling, or disposing of; causing to be made, sold or disposed of; keeping in possession, control or custody; or concealing any punch, die, plate, stone, or other thing designed to print, imprint, or reproduce the trademark, trade name, or other identifying mark, imprint, or device of another or any likeness of any of the foregoing upon any drug or container or labeling thereof so as to render such drug a counterfeit drug.

(17) The doing of any act which causes a drug to be a counterfeit drug, or the sale or dispensing, or the holding for sale or dispensing of a counterfeit drug.

(18) Dispensing or causing to be dispensed a different drug in place of the drug ordered or prescribed without the express permission of the person ordering or prescribing.

(19) The acquiring or obtaining or attempting to acquire or obtain any drug subject to the provisions of G.S. 106-134.1(a)(3) or (4) by fraud, deceit, misrepresentation, or subterfuge, or by forgery or alteration of a prescription, or

by the use of a false name, or the giving of a false address. (1939, c. 320, s. 3; 1975, c. 614, ss. 3-5.)

§ 106-123. Injunctions restraining violations.

In addition to the remedies hereinafter provided, the Commissioner of Agriculture is hereby authorized to apply to the superior court for, and such court shall have jurisdiction upon hearing and for cause shown to grant, a temporary or permanent injunction restraining any person from violating any provision of G.S. 106-122, irrespective of whether or not there exists an adequate remedy at law. (1939, c. 320, s. 4.)

§ 106-124. Violations made misdemeanor.

(a)   Any person, firm or corporation violating any provision of this Article, or any regulation of the Board adopted pursuant to this Article, shall be guilty of a Class 2 misdemeanor. In addition, if any person continues to violate or further violates any provision of this Article after written notice from the Commissioner, or his duly designated agent, the court may determine that each day during which the violation continued or is repeated constitutes a separate violation subject to the foregoing penalties.

(b)   No person shall be subject to the penalties of subsection (a) of this section, for having violated G.S. 106-122, subdivision (1) or (3) if he establishes a guaranty or undertaking signed by, and containing the name and address of, the person residing in the State of North Carolina from whom he received in good faith the article, to the effect that such article is not adulterated or misbranded within the meaning of this Article, designating this article.

(c)   No publisher, radio-broadcast licensee, or agency or medium for the dissemination of an advertisement, except the manufacturer, packer, distributor, or seller of the article to which a false advertisement relates, shall be liable under this section by reason of the dissemination by him of such false advertisement, unless he has refused on the request of the Commissioner of Agriculture to furnish the Commissioner the name and post-office address of the manufacturer, packer, distributor, seller or advertising agency residing in the State of North Carolina who caused him to disseminate such advertisement. (1939, c. 320, s. 5; 1975, c. 614, s. 6; 1993, c. 539, s. 744; 1994, Ex. Sess., c. 24, s. 14(c).)

§ 106-124.1. Civil penalties.

(a) The Commissioner may assess a civil penalty of not more than two thousand dollars ($2,000) against any person who violates a provision of this Article or any rule adopted pursuant to this Article. In determining the amount of the penalty, the Commissioner shall consider the degree and extent of harm caused by the violation.

(b) Prior to assessing a civil penalty, the Commissioner shall give the person written notice of the violation and a reasonable period of time in which to correct the violation. However, the Commissioner shall not be required to give a person time to correct a violation before assessing a penalty if the Commissioner determines the violation is likely to cause future physical injury or illness.

(c) The Commissioner shall consider the training and management practices implemented by the person for the purpose of complying with this Article as a mitigating factor when determining the amount of the civil penalty.

(d) The Commissioner shall remit the clear proceeds of civil penalties assessed pursuant to this section to the Civil Penalty and Forfeiture Fund in accordance with G.S. 115C-457.2. (2003-389, s. 1.)

§ 106-125. Detention of product or article suspected of being adulterated or misbranded.

(a) Whenever a duly authorized agent of the Department of Agriculture and Consumer Services finds or has probable cause to believe, that any food, drug, device, cosmetic or consumer commodity is adulterated, or so misbranded as to be dangerous or fraudulent within the meaning of this Article or is in violation of G.S. 106-131 or 106-135 of this Article, he shall affix to such article a tag or other appropriate marking giving notice that such article is, or is suspected of being, adulterated or misbranded and has been detained or embargoed, and warning all persons not to remove or dispose of such article by sale or otherwise until permission for removal or disposal is given by such agent or the court. It shall be unlawful for any person to remove or dispose of such detained or embargoed article by sale or otherwise without such permission.

(b)   When an article detained or embargoed under subsection (a) has been found by such agent to be adulterated, or misbranded or to be in violation of G.S. 106-131 or 106-135 of this Article, he shall petition a judge of the district, or superior court in whose jurisdiction the article is detained or embargoed for an order for condemnation of such article. When such agent has found that an article so detained or embargoed is not adulterated or misbranded, he shall remove the tag or other marking.

(c)   If the court finds that a detained or embargoed article is adulterated or misbranded, such article shall, after entry of the decree, be destroyed at the expense of the claimant thereof, under the supervision of such agent; and all court costs and fees, and storage and other proper expenses, shall be taxed against the claimant of such article or his agent: Provided, that when the adulteration or misbranding can be corrected by proper labeling or processing of the article, the court, after entry of the decree and after such costs, fees, and expenses have been paid and a good and sufficient bond, conditioned that such article shall be so labeled or processed, has been executed, may by order direct that such article be delivered to the claimant thereof for such labeling or processing under the supervision of an agent of the Department of Agriculture and Consumer Services. The expense of such supervision shall be paid by the claimant. Such bond shall be returned to the claimant of the article on representation to the court by the Department of Agriculture and Consumer Services that the article is no longer in violation of this Article, and that the expenses of such supervision have been paid.

(d)   Whenever any duly authorized agent of the Department of Agriculture and Consumer Services shall find in any room, building, vehicle of transportation or other structure, any meat, seafood, poultry, vegetable, fruit or other perishable articles which are unsound, or contain any filthy, decomposed or putrid substance, or that may be poisonous or deleterious to health or otherwise unsafe, the same being hereby declared to be a nuisance, the agent shall forthwith condemn or destroy the same, or in any other manner render the same unsalable as human food. (1939, c. 320, s. 6; 1973, c. 108, s. 53; 1975, c. 614, ss. 7-9; 1997-261, s. 109.)

§ 106-126. Prosecutions of violations.

It shall be the duty of the solicitors and district attorneys of this State to promptly prosecute all violations of this Article. (1939, c. 320, s. 7; 1973, c. 47, s. 2; c. 108, s. 54; 1975, c. 614, s. 10.)

§ 106-127. Report of minor violations in discretion of Commissioner.

Nothing in this Article shall be construed as requiring the Commissioner of Agriculture to report for the institution of proceedings under this Article, minor violations of this Article, whenever the Commissioner believes that the public interest will be adequately served in the circumstances by a suitable written notice or warning. (1939, c. 320, s. 8.)

§ 106-128. Establishment of reasonable standards of quality by Board of Agriculture.

Whenever in the judgment of the Board of Agriculture such action will promote honesty and fair dealing in the interest of consumers, the Board shall promulgate regulations fixing and establishing for any food or class of food a reasonable definition and standard of identity, and/or reasonable standard of quality and/or fill of container. In prescribing a definition and standard of identity for any food or class of food in which optional ingredients are permitted, the Board shall, for the purpose of promoting honesty and fair dealing in the interest of consumers, designate the optional ingredients which shall be named on the label. The definitions and standards so promulgated shall conform so far as practicable to the definitions and standards promulgated by the Commissioner of the Federal Food and Drug Administration under authority conferred by section 401 of the federal act.

Temporary permits now or hereafter granted for interstate shipment of experimental packs of food varying from the requirements of federal definitions and standards of identity are automatically effective in this State under the conditions provided in such permits. In addition, the Board of Agriculture may cause to be issued additional permits where they are necessary to the completion or conclusiveness of an otherwise adequate investigation and where the interests of consumers are safeguarded. Such permits are subject to the terms and conditions the Board of Agriculture may prescribe by regulation. (1939, c. 320, s. 9; 1975, c. 614, ss. 11, 12.)

§ 106-129. Foods deemed to be adulterated.

A food shall be deemed to be adulterated:

(1) a. If it bears or contains any poisonous or deleterious substance which may render it injurious to health; but in case the substance is not an added substance such food shall not be considered adulterated under this paragraph if the quantity of such substance in such food does not ordinarily render it injurious to health; or

b. 1. If it bears or contains any added poisonous or added deleterious substance, other than one which is

I. A pesticide chemical in or on a raw agricultural commodity;

II. A food additive; or

III. A color additive, which is unsafe within the meaning of G.S. 106-132; or

2. If it is a raw agricultural commodity and it bears or contains a pesticide chemical which is unsafe within the meaning of G.S. 106-132; or

3. If it is or it bears or contains any food additive which is unsafe within the meaning of G.S. 106-132;

provided, that where a pesticide chemical has been used in or on a raw agricultural commodity in conformity with an exemption granted or tolerance prescribed under G.S. 106-132 of this Article, and such raw agricultural commodity has been subjected to processing such as canning, cooking, freezing, dehydrating, or milling, the residue of such pesticide chemical remaining in or on such processed food shall, notwithstanding the provisions of G.S. 106-132 and clause 3 of this section, not be deemed unsafe if such residue in or on the raw agricultural commodity has been removed to the extent possible in good manufacturing practice, and the concentration of such residue in the processed food when ready-to-eat, is not greater than the tolerance prescribed for the raw agricultural commodity; or

c. If it consists in whole or in part of a diseased, contaminated, filthy, putrid or decomposed substance, or if it is otherwise unfit for food; or

d. If it has been produced, prepared, packed or held under insanitary conditions whereby it may have become contaminated with filth, or whereby it may have been rendered diseased, unwholesome or injurious to health; or

e. If it is the product of a diseased animal or an animal which has died otherwise than by slaughter, or that has been fed upon the uncooked offal from a slaughterhouse; or

f. If its container is composed, in whole or in part, of any poisonous or deleterious substance which may render the contents injurious to health;

g. If it has been intentionally subjected to radiation, unless the use of the radiation was in conformity with a regulation or exemption in effect pursuant to G.S. 106-132 of this Article; or

h. If a retail or wholesale establishment has added sulfiting agents, including sulfur dioxide, sodium sulfite, sodium or potassium bisulfite, and sodium or potassium metabisulfite, separately or in combination, to fresh fruits and fresh vegetables intended for retail sale as fresh food products.

(2) a. If any valuable constituent has been in whole or in part omitted or abstracted therefrom; or

b. If any substance has been substituted wholly or in part therefor; or

c. If damage or inferiority has been concealed in any manner; or

d. If any substance has been added thereto or mixed or packed therewith so as to increase its bulk or weight, or reduce its quality or strength or make it appear better or of greater value than it is.

(3) If it is confectionery, and:

a. Has partially or completely imbedded therein any nonnutritive object: Provided, that this clause shall not apply in the case of any nonnutritive object if, in the judgment of the Board of Agriculture as provided by regulations, such object is of practical functional value to the confectionery product and would not render the product injurious or hazardous to health; or

b. Bears or contains more than five percent (5%) alcohol by volume. Confectionery that contains more than five-tenths of one percent (0.5%) alcohol by volume shall conspicuously bear a label indicating alcohol content; or

c. Bears or contains any nonnutritive substance: Provided, that this clause shall not apply to a safe nonnutritive substance which is in or on confectionery by reason of its use for some practical functional purpose in the manufacture, packaging, or storing of such confectionery if the use of the substance does not promote deception of the consumer or otherwise result in adulteration or misbranding in violation of any provision of this Article; and provided further, that the Board may, for the purpose of avoiding or resolving uncertainty as to the application of this clause, issue regulations allowing or prohibiting the use of particular nonnutritive substances.

(4) If it is or bears or contains any color additive which is unsafe within the meaning of G.S. 106-132. (1939, c. 320, s. 10; 1975, c. 614, ss. 13-16; 1985, c. 399; 2011-26, s. 1.)

§ 106-130. Foods deemed misbranded.

A food shall be deemed to be misbranded:

(1) a. If its labeling is false or misleading in any particular, or

b. If its labeling or packaging fails to conform with the requirements of G.S. 106-139 and 106-139.1 of this Article.

(2) If it is offered for sale under the name of another food.

(3) If it is an imitation of another food, unless its label bears, in type of uniform size and prominence, the word "imitation" and, immediately thereafter, the name of the food imitated.

(4) If its container is so made, formed or filled as to be misleading.

(5) If in package form, unless it bears a label containing

a. The name and place of business of the manufacturer, packer, or distributor; and

b. An accurate statement of the quantity of the contents in terms of weight, measure, or numerical count, which statement shall be separately and accurately stated in a uniform location upon the principal display panel of the label:

Provided, that under paragraph b of this subdivision reasonable variations shall be permitted, and exemptions as to small packages shall be established, by regulations prescribed by the Board of Agriculture.

(6) If any word, statement, or other information required by or under authority of this Article to appear on the label or labeling is not prominently placed thereon with such conspicuousness (as compared with other words, statements, designs, or devices, in the labeling) and in such terms as to render it likely to be read and understood by the ordinary individual under customary conditions of purchase and use.

(7) If it purports to be or is represented as a food for which a definition and standard of identity has been prescribed by regulations as provided by G.S. 106-128, unless

a. It conforms to such definition and standard, and

b. Its label bears the name of the food specified in the definition and standard, and, insofar as may be required by such regulations, the common names of optional ingredients (other than spices, flavoring, and coloring) present in such food.

(8) If it purports to be or is represented as

a. A food for which a standard of quality has been prescribed by regulations as provided by G.S. 106-128 and its quality falls below such standard unless its label bears, in such manner and form as such regulations specify, a statement that it falls below such standard; or

b. A food for which a standard or standards of fill of container have been prescribed by regulation as provided by G.S. 106-128, and it falls below the standard of fill of container applicable thereto, unless its label bears, in such manner and form as such regulations specify, a statement that it falls below such standard.

(9) If it is not subject to the provisions of subdivision (7) of this section, unless its label bears

    a. The common or usual name of the food, if any there be, and

    b. In case it is fabricated from two or more ingredients, the common or usual name of each such ingredient; except that spices, flavorings, and colorings, other than those sold as such, may be designated as spices, flavorings, and colorings without naming each:

Provided, that, to the extent that compliance with the requirements of paragraph b of this subdivision is impracticable or results in deception or unfair competition, exemptions shall be established by regulations promulgated by the Board of Agriculture.

(10) If it purports to be or is represented for special dietary uses, unless its label bears such information concerning its vitamin, mineral, and other dietary properties as the Board of Agriculture determines to be, and by regulations prescribes as, necessary in order to fully inform purchasers as to its value for such uses.

(11) If it bears or contains any artificial flavoring, artificial coloring, or chemical preservatives, unless it bears labeling stating that fact: Provided, that to the extent that compliance with the requirements of this subdivision are impracticable, exemptions shall be established by regulations promulgated by the Board of Agriculture. The provisions of this subdivision and subdivisions (7) and (9) with respect to artificial coloring do not apply to butter, cheese, or ice cream. The provisions of this subdivision with respect to chemical preservatives do not apply to a pesticide chemical when used in or on a raw agricultural commodity which is the product of the soil.

(12) If it is a raw agricultural commodity which is the produce of the soil, bearing or containing a pesticide chemical applied after harvest, unless the shipping container of such commodity bears labeling which declares the presence of such chemical in or on such commodity and the common or usual name and the function of such chemical: Provided, however, that no such declaration shall be required while such commodity, having been removed from the shipping container, is being held or displayed for sale at retail out of such container in accordance with the custom of the trade.

(13)   If it is a product intended as an ingredient of another food and when used according to the directions of the purveyor will result in the final food product being adulterated or misbranded.

(14)   If it is a color additive unless its packaging and labeling are in conformity with such packaging and labeling requirements applicable to such color additive prescribed under the provisions of G.S. 106-132 of this Article.

(15)   If the labeling provided by the manufacturer, packer, distributor, or retailer on meat, meat products, poultry, or seafood includes a "sell-by" date or other indicator of a last recommended day of sale, and the date has been removed, obscured, or altered by any person other than the customer. This subdivision does not prohibit the removal of a label for the purpose of repackaging and relabeling a food item so long as the new package or new label does not bear a "sell-by" date or other indicator of a last recommended day of sale later than the original package. This subdivision does not prohibit relabeling of meat, meat products, poultry, or seafood that has had its shelf life extended through freezing, cooking, or other additional processing that extends the shelf life of the product. (1939, c. 320, s. 11; 1975, c. 614, ss. 17-20; 2000-67, s. 7.10.)

§ 106-131. Permits governing manufacture of foods subject to contamination with microorganisms.

(a)   Whenever the Commissioner of Agriculture finds after investigation by himself or his duly authorized agents, that the distribution in North Carolina of any class of food may, by reason of contamination with microorganisms during manufacture, processing, or packing thereof in any locality in this State, be injurious to health, and that such injurious nature cannot be adequately determined after such articles have entered commerce, the Commissioner, then, and in such case only, shall promulgate regulations providing for the issuance, to manufacturers, processors, or packers of such class of food in such locality, of permits to which shall be attached such conditions governing the manufacture, processing, or packing of such class of food, for such temporary period of time, as may be necessary to protect the public health; and after the effective date of such regulations, and during such temporary period, no person shall introduce or deliver for introduction into commerce any such food manufactured, processed, or packed by any such manufacturer, processor, or packer unless such manufacturer, processor, or packer holds a permit issued by the Commissioner as provided by such regulations.

(b)   The Commissioner of Agriculture is authorized to suspend immediately upon notice any permit issued under authority of this section if it is found that any of the conditions of the permit have been violated. The holder of a permit so suspended shall be privileged at any time to apply for the reinstatement of such permit, and the Commissioner shall immediately after prompt hearing and an inspection of the establishment, reinstate such permit if it is found that adequate measures have been taken to comply with and maintain the conditions of the permit, as originally issued, or as amended.

(c)   Any officer or employee duly designated by the Commissioner of Agriculture shall have access to any factory or establishment, the operator of which holds a permit from the Commissioner of Agriculture for the purpose of ascertaining whether or not the conditions of the permit are being complied with, and denial of access for such inspection shall be ground for suspension of the permit until such access is freely given by the operator. (1939, c. 320, s. 12.)

§ 106-132. Additives, etc., deemed unsafe.

Any added poisonous or added deleterious substance, any food additive, any pesticide chemical in or on a raw agricultural commodity or any color additive, shall with respect to any particular use or intended use be deemed unsafe for the purpose of application of G.S. 106-129(1), paragraphs b and g and 106-129(4) with respect to any food, 106-133(1) with respect to any drug or device, or 106-136(1) and (5) with respect to any cosmetic, unless there is in effect a regulation pursuant to G.S. 106-139 of this Article limiting the quantity of substance, and the use or intended use of such substance conforms to the terms prescribed by such regulation. While such regulations relating to such substance are in effect, a food, drug, or cosmetic shall not, by reason of bearing or containing such substance in accordance with the regulations be considered adulterated within the meaning of G.S. 106-129(1)a, 106-133(1) and 106-136(1). (1939, c. 320, s. 13; 1975, c. 614, s. 21.)

§ 106-133. Drugs deemed to be adulterated.

A drug or device shall be deemed to be adulterated:

(1) a. If it consists in whole or in part of any filthy, putrid or decomposed substance; or

b. If it has been produced, prepared, packed, or held under insanitary conditions whereby it may have been contaminated with filth, or whereby it may have been rendered injurious to health; or

c. If it is a drug and its container is composed, in whole or in part, of any poisonous or deleterious substance which may render the contents injurious to health; or

d. If

1. It is a drug and it bears or contains, for purposes of coloring only, a color additive which is unsafe within the meaning of G.S. 106-132, or

2. If it is a color additive, the intended use of which in or on drugs is for purposes of coloring only, and is unsafe within the meaning of G.S. 106-132;

e. If it is a drug and the methods used in, or the facilities or controls used for, its manufacture, processing, packing, or holding do not conform to or are not operated or administered in conformity with current good manufacturing practice to assure that such drug meets the requirements of this Article as to safety and has the identity and strength, and meets the quality and purity characteristics, which it purports or is represented to possess.

(2) If it purports to be or is represented as a drug the name of which is recognized in an official compendium, and its strength differs from, or its quality or purity falls below, the standard set forth in such compendium. Such determination as to strength, quality, or purity shall be made in accordance with the tests or methods of assay set forth in such compendium, or in the absence of or inadequacy of such tests or methods of assay, those so prescribed under authority of the federal act. No drug defined in an official compendium shall be deemed to be adulterated under this subdivision because it differs from the standard of strength, quality, or purity therefor set forth in such compendium, if its difference in strength, quality, or purity from such standard is plainly stated on its label. Whenever a drug is recognized in both the United States Pharmacopoeia and the Homeopathic Pharmacopoeia of the United States it shall be subject to the requirements of the United States Pharmacopoeia unless it is labeled and offered for sale as a homeopathic drug, in which case it shall

be subject to the provisions of the Homeopathic Pharmacopoeia of the United States and not to those of the United States Pharmacopoeia.

(3) If it is not subject to the provisions of subdivision (2) of this section and its strength differs from, or its purity or quality falls below, that which it purports or is represented to possess.

(4) If it is a drug and any substance has been

a. Mixed or packed therewith so as to reduce its quality or strength; or

b. Substituted wholly or in part therefor. (1939, c. 320, s. 14; 1975, c. 614, ss. 22-24.)

§ 106-134. Drugs deemed misbranded.

A drug or device shall be deemed to be misbranded:

(1) If its labeling is false or misleading in any particular, or if its labeling or packaging fails to conform with the requirements of G.S. 106-139 or 106-139.1 of this Article.

(2) If in package form unless it bears a label containing

a. The name and place of business of the manufacturer, packer, or distributor; and

b. An accurate statement of the quantity of the contents in terms of weight, measure, or numerical count, which statement shall be separately and accurately stated in a uniform location upon the principal display panel of the label, except as exempted with respect to this clause by G.S. 106-121(2a)c of this Article; provided, that under paragraph b of this subdivision reasonable variations shall be permitted, and exemptions as to small packages shall be established, by regulations prescribed by the Board of Agriculture.

(3) If any word, statement, or other information required by or under authority of this Article to appear on the label or labeling is not prominently placed thereon with such conspicuousness (as compared with other words, statements, designs or devices, in the labeling) and in such terms as to render it

likely to be read and understood by the ordinary individual under customary conditions of purchase and use.

(4)   If it is for use by man and contains any quantity of the narcotic or hypnotic substance alphaeucaine, barbituric acid, betaeucaine, bromal, cannabis, carbromal, chloral, coca, cocaine, codeine, heroin, marijuana, morphine, opium, paraldehyde, peyote, or sulphonmethane; or any chemical derivative of such substances, which derivative has been by the Board after investigation, found to be, and by regulations under this Article, designated as, habit forming; unless its label bears the name and quantity or proportion of such substance or derivative and in juxtaposition therewith the statement "Warning - May be habit forming."

(5)   a.   If it is a drug, unless:

1.   Its label bears, to the exclusion of any other nonproprietary name (except the applicable systematic chemical name or the chemical formula),

I.   The established name (as defined in paragraph b of this subdivision) of the drug, if such there be, and

II.   In case it is fabricated from two or more ingredients the established name and quantity of each active ingredient, including the kind and quantity or proportion of any alcohol and also including, whether active or not, the established name and quantity or proportion of any bromides, ether, chloroform, acetanilid, acetphenetidin, amidopyrine, antipyrine, atropine, hyoscine, hyoscyamine, arsenic, digitalis, digitalis glucosides, mercury, ouabain, strophanthin, strychnine, thyroid, or any derivative or preparation of any such substances, contained therein: Provided, that the requirement for stating the quantity of the active ingredients, other than the quantity of those specifically named in this subdivision, shall apply only to prescription drugs; and

2.   For any prescription drug the established name of such drug or ingredient, as the case may be, on such label (and on any labeling on which a name for such drug or ingredient is used) is printed prominently and in type at least half as large as that used thereon for any proprietary name or designation for such drug or ingredient; and provided, that to the extent that compliance with the requirements of 1 II or 2 of this subdivision is impracticable, exemptions shall be allowed under regulations promulgated by the Board.

b. As used in this subdivision (5), the term "established name," with respect to a drug or ingredient thereof, means:

1. The applicable official name designated pursuant to section 508 of the federal act, or

2. If there is no such name and such drug, or such ingredient, is an article recognized in an official compendium, then the official title thereof, in such compendium, or

3. If neither 1 nor 2 of this paragraph applies, then the common or usual name, if any, of such drug or of such ingredient:

Provided further, that where 2 of this sub-subdivision applies to an article recognized in the United States Pharmacopoeia and in the Homeopathic Pharmacopoeia under different official titles, the official title used in the United States Pharmacopoeia shall apply unless it is labeled and offered for sale as a homeopathic drug, in which case the official title used in the Homeopathic Pharmacopoeia shall apply.

(6) Unless its labeling bears

a. Adequate directions for use; and

b. Such adequate warnings against use in those pathological conditions or by children where its use may be dangerous to health, or against unsafe dosage or methods or duration of administration or application, in such manner and form, as are necessary for the protection of users: Provided, that where any requirement of paragraph a of this subdivision, as applied to any drug or device, is not necessary for the protection of the public health, the Board of Agriculture shall promulgate regulations exempting such drug or device from such requirements.

(7) If it purports to be a drug the name of which is recognized in an official compendium, unless it is packaged and labeled as prescribed therein: Provided, that the method of packing may be modified with the consent of the Board of Agriculture. Whenever a drug is recognized in both the United States Pharmacopoeia and the Homeopathic Pharmacopoeia of the United States, it shall be subject to the requirements of the United States Pharmacopoeia with respect to packaging and labeling unless it is labeled and offered for sale as a homeopathic drug, in which case it shall be subject to the provisions of the

Homeopathic Pharmacopoeia of the United States and not to those of the United States Pharmacopoeia.

(8) If it has been found by the Department of Agriculture and Consumer Services to be a drug liable to deterioration, unless it is packaged in such form and manner, and its label bears a statement of such precautions, as the Board of Agriculture shall by regulations require as necessary for the protection of public health. No such regulation shall be established for any drug recognized in an official compendium until the Commissioner of Agriculture shall have informed the appropriate body charged with the revision of such compendium of the need for such packaging or labeling requirements and such body shall have failed within a reasonable time to prescribe such requirements.

(9) a. If it is a drug and its container is so made, formed, or filled as to be misleading; or

b. If it is an imitation of another drug; or

c. If it is offered for sale under the name of another drug.

(10) If it is dangerous to health when used in the dosage, or with the frequency or duration prescribed, recommended, or suggested in the labeling thereof.

(11), (12) Repealed by Session Laws 1975, c. 614, s. 28.

(13) If it is, or purports to be, or is represented as a drug composed wholly or partly of insulin, unless:

a. It is from a batch with respect to which a certificate or release has been issued pursuant to section 506 of the federal act, and

b. Such certificate or release is in effect with respect to such drug.

(14) If it is, or purports to be, or is represented as a drug composed wholly or partly of any kind of penicillin, streptomycin, chlortetracycline, chloramphenicol, bacitracin, or any other antibiotic drug, or any derivative thereof, unless

a. It is from a batch with respect to which a certificate or release has been issued pursuant to section 507 of the federal act, and

b. Such certificate or release is in effect with respect to such drug:

Provided, that this subsection shall not apply to any drug or class of drugs exempted by regulations promulgated under section 507(c) or (d) of the federal act. For the purpose of this subsection the term "antibiotic drug" means any drug intended for use by man containing any quantity of any chemical substance which is produced by microorganisms and which has the capacity to inhibit or destroy microorganisms in dilute solution (including the chemically synthesized equivalent of any such substance).

(15) If it is a color additive, the intended use of which in or on drugs is for the purpose of coloring only, unless its packaging and labeling are in conformity with such packaging and labeling requirements applicable to such color additive, prescribed under the provisions of G.S. 106-132 of this Article.

(16) In the case of any prescription drug distributed or offered for sale in this State, unless the manufacturer, packer, or distributor thereof includes in all advertisements and other descriptive printed matter issued or caused to be issued by the manufacturer, packer, or distributor with respect to that drug a true statement of

a. The established name, as defined in G.S. 106-134(5)b of this Article, printed prominently and in type at least half as large as that used for any trade or brand name thereof,

b. The formula showing quantitatively each ingredient of such drug to the extent required for labels under section 502(e) of the federal act, and

c. Such other information in brief summary relating to side effects, contraindications, and effectiveness as shall be required in regulations issued under the federal act.

(17) If a trademark, trade name or other identifying mark, imprint or device of another or any likeness of the foregoing has been placed thereon or upon its container with intent to defraud.

(18) If it is a drug and its packaging or labeling is in violation of an applicable regulation issued pursuant to section 3 or 4 of the Federal Poison Prevention Packaging Act of 1970. (1939, c. 320, s. 15; 1949, c. 370; 1973, c. 831, s. 1; 1975, c. 614, ss. 25-28, 30; 1997-261, s. 33.)

§ 106-134.1. Prescriptions required; label requirements; removal of certain drugs from requirements of this section.

(a)   A drug intended for use by man which:

(1)   Is a habit-forming drug to which G.S. 106-134(4) applies; or

(2)   Because of its toxicity or other potentiality for harmful effect, or the method of its use, or the collateral measures necessary to its use, is not safe for use except under the supervision of a practitioner licensed by law to administer such drug in the course of his normal practice; or

(3)   Is limited by an approved application under section 505 of the federal act to use under the professional supervision of a practitioner licensed by law to administer such drug; or

(4)   Is a drug the label of which bears the statement "Caution: Federal law prohibits dispensing without a prescription," shall be dispensed only

a.   Upon a written prescription of a practitioner licensed by law to administer such drug, or authorized to issue orders pursuant to G.S. 90-87(23)(a), provided that the written prescription must bear the printed or stamped name, address, telephone number and DEA number of the prescriber in addition to his legal signature, or

b.   Upon an oral prescription of such practitioner which is reduced promptly to writing and filed by the pharmacist, or

c.   By refilling any such written or oral prescription if such refilling is authorized by the prescriber either in the original prescription or by oral order which is reduced promptly to writing and filed by the pharmacist. If any prescription for such drug does not indicate the times it may be refilled, if any, such prescription may not be refilled unless the pharmacist is subsequently authorized to do so by the practitioner.

The act of dispensing a drug contrary to the provisions of this subdivision shall be deemed to be an act which results in a drug being misbranded while held for sale.

(b)   Any drug dispensed by filling or refilling a written or oral prescription of a practitioner licensed by law to administer such drug shall be exempt from the requirements of G.S. 106-134, except subsections (1), (9)b and c, (13) and (14), and the packaging requirements of subsections (7) and (8), if the drug bears an affixed label containing the name of the patient, the name and address of the pharmacy, the phrase "Filled by _____" or "Dispensed by_____," with the name of the practitioner who dispenses the prescription appearing in the blank, the serial number and date of the prescription or of its filling, the name of the prescriber, the directions for use, and unless otherwise directed by the prescriber of such drug, the name and strength of such drug. This exemption shall not apply to any drugs dispensed in the course of the conduct of a business of dispensing drugs pursuant to diagnosis by mail, or to a drug dispensed in violation of subsection (a) of this section.

Any tranquilizer or sedative dispensed by filling or refilling a written or oral prescription of a practitioner licensed by law to administer such drug shall be labelled by the pharmacist, if the prescriber so directs on the prescription, with a warning that: "The consumption of alcoholic beverages while on this medication can be harmful to your health."

(c)   The Board may, by regulation, remove drugs subject to G.S. 106-134(4) and G.S. 106-135 from the requirements of subsection (a) of this section when such requirements are not necessary for the protection of the public health. Drugs removed from the prescription requirements of the federal act by regulations issued thereunder shall also, by regulations issued by the Board, be removed from the requirement of subsection (a).

(d)   A drug which is subject to subsection (a) of this section shall be deemed to be misbranded if at any time prior to dispensing its label fails to bear the statement "Caution: Federal Law Prohibits Dispensing Without Prescription." A drug to which subsection (a) of this section does not apply shall be deemed to be misbranded if at any time prior to dispensing its label bears the caution statement quoted in the preceding sentence.

(e)   Nothing in this section shall be construed to relieve any person from any requirement prescribed by or under authority of law with respect to drugs now included or which may hereafter be included within the classification of "controlled substances" as this term is defined in applicable federal and State controlled substance acts. (1975, c. 614, s. 29; 1977, c. 421; 1979, c. 626; 1981, c. 75, s. 2.)

§ 106-135. Regulations for sale of new drugs.

(a) No person shall sell, deliver, offer for sale, hold for sale or give away any new drug unless:

(1) An application with respect thereto has been approved and said approval has not been withdrawn under section 505 of the federal act, or

(2) When not subject to the federal act, by virtue of not being a drug in interstate commerce, unless such drug has been tested and has been found to be safe for use and effective in use under the conditions prescribed, recommended, or suggested in the labeling thereof, and prior to selling or offering for sale such drug, there has been filed with the Commissioner an application setting forth

a. Full reports of investigations which have been made to show whether or not such drug is safe for use and whether such drug is effective in use;

b. A full list of the articles used as components of such drug;

c. A full statement of the composition of such drug;

d. A full description of the methods used in, and the facilities and controls used for, the manufacture, processing, and packing of such drug;

e. Such samples of such drug and of the articles used as components thereof as the Commissioner may require; and

f. Specimens of the labeling proposed to be used for such drug.

(b) An application provided for in subdivision (a)(2) of this section shall become effective on the one hundred eightieth day after the filing thereof, except that if the Commissioner finds, after due notice to the applicant and giving him an opportunity for hearing,

(1) That the drug is not safe or not effective for use under the conditions prescribed, recommended or suggested in the proposed labeling thereof; or

(2) The methods used in, and the facilities and controls used for, the manufacture, processing and packing of such drug is inadequate to preserve its identity, strength, quality, and purity; or

(3) Based on a fair evaluation of all material facts, such labeling is false or misleading in any particular; he shall, prior to the effective date of the application, issue an order refusing to permit the application to become effective.

(c) An order refusing to permit an application under this section to become effective may be revoked by the Commissioner.

(d) The Commissioner shall promulgate regulations for exempting from the operation of the foregoing subsections and subdivisions of this section drugs intended solely for investigational use by experts qualified by scientific training and experience to investigate the safety and effectiveness of drugs. Such regulations may, within the discretion of the Commissioner among other conditions relating to the protection of the public health, provide for conditioning such exemption upon

(1) The submission to the Commissioner, before any clinical testing of a new drug is undertaken, of reports, by the manufacturer or the sponsor of the investigation of such drug, of preclinical tests (including tests on animals) of such drug adequate to justify the proposed clinical testing;

(2) The manufacturer or the sponsor of the investigation of a new drug proposed to be distributed to investigators for clinical testing obtaining a signed agreement from each of such investigators that patients to whom the drug is administered will be under his personal supervision, or under the supervision of investigators responsible to him, and that he will not supply such drug to any other investigator, or to clinics, for administration to human beings; and

(3) The establishment and maintenance of such records, and the making of such reports to the Commissioner, by the manufacturer or the sponsor of the investigation of such drug, of data (including but not limited to analytical reports by investigators) obtained as the result of such investigational use of such drug, as the Commissioner finds will enable him to evaluate the safety and effectiveness of such drug in the event of the filing of an application pursuant to subsection (b).

Such regulations shall provide that such exemption shall be conditioned upon the manufacturer, or the sponsor of the investigation, requiring that experts using such drugs for investigational purposes certify to such manufacturer or sponsor that they will inform any human beings to whom such drugs, or any controls used in connection therewith, are being administered, or their representatives, that such drugs are being used for investigational purposes and will obtain the consent of such human beings or their representatives, except where they deem it not feasible, or, in their professional judgment, contrary to the best interests of such human beings. Nothing in this subsection shall be construed to require any clinical investigator to submit directly to the Commissioner reports on the investigational use of drugs; provided, that regulations adopted under section 505(i) of the federal act may be adopted by the Commissioner as the regulations in this State.

(e)   (1)   In the case of any drug for which an approval of an application filed pursuant to this section is in effect, the applicant shall establish and maintain such records, and make such reports to the Commissioner, of data relating to clinical experience and other data or information, received or otherwise obtained by such applicant with respect to such drug, as the Commissioner may by general regulation, or by order with respect to such application, prescribe: Provided, however, that regulations and orders issued under this subsection and under subsection (d) shall have due regard for the professional ethics of the medical profession and the interests of patients and shall provide, where the Commissioner deems it to be appropriate, for the examination, upon request, by the persons to whom such regulations or orders are applicable, of similar information received or otherwise obtained by the Commissioner.

(2)   Every person required under this section to maintain records, and every person in charge or custody thereof, shall, upon request of an officer or employee designated by the Commissioner, permit such officer or employee at all reasonable times to have access to and copy and certify such records.

(f)   The Commissioner may, after affording an opportunity for public hearing, revoke an application approved pursuant to this section if he finds that the drug, based on evidence acquired after such approval, may not be safe or effective for its intended use, or that the facilities or controls used in the manufacture, processing, or labeling of such drug may present a hazard to the public health.

(g)   This section shall not apply:

(1)   To a drug sold in this State or introduced into interstate commerce at any time prior to the enactment of the federal act, if its labeling contained the same representations concerning the conditions of its use; or

(2) To any drug which is licensed under the Public Health Service Act of July 1, 1944 (58 Stat. 682, as amended; 42 U.S.C. 201 et seq.) or under the Animal Virus-Serum-Toxin Act of March 4, 1913 (13 Stat. 832; 21 U.S.C. 151 et seq.); or

(3) To any drug which is subject to G.S. 106-134 (14) of this Article. (1939, c. 320, s. 16; 1975, c. 614, s. 31.)

§ 106-136. Cosmetics deemed adulterated.

A cosmetic shall be deemed to be adulterated:

(1) If it bears or contains any poisonous or deleterious substance which may render it injurious to users under the conditions of use prescribed in the labeling or advertisement thereof, or under such conditions of use as are customary or usual: Provided, that this provision shall not apply to coal-tar hair dye, the label of which bears the following legend conspicuously displayed thereon: "Caution - This product contains ingredients which may cause skin irritation on certain individuals and a preliminary test according to accompanying directions should first be made. This product must not be used for dyeing the eyelashes or eyebrows; to do so may cause blindness," and the labeling of which bears adequate directions for such preliminary testing. For the purposes of this subdivision and subdivision (5) the term "hair dye" shall not include eyelash dyes or eyebrow dyes.

(2) If it consists in whole or in part of any filthy, putrid, or decomposed substance.

(3) If it has been produced, prepared, packed, or held under insanitary conditions whereby it may have become contaminated with filth, or whereby it may have been rendered injurious to health.

(4) If its container is composed, in whole or in part, of any poisonous or deleterious substance which may render the contents injurious to health.

(5) If it is not a hair dye and it is, or it bears or contains a color additive which is unsafe within the meaning of G.S. 106-132. (1939, c. 320, s. 17; 1975, c. 614, s. 32.)

§ 106-137. Cosmetics deemed misbranded.

A cosmetic shall be deemed to be misbranded:

(1)   a.   If its labeling is false or misleading in any particular; or

b.   If its labeling or packaging fails to conform with the requirements of G.S. 106-139 and 106-139.1 of this Article.

(2)   If in package form unless it bears a label containing

a.   The name and place of business of the manufacturer, packer, or distributor; and

b.   An accurate statement of the quantity, of the contents in terms of weight, measure, or numerical count, which statement shall be separately and accurately stated in a uniform location upon the principal display panel of the label: Provided, that under paragraph b of this subdivision reasonable variations shall be permitted, and exemptions as to small packages shall be established by regulations prescribed by the Board of Agriculture.

(3)   If any word, statement, or other information required by or under authority of this Article to appear on the label or labeling is not prominently placed thereon with such conspicuousness (as compared with other words, statements, designs, or devices, in the labeling) and in such terms as to render it likely to be read and understood by the ordinary individual under customary conditions of purchase and use.

(4)   If its container is so made, formed, or filled as to be misleading.

(5)   If it is a color additive, unless its packaging and labeling are in conformity with such packaging and labeling requirements applicable to such color additive prescribed under the provisions of G.S. 106-132 of this Article. This subdivision shall not apply to packages of color additives which, with respect to their use for cosmetics, are marketed and intended for use only in or on hair dyes (as defined in the last sentence of G.S. 106-136(1)). (1939, c. 320, s. 18; 1975, c. 614, ss. 33-35.)

§ 106-138. False advertising.

(a) An advertisement of a food, drug, device or cosmetic shall be deemed to be false if it is false or misleading in any particular.

(b) For the purpose of this Article the advertisement of a drug or device representing it to have any effect in albuminuria, appendicitis, arteriosclerosis, blood poison, bone disease, Bright's disease, cancer, carbuncles, cholecystitis, diabetes, diphtheria, dropsy, erysipelas, gallstones, heart and vascular diseases, high blood pressure, mastoiditis, measles, meningitis, mumps, nephritis, otitis, media, paralysis, pneumonia, poliomyelitis, (infantile paralysis), prostate gland disorders, pyelitis, scarlet fever, sexual impotence, sinus infection, smallpox, tuberculosis, tumors, typhoid, uremia, or venereal diseases, shall also be deemed to be false; except that no advertisement not in violation of subsection (a) shall be deemed to be false under this subsection if it is disseminated only to members of the medical, dental, pharmaceutical, or veterinary professions, or appears only in the scientific periodicals of these professions, or is disseminated only for the purpose of public health education by persons not commercially interested, directly or indirectly, in the sale of such drugs or devices: Provided, that whenever the Department of Agriculture and Consumer Services determines that an advance in medical science has made any type of self-medication safe as to any of the diseases named above, the Board shall by regulation authorize the advertisement of drugs having curative or therapeutic effect for such disease, subject to such conditions and restrictions as the Board may deem necessary in the interest of public health: Provided, that this subsection shall not be construed as indicating that self-medication for diseases other than those named herein is safe or efficacious. (1939, c. 320, s. 19; 1997-261, s. 109.)

§ 106-139. Regulations by Board of Agriculture.

(a) The authority to promulgate regulations for the efficient enforcement of this Article is hereby vested in the Board of Agriculture, except the Commissioner of Agriculture is hereby authorized to promulgate regulations under G.S. 106-131 and 106-135. The Board and Commissioner are hereby authorized to make the regulations promulgated under this Article conform, insofar as practicable, with those promulgated for foods, drugs, devices, cosmetics and consumer commodities under the federal act, including but not limited to pesticide chemical residues on or in foods, food additives, color additives, special dietary foods, labeling of margarine for retail sale or distribution, nutritional labeling of foods, the fair packaging and labeling of consumer commodities and new drug clearance. Notwithstanding the provisions of subsection (e) of this section, a federal regulation adopted by the Board or Commissioner pursuant to this Article shall take effect in this State on the date it becomes effective as a federal regulation.

(b) The Board may promulgate regulations exempting from any affirmative labeling requirement of this Article consumer commodities which are, in accordance with the practice of the trade, to be processed, labeled or repacked in substantial quantities at establishments other than those where originally processed or packed, on condition that such consumer commodities are not adulterated or misbranded under the provisions of this Article upon removal from such processing, labeling or repacking establishment. The Board may additionally promulgate regulations exempting from any labeling requirement of this Article foods packaged or dispensed at the direction of the retail purchaser at the time of sale, whether or not for immediate consumption by the purchaser on the premises of the seller.

(c) Whenever the Board determines that regulations containing prohibitions or requirements other than those prescribed by G.S. 106-139.1(a) are necessary to prevent the deception of consumers or to facilitate value comparisons as to any consumer commodity, the Board shall promulgate with respect to that commodity regulations effective to:

(1) Establish and define standards for the characterization of the size of a package enclosing any consumer commodity, which may be used to supplement the label statement of net quantity of contents of packages containing such commodity, but this paragraph shall not be construed as authorizing any limitation of the size, shape, weight, dimensions, or number of packages which may be used to enclose any commodity;

(2) Regulate the placement upon any package containing any commodity or upon any label affixed to such commodity, of any printed matter stating or representing by implication that such commodity is offered for retail sale at a price lower than the ordinary and customary retail sale price or that a retail sale price advantage is accorded to purchasers thereof by reason of the size of that package or the quantity of its contents;

(3) Require that the label on each package of a consumer commodity bear

a. The common or usual name of such consumer commodity, if any, and

b. In case such consumer commodity consists of two or more ingredients, the common or usual name of each such ingredient listed in order of decreasing predominance, but nothing in this paragraph shall be deemed to require that any trade secret be divulged; or

(4) Prevent the nonfunctional slack-fill of packages containing consumer commodities.

For the purposes of subdivision (4) of this subsection, a package shall be deemed to be nonfunctionally slack-filled if it is filled of substantially less than its capacity for reasons other than

a. Protection of the contents of such package, or

b. The requirements of machines used for enclosing the contents in such package;

provided, the Board may adopt any regulations promulgated pursuant to the Federal Fair Packaging and Labeling Act which shall have the force and effect of law in this State.

(d) Hearings authorized or required by G.S. 106-131 or G.S. 106-135 shall be conducted in accordance with Chapter 150B of the General Statutes.

(e) Repealed by Session Laws 1987, c. 827, s. 30 (1939, c. 320, s. 20; 1973, c. 476, s. 128; 1975, c. 614, s. 36; 1987, c. 827, s. 30.)

§ 106-139.1. Declaration of net quantity of contents.

(a) All labels of consumer commodities, as defined by this Article, shall conform with the requirement for the declaration of net quantity of contents of section 4 of the Federal Fair Packaging and Labeling Act (15 U.S.C. 1451, et seq.) and the regulations promulgated pursuant thereto: Provided, that consumer commodities exempted from such requirements of section 4 of the Federal Fair Packaging and Labeling Act shall also be exempt from this subsection.

(b) The label of any package of a consumer commodity which bears a representation as to the number of servings of such commodity contained in such package shall bear a statement of the net quantity (in terms of weight, measure, or numerical count) of each such serving.

(c) No person shall distribute or cause to be distributed in commerce any packaged consumer commodity if any qualifying words or phrases appear in conjunction with the separate statement of the net quantity of contents required by subsection (a) of this section, but nothing in this section shall prohibit supplemental statements, at other places on the package, describing in nondeceptive terms the net quantity of contents: Provided, that such supplemental statements of net quantity of contents shall not include any term qualifying a unit of weight, measure, or count that tends to exaggerate the amount of the commodity contained in the package. (1975, c. 614, s. 37.)

§ 106-140. Further powers of Commissioner of Agriculture for enforcement of Article; report by inspector to owner of establishment.

(a) For purposes of enforcement of this Article, the Commissioner or any of his authorized agents, are authorized upon presenting appropriate credentials and a written notice to the owner, operator or agent in charge,

(1) To enter at reasonable times any factory, warehouse or establishment in which food, drugs, devices or cosmetics are manufactured, processed, or packed or held for introduction into commerce or after such introduction or to enter any vehicle being used to transport or hold such food, drugs, devices or cosmetics in commerce; and

(2) To inspect at reasonable times and in a reasonable manner such factory, warehouse, establishment or vehicle and all pertinent equipment, finished or unfinished materials, containers and labeling therein, and to obtain samples necessary to the endorsement of this Article. In the case of any factory, warehouse, establishment, or consulting laboratory in which any food, drug, device or cosmetic is manufactured, processed, analyzed, packed or held, the inspection shall extend to all things therein (including records, files, papers, processes, controls and facilities) bearing on whether any food, drug, device or cosmetic which is adulterated or misbranded within the meaning of this Article or which may not be manufactured, introduced into commerce or sold or offered for sale by reason of any provision of this Article, has been or is being manufactured, processed, packed, transported or held in any such place or

otherwise bearing on violation of this Article. No inspection authorized by the preceding sentence shall extend to

a. Financial data,

b. Sales data other than shipment data,

c. Personnel data (other than data as to qualifications of technical and professional personnel performing functions subject to this Article),

d. Pricing data, and

e. Research data (other than data relating to new drugs and antibiotic drugs, subject to reporting and inspection under lawful regulations issued pursuant to section 505(i) or (j) or section 507 (d) or (g) of the federal act, and data, relating to other drugs, which in the case of a new drug would be subject to reporting or inspection under lawful regulations issued pursuant to section 505(j) of the federal act).

Such inspection shall be commenced and completed with reasonable promptness. The provisions of the second sentence of this subsection shall not apply to such classes of persons as the Board may by regulation exempt from the application of this section upon a finding that inspection as applied to such classes of persons in accordance with this section is not necessary for the protection of the public health.

(3) To have access to and to copy all records of carriers in commerce showing the movement in commerce of any food, drug, device, or cosmetic, or the holding thereof during or after such movement, and the quantity, shipper and consignee thereof: Provided, that evidence obtained under this subsection shall not be used in a criminal prosecution of the person from whom obtained; and provided further, that carriers shall not be subject to the other provisions of this Article by reason of their receipt, carriage, holding, or delivery of food, drugs, devices or cosmetics in the usual course of business as carriers.

(b) Upon completion of any such inspection of a factory, warehouse, consulting laboratory or other establishment and prior to leaving the premises, the authorized agent making the inspection shall give to the owner, operator, or agent-in-charge a report in writing setting forth any conditions or practices observed by him which in his judgment indicate that any food, drug, device or cosmetic in such establishment:

(1) Consists in whole or in part of any filthy, putrid, or decomposed substance; or

(2) Has been prepared, packed or held under insanitary conditions whereby it may have become contaminated with filth or whereby it may have been rendered injurious to health.

(c) If the authorized agent making any such inspection of a factory, warehouse or other establishment has obtained any salable product samples in the course of the inspection, upon completion of the inspection and prior to leaving the premises he shall offer reasonable payment for any such product samples.

(d) It shall be the duty of the Commissioner of Agriculture to make or cause to be made examination of samples secured under the provisions of this section to determine whether or not any provision of this Article is being violated. (1939, c. 320, s. 21; 1975, c. 614, s. 38.)

§ 106-140.1. Registration of producers of prescription drugs and devices.

(a) On or before December 31 of each year, every person doing business in North Carolina and operating as a wholesaler, manufacturer, or repackager, as those terms are defined in subsection (j) of this section, shall register with the Commissioner his name and business location(s) in North Carolina. If said person has no business locations in North Carolina, he shall register his name and location of his corporate offices.

(b) Every person, upon first operating as a wholesaler, manufacturer or repackager in North Carolina shall immediately register with the Commissioner his name, place of business, and such establishment. If said person has no business locations in North Carolina, he shall register his name and location of his corporate offices.

(c) Every person duly registered in accordance with subsections (a) and (b) of this section shall register with the Commissioner any additional establishment that he owns or operates in the State of North Carolina prior to doing business as a manufacturer, wholesaler or repackager.

(d) The Commissioner may assign a registration number to any person or any establishment registered in accordance with this section.

(e) The Commissioner shall make available for inspection to any person so requesting any registration filed pursuant to this section.

(f) The following classes of people are exempt from the registration requirements of this section:

(1) Pharmacists as defined in G.S. 90-85.3(q) holding a valid permit as defined in G.S. 90-85.3(m);

(2) Practitioners licensed or registered by law to prescribe or administer drugs and who manufacture, prepare, compound, or process drugs or devices solely for use in the course of their professional practice.

(3) Persons who manufacture, prepare, compound, or process drugs solely for use in research, teaching, or chemical analysis and not for sale.

(4) Other classes of persons the Commissioner may by rule exempt from the application of this section upon a finding that registration by these classes of persons in accordance with this section is not necessary for the protection of the public health.

(5) Wholesale distributors of prescription drugs licensed under G.S. 106-145.3.

(g) Every establishment in the State of North Carolina registered with the Commissioner pursuant to this section shall be subject to inspection pursuant to G.S. 106-140.

(h) The Commissioner shall adopt rules to implement the registration requirements of this section. These rules may provide for an annual registration fee of up to five hundred dollars ($500.00) for companies operating as manufacturers, wholesalers, or repackagers. The Department of Agriculture and Consumer Services shall use these funds for the implementation of the North Carolina Food, Drug and Cosmetic Act.

(i) For the purposes of this act, name means the name of the partnership if a partnership and the name of the corporation if a corporation.

(j) As used in this section:

(1) The term "manufacturer" means a person who prepares, derives, or produces a prescription drug. Pharmacists are specifically excluded from this definition if they are acting in the course of their professional practice as defined in Chapter 90 and rules adopted pursuant to it.

(2) The term "prescription drug" means a drug that under federal law is required, prior to being dispensed or delivered, to be labeled with the following statement: "Caution: Federal law prohibits dispensing without a prescription."

(3) The term "repackager" means a person who repacks, relabels, or manipulates a prescription drug which was in a unit packaged and sealed by a manufacturer. Pharmacists are specifically exempted from this definition if they are acting in the course of their professional practice as defined in Chapter 90 and rules adopted pursuant to it.

(4) The term "wholesaler" means a person acting as a jobber, wholesale merchant, salvager, or broker, or agent thereof, who sells or distributes for resale a prescription drug. Pharmacists are specifically exempted from this definition if they are acting in the course of their professional practice as defined in Chapter 90 and rules adopted pursuant to it. (1987, c. 737, s. 2; 1989, c. 226, s. 2; 1989 (Reg. Sess., 1990), c. 1024, s. 20; 1991, c. 699, ss. 3, 4; 1997-261, s. 109.)

§ 106-141. Examinations and investigations.

(a) Repealed by Session Laws 1975, c. 614, s. 39.

(b) The Commissioner of Agriculture is authorized to conduct the examinations and investigations for the purposes of this Article through officers and employees of the Department or through any health, food or drug officer or employee of the State, or any political subdivision thereof: Provided, that when examinations and investigations are to be conducted through any officer or employee of any agency other than the Department of Agriculture and Consumer Services the arrangements for such examinations and investigations shall be approved by the directing head of such agency.

(c) The Commissioner of Agriculture is authorized to delegate embargo authority concerning food and drink pursuant to G.S. 106-125 to the Secretary of Health and Human Services and to local health directors. (1939, c. 320, s. 22; 1975, c. 614, s. 39; 1983, c. 891, s. 12; 1997-261, s. 109; 1997-443, s. 11A.118(a).)

§ 106-141.1. Inspections of donated food.

(a) The Department of Agriculture and Consumer Services is authorized to inspect for compliance with the provisions of Article 12 of Chapter 106 of the North Carolina General Statutes, food items donated for use or distribution by nonprofit organizations or nonprofit corporations, and may establish procedures for the handling of the food items, including reporting procedures concerning the donation of food.

(b) The Department of Agriculture and Consumer Services may apply to Superior Court for injunctive relief restraining the violation of this section.

(c) Nothing in this section shall limit the duties or responsibilities of the Commission for Public Health or the local boards of health. (1979, 2nd Sess., c. 1188, s. 3; 1997-261, s. 34; 2007-182, s. 2.)

§ 106-142. Publication of reports of judgments, decrees, etc.

(a) The Commissioner of Agriculture may cause to be published from time to time reports summarizing all judgments, decrees, and court orders which have been rendered under this Article, including the nature of the charge and the disposition thereof.

(b) The Commissioner of Agriculture may also cause to be disseminated such information regarding food, drugs, devices, and cosmetics as he deems necessary in the interest of public health and the protection of the consumer against fraud. Nothing in this section shall be construed to prohibit the Commissioner of Agriculture from collecting, reporting, and illustrating the results of the investigations of the Department. (1939, c. 320, s. 23.)

§ 106-143. Article construed supplementary.

Nothing in this Article shall be construed as in any way amending, abridging, or otherwise affecting the validity of any law or ordinance relating to the Commission for Public Health or the Department of Environment and Natural Resources or any local health department in their sanitary work in connection with public and private water supplies, sewerage, meat, or other foods, or food products, or the production, handling, or processing of these items. (1939, c. 320, s. 241/2; 1973, c. 476, s. 128; 1975, c. 19, s. 31; 1997-443, s. 11A.41; 2007-182, s. 2; 2011-145, s. 13.3(u).)

§ 106-144. Exemptions.

Meats and meat products subject to the Federal Meat Inspection Act of March 4, 1907 (34 Stat. 1260), as amended and extended (21 U.S.C. 71 et seq.), and poultry and poultry products subject to the Federal Poultry Products Inspection Act (21 U.S.C. 451 et seq.) are exempted from the provisions of this Article so long as such meat, meat products, poultry, and poultry products remain in the possession of the processor. (1939, c. 320, s. 24 2/3; 1975, c. 614, s. 40.)

§ 106-145. Effective date.

This Article shall be in full force and effect from and after January 1, 1940: Provided, that the provisions of G.S. 106-139 shall become effective on April 3, 1939, and thereafter the Commissioner of Agriculture is authorized hereby to conduct hearings, and the Board is authorized to promulgate regulations which shall become effective on and after the effective date of this Article as the Board shall direct. (1939, c. 320, s. 25.)

Article 12A.

Wholesale Prescription Drug Distributors.

§ 106-145.1. Purpose and interpretation of Article.

This Article establishes a State licensing program for wholesale distributors to enable wholesale distributors to comply with federal law. This Article shall be construed to do only that required for compliance with 21 U.S.C. § 353(e) and 21 C.F.R. Part 205. This Article shall be interpreted to be consistent with 21 C.F.R. Part 205, Guidelines for State Licensing of Wholesale Prescription Drug Distributors. In the event of a conflict, the federal law controls. (1991, c. 699, s. 2.)

§ 106-145.2. Definitions.

The following definitions apply in this Article:

(1)   Blood. - Whole blood collected from a single donor and processed either for transfusion or further manufacturing.

(2)   Blood component. - That part of blood separated by physical or mechanical means.

(3)   Commissioner. - The Commissioner of Agriculture.

(4)   Common control. - The power to direct or cause the direction of the management and policies of a person, whether by ownership of stock, by voting rights, by contract, or otherwise.

(5)   Department. - The Department of Agriculture and Consumer Services.

(6)   Drug sample. - A unit of a prescription drug that is not intended to be sold and is intended to promote the sale of the drug.

(7)   Manufacturer. - A person who is engaged in manufacturing, preparing, propagating, compounding, processing, packaging, repackaging, or labeling a prescription drug.

(8)   Person. - An individual, a corporation, a partnership, or any other entity.

(9)   Prescription drug. - A human drug required by federal law or regulation to be dispensed only by a prescription, including finished dosage forms and active ingredients subject to 21 U.S.C. § 353(b). Only for the purposes of the provisions of this Article, the term "prescription drug" shall include

pseudoephedrine products as defined in G.S. 90-113.51 that may be dispensed without a prescription.

(10) Wholesale distribution. - Distribution of a prescription drug to a person who is not a consumer or patient, other than any of the following types of distributions:

a. Intracompany sales. An intracompany sale is a transaction or transfer between any divisions, subsidiary and parent companies, or affiliated companies under common control of the same corporate entity.

b. The purchase or other acquisition of a prescription drug by a hospital or other health care entity that is a member of a group purchasing organization for its own use from the group purchasing organization or from other hospitals or other health care entities that are members of these organizations.

c. The sale, purchase, or trade of a prescription drug or an offer to sell, purchase, or trade a prescription drug by a charitable organization described in section 501(c)(3) of the Internal Revenue Code to a nonprofit affiliate of the organization to the extent otherwise permitted by law.

d. The sale, purchase, or trade of a prescription drug or an offer to sell, purchase, or trade a prescription drug among hospitals or other health care entities that are under common control.

e. The sale, purchase, or trade of a prescription drug or an offer to sell, purchase, or trade a prescription drug for emergency medical reasons. Emergency medical reasons include transfers of prescription drugs by a retail pharmacy to another retail pharmacy to alleviate a temporary shortage when the gross dollar value of the transfers does not exceed five percent (5%) of the total prescription drug sales revenue of either the transferor or transferee pharmacy during any 12-consecutive-month period.

f. The sale, purchase, or trade of a prescription drug; an offer to sell, purchase, or trade a prescription drug; or the dispensing of a prescription drug pursuant to a prescription.

g. The distribution of drug samples by a representative of a manufacturer or a wholesale distributor.

h.   The sale, purchase, or trade of blood and blood components intended for transfusion.

(11)   Wholesale distributor. - A person who is engaged in the wholesale distribution of prescription drugs. The term includes manufacturers, repackers, own-label distributors, private-label distributors, jobbers, brokers, warehouses, independent wholesale drug traders, and retail pharmacies that conduct wholesale distributions. The term does not include a person who acquires prescription drugs commingled with other goods as part of a recovery operation and who disposes of such drugs under the supervision of the Department. A warehouse includes a warehouse of a manufacturer or wholesale distributor, a chain drug warehouse, and a wholesale drug warehouse. (1991, c. 699, s. 2; 1997-261, s. 35; 2005-434, s. 2.)

§ 106-145.3. Wholesale distributor must have license.

(a)   Requirement. - Every wholesale distributor engaged in the wholesale distribution of prescription drugs in interstate commerce in this State shall obtain a license from the Commissioner for each location from which prescription drugs are distributed and shall renew each license annually. A license may cover multiple buildings and multiple operations at a single location, at the wholesale distributor's discretion. A license expires on December 31 of the year in which it is issued. A wholesale distributor licensed under this section is not required to register under G.S. 106-140.1. In lieu of licensing under this section, a wholesale distributor who has no facilities in this State may register under G.S. 106-140.1 if the wholesale distributor possesses a valid license granted by another state that has requirements substantially similar to this Article.

(b)   Reciprocity. - The Commissioner may license an out-of-State wholesale distributor on the basis of reciprocity with another state when the following conditions apply:

(1)   The out-of-State wholesale distributor possesses a valid license granted by another state pursuant to requirements substantially equivalent to the license requirements of this State.

(2)   The other state extends reciprocal treatment under its own laws to wholesale distributors licensed in this State. (1991, c. 699, s. 2.)

§ 106-145.4. Application and fee for license.

(a) Application. - An application for a wholesale distributor license or for renewal of a wholesale distributor license shall be on a form prescribed by the Commissioner and shall include the following information:

(1) The name, full business address, and telephone number of the applicant.

(2) All trade or business names used by the applicant.

(3) Addresses, telephone numbers, and names of contact persons for all facilities used by the applicant for the storage, handling, and distribution of prescription drugs.

(4) The type of ownership or operation of the applicant, such as a partnership, a corporation, or a sole proprietorship.

(5) The name of each owner and operator of the applicant, including:

a. If the applicant is an individual, the individual's name.

b. If the applicant is a partnership, the name of each partner and the name of the partnership.

c. If the applicant is a corporation, the name and title of each corporate officer and director, the corporate name of the corporation, and the state of incorporation.

d. If the applicant is a sole proprietorship, the full name of the sole proprietor and the name of the business entity.

(6) Any other information required by the Commissioner to determine if the applicant is qualified to receive a license.

When a change occurs in any information listed in this subsection after a license is issued, the license holder shall report the change to the Commissioner within 90 days after the change.

(b) Fee. - An application for an initial license or a renewed license as a wholesale distributor shall be accompanied by a nonrefundable fee of five hundred dollars ($500.00) for a manufacturer or three hundred fifty dollars ($350.00) for any other person. (1991, c. 699, s. 2.)

§ 106-145.5. Review of application and qualifications of applicant.

The Commissioner shall determine whether to issue or deny a wholesale distributor license within 90 days after an applicant files an application for a license with the Commissioner. In reviewing an application, the Commissioner shall consider the factors listed in this subsection. In the case of a partnership or corporation, the Commissioner shall consider the factors as applied to each individual whose name is required to be included in the license application.

The factors to be considered are:

(1)   Any convictions of the applicant under any federal, state, or local law relating to drug samples, wholesale or retail drug distribution, or distribution of controlled substances.

(2)   Any felony convictions of the applicant under federal, state, or local law.

(3)   The applicant's past experience in the manufacture or distribution of controlled substances and other prescription drugs.

(4)   Whether the applicant has previously given any false or fraudulent information in an application made in connection with drug manufacturing or distribution.

(5)   Suspension or revocation by the federal government or a state or local government of any license currently or previously held by the applicant for the manufacture or distribution of any controlled substances or other prescription drugs.

(6)   Compliance with the licensing requirements under any previously granted license.

(7)   Compliance with the requirements to maintain or make available to the Commissioner or to a federal, state, or local law enforcement official those records required under G.S. 106-145.8.

(8) Whether the applicant requires employees of the applicant who are involved in any prescription drug wholesale distribution activity to have education, training, experience, or any combination of these factors sufficient to enable the employee to perform assigned functions in a manner that ensures that prescription drug quality, safety, and security will be maintained at all times as required by law.

(9) Any other factors or qualifications the Commissioner considers relevant to and consistent with the public health and safety.

The Commissioner shall inspect the facility of an applicant at which prescription drugs will be stored, handled, or distributed before issuing the applicant a license. (1991, c. 699, s. 2.)

§ 106-145.6. Denial, revocation, and suspension of license; penalties for violations.

(a) Adverse Action. - The Commissioner may deny a license to an applicant if the Commissioner determines that granting the applicant a license would not be in the public interest. Public interest considerations shall be limited to factors and qualifications that are directly related to the protection of public health and safety. The Commissioner may deny, suspend, or revoke a license for substantial or repeated violations of this Article or for conviction of a violation of any other federal, state, or local prescription drug law or regulation. Chapter 150B of the General Statutes governs the denial, suspension, or revocation of a license under this Article.

(b) Criminal Sanctions. - It is unlawful to engage in wholesale distribution in this State without a wholesale distributor license or to violate any other provision of this Article. A person who violates this Article commits a Class H felony. A fine imposed for a violation of this Article may not exceed two hundred fifty thousand dollars ($250,000).

(c) Civil Penalty. - The Commissioner may assess a civil penalty of not more than ten thousand dollars ($10,000) against a person who violates any provision of this Article. In determining the amount of a civil penalty, the Commissioner shall consider the degree and extent of harm caused by the violation. Chapter 150B of the General Statutes governs the assessment of a civil penalty under this subsection. If a civil penalty is not paid within 30 days after the completion of judicial review of a final agency decision by the Commissioner, the penalty may be collected in any manner by which a debt may be collected. The clear proceeds of civil penalties assessed pursuant to this section shall be remitted to the Civil Penalty and Forfeiture Fund in accordance with G.S. 115C-457.2. (1991, c. 699, s. 2; 1993, c. 539, s. 1294; 1994, Ex. Sess., c. 24, s. 14(c); 1998-215, s. 7.)

§ 106-145.7. Storage, handling, and records of prescription drugs.

(a) Facilities. - All facilities at which prescription drugs are stored, warehoused, handled, held, offered, marketed, or displayed for wholesale distribution shall meet the following requirements:

(1) Be of suitable size and construction to facilitate cleaning, maintenance, and proper operations.

(2) Have storage areas designed to provide adequate lighting, ventilation, temperature, sanitation, humidity, space, equipment, and security conditions.

(3) Have a quarantine area for the storage of prescription drugs that are outdated, damaged, deteriorated, misbranded, or adulterated, or that are in immediate or sealed secondary containers that have been opened.

(4) Be maintained in a clean and orderly condition.

(5) Be free from infestation by insects, rodents, birds, or vermin of any kind.

(b) Security. - All facilities used for wholesale distribution shall be secure from unauthorized entry. Access from outside the premises shall be kept to a minimum and be well-controlled. The outside perimeter of the premises shall be well-lighted. Entry into areas where prescription drugs are held shall be limited to authorized personnel. The facilities shall be equipped with the following:

(1) An alarm system to detect entry after hours.

(2) A security system that will provide suitable protection against theft and diversion. When appropriate, the security system shall provide protection against theft or diversion that is facilitated or hidden by tampering with computers or electronic records.

(c) Storage. - All prescription drugs for wholesale distribution shall be stored at appropriate temperatures and under appropriate conditions in accordance with any requirements stated in the labeling of the prescription drugs or with requirements in the current edition of an official compendium, such as the United States Pharmacopeia/National Formulary (USP/NF). If the labeling of a prescription drug or a compendium do not establish storage requirements for a prescription drug, the drug may be held at "controlled" room temperature, as defined in an official compendium, to help ensure that its identity, strength, quality, and purity are not adversely affected.

(d) Examination of Materials. - A wholesale distributor shall visually examine each outside shipping container upon receipt for identity and to prevent the acceptance of contaminated prescription drugs or prescription drugs that are otherwise unfit for distribution. The examination shall be adequate to reveal container damage that would suggest possible contamination or other damage to the contents. A wholesale distributor shall carefully inspect each outgoing shipment for identity of the prescription drugs and to ensure that no prescription drugs that have been damaged in storage or held under improper conditions are delivered.

(e) Returned, Damaged, and Outdated Prescription Drugs. - A wholesale distributor shall quarantine and physically separate prescription drugs that are outdated, damaged, deteriorated, misbranded, or adulterated from other prescription drugs until their destruction or their return to their supplier. A prescription drug whose immediate or sealed outer or sealed secondary container has been opened or used shall be identified as having been opened or used and shall be treated in the same manner as outdated prescription drugs.

If the conditions under which a prescription drug has been returned to a wholesale distributor cast doubt on the drug's safety, identity, strength, quality, or purity, then the drug shall be destroyed or returned to its supplier unless examination, testing, or other investigation proves that the drug meets appropriate standards of safety, identity, strength, quality, and purity. In determining whether the conditions under which a prescription drug has been returned cast doubt on the drug's safety, identity, strength, quality, or purity, the wholesale distributor shall consider, among other things, the conditions under which the drug has been held, stored, or shipped before or during its return and the condition of the drug and its container, carton, or labeling as a result of storage or shipping. (1991, c. 699, s. 2.)

§ 106-145.8. Records of prescription drugs.

(a) Records. - A wholesale distributor shall establish and maintain inventories and records of all transactions regarding the receipt and distribution or other disposition of prescription drugs, including all stored prescription drugs, all incoming and outgoing prescription drugs, and all outdated, damaged, deteriorated, misbranded, or adulterated prescription drugs. A wholesale distributor is not required, however, to keep a record of the lot number or expiration date of a prescription drug disposed of or distributed by the distributor.

A record of a prescription drug shall include all of the following information:

(1) The source of the prescription drug, including the name and principal address of the seller or transferor and the address of the location from which the drug was shipped.

(2) The identity and quantity of the prescription drug received and distributed or disposed of through another method.

(3) The date the wholesale distributor received the prescription drug and the date the wholesale distributor distributed or otherwise disposed of the drug.

(4) Documentation of the proper storage of prescription drugs. Documentation may be by manual, electromechanical, or electronic temperature and humidity recording equipment, devices, or logs.

A wholesale distributor shall keep a record of a prescription drug for two years after its disposition.

(b) Inspection. - A wholesale distributor shall make inventories and records of prescription drugs available for inspection and photocopying by representatives of the Department or authorized federal, State, or local law enforcement officials. A wholesale drug distributor shall permit the Department or an authorized federal, State, or local law enforcement official to enter and inspect the distributor's premises and delivery vehicles and to audit the distributor's records and written operating procedures at reasonable times and in a reasonable manner.

A record that is kept at the inspection site or is immediately retrievable by computer or other electronic means shall be readily available for authorized inspection during the two-year retention period. A record kept at a central location apart from the inspection site and not electronically retrievable shall be made available for inspection within two working days of a request by an authorized official of a federal, State, or local law enforcement agency. (1991, c. 699, s. 2.)

§ 106-145.9. Written procedures concerning prescription drugs and lists of responsible persons.

(a) Procedures. - A wholesale distributor shall establish, maintain, and adhere to written procedures for the receipt, security, storage, inventory, and distribution of prescription drugs. These shall include all of the following:

(1) A procedure for identifying, recording, and reporting a loss or theft of a prescription drug.

(2) A procedure for correcting all errors and inaccuracies in inventories of prescription drugs.

(3) A procedure whereby the oldest approved stock of a prescription drug is distributed first. The procedure may permit deviation from this requirement, if the deviation is temporary and appropriate.

(4) A procedure for handling recalls and withdrawals of prescription drugs that adequately addresses recalls and withdrawals due to any of the following:

a. An action initiated at the request of the Food and Drug Administration or other federal, State, or local law enforcement or other governmental agency, including the Department.

b. Any voluntary action by the manufacturer to remove defective or potentially defective prescription drugs from the market.

c. Any action undertaken to promote public health and safety by replacing existing prescription drugs with an improved product or new package design.

(5) A procedure to ensure that the wholesale distributor prepares for, protects against, and handles any crisis that affects security or operation of any facility in the event of a strike, a fire, flood, or other natural disaster, or another emergency.

(6) A procedure to ensure that any outdated prescription drugs are segregated from other prescription drugs and either returned to the manufacturer or destroyed.

(b) Responsible Persons. - A wholesale distributor shall establish and maintain lists of officers, directors, managers, and other persons in charge of the distribution, storage, or handling of prescription drugs. The lists shall include a description of the duties of those on the list and a summary of their qualifications. (1991, c. 699, s. 2.)

§ 106-145.10. Application of other laws.

A wholesale drug distributor shall comply with applicable federal, State, and local laws and regulations. A wholesale distributor that deals in controlled substances shall register with the federal Drug Enforcement Administration (DEA) and shall comply with all applicable federal, State, and local laws and regulations. A wholesale drug distributor is subject to any applicable federal, State, or local laws or regulations that relate to prescription drug salvaging or reprocessing. (1991, c. 699, s. 2.)

§ 106-145.11. Wholesale Distributor Advisory Committee.

(a) Organization. - The Wholesale Distributor Advisory Committee is created in the Department. The Committee shall consist of five members appointed by the Commissioner as follows:

(1) Two members shall be representatives of wholesale distributors.

(2) One member shall be a representative of a manufacturer.

(3) One member shall be a representative of practicing pharmacists.

(4)   One member shall be a representative of the consuming public not included in the three categories above.

The Committee shall elect a chair and other officers it finds necessary. The committee shall meet at the call of the chair or upon written notice to all Committee members signed by at least three members. A majority of the Committee is a quorum for the purpose of conducting business. The Department shall provide administrative and clerical support services to the Committee. Members shall be entitled to per diem and reimbursement of expenses as provided in Chapter 138 of the General Statutes.

(b)   Duties. - The Committee shall do the following:

(1)   Review all rules to implement this Article that are proposed for adoption by the Commissioner.

(2)   Advise the Commissioner on the implementation and enforcement of this Article. (1991, c. 699, s. 2.)

§ 106-145.12. Enforcement and implementation of Article.

The Commissioner shall enforce this Article by using employees of the Department. The Commissioner may enter into agreements with federal, State, or local agencies to facilitate enforcement of this Article. The Commissioner may adopt rules to implement this Article. (1991, c. 699, s. 2.)

§ 106-145.13. Submittal of reports by wholesale distributors of transactions involving pseudoephedrine products.

Every 30 calendar days, a wholesale distributor of pseudoephedrine products licensed as provided in this Article shall submit a report electronically to the State Bureau of Investigation that accounts for all transactions involving pseudoephedrine products with persons or firms located within this State for the preceding month. The report shall be submitted on a form and in a manner approved by the State Bureau of Investigation. A wholesale distributor shall maintain each monthly report for a period of two years from the date of submittal to the State Bureau of Investigation. The records shall be readily available for inspection by an authorized official of a federal, State, or local law enforcement agency or the Department of Agriculture and Consumer Services. (2005-434, s. 3.)

Article 13.

Canned Dog Foods.

§§ 106-146 through 106-158: Repealed by Session Laws 1973, c. 771, s. 19.

Article 14.

State Inspection of Slaughterhouses.

§§ 106-159 through 106-168. Repealed by Session Laws 1981, c. 284.

Article 14A.

Licensing and Regulation of Rendering Plants, Rendering Operations, and Waste Kitchen Grease Collection.

§ 106-168.1. Definitions.

For the purposes of this Article, unless the context or subject matter otherwise clearly requires,

(1)   "Collector" means any person, as defined in this section, who collects raw material for the purpose of selling the same to any renderer for further processing.

(2)   "Person" means any individual, partnership, firm, association or corporation.

(3)   "Raw material" means inedible whole or portion of animal or poultry carcasses.

(4) "Rendering operation" means the processing of inedible whole or portion of animal or poultry carcasses and includes collection of such raw material for the purpose of processing.

(5) "Rendering plant" means the building or buildings in which raw material is processed and the premises upon which said building or buildings used in connection with such processing are located.

(6) "Waste kitchen grease" means animal fats or vegetable oils that have been used, and will not be reused, for cooking in a food establishment. "Waste kitchen grease" does not include grease septage as defined in G.S. 130A-290. (1953, c. 732; 2012-127, s. 2.)

§ 106-168.2. License required.

No person shall engage in rendering operations unless such person shall hold a valid license to do so issued as hereinafter provided. (1953, c. 732.)

§ 106-168.3. Exemptions.

Nothing in this Article shall apply to the premises or the rendering operations on the premises of any establishment operating under a numbered permit from the North Carolina Department of Agriculture and Consumer Services as provided by the North Carolina Meat Inspection Act, or under United States government inspection. (1953, c. 732; 1997-261, s. 109.)

§ 106-168.4. Application for license.

Application for license shall be made to the Commissioner of Agriculture, hereinafter called the "Commissioner," on forms provided by him. The application shall set forth the name and residence of the applicant, his present or proposed place of business, the particular method which he intends to employ or employs in the processing of raw material, and such other information as the Commissioner may require, except that the Commissioner shall not require the submission of blueprints, plans, or specifications of the existing plant or equipment of any person owning and operating a rendering plant in North Carolina on January 1, 1953. The applicant shall pay a fee of fifty dollars ($50.00) with each application, which said fee shall be the only charge made in connection with licensure. (1953, c. 732.)

§ 106-168.5. Duties of Commissioner upon receipt of application; inspection committee.

Upon receipt of the application, the Commissioner shall promptly cause the rendering plant and equipment, or the plans, specifications, and selected site, of the applicant to be inspected by an inspection committee hereinafter called the "committee," which shall be composed of three members: One member who shall be designated by the Commissioner of Agriculture and who shall be an employee of the Department of Agriculture and Consumer Services, one member who shall be designated by the Secretary of Health and Human Services and who shall be an employee of the Department of Health and Human Services, and one member who shall be designated by the board of directors of the North Carolina Renderers Association, and who shall be a person having practical knowledge of rendering operations. Each member may be designated and relieved from time to time at the discretion of the designating authority. No State employee designated as a member of the committee shall receive any additional compensation therefor and no compensation shall be paid by the State to any other member. (1953, c. 732; 1957, c. 1357, s. 13; 1973, c. 476, s. 128; 1989, c. 727, s. 219(31); 1997-261, s. 109; 1997-443, s. 11A.42; 2012-127, s. 3.)

§ 106-168.6. Inspection by committee; certificate of specific findings.

The committee upon notification by the Commissioner shall promptly inspect the plans, specifications, and selected site in the case of proposed rendering plants and shall inspect the buildings, grounds, and equipment of established rendering plants. If the committee finds that the plans, specifications, and selected site in the case of proposed plants, or the buildings, grounds, and equipment in the case of established plants, comply with the requirements of this Article and the rules and regulations promulgated by the Commissioner not inconsistent therewith, it shall certify its findings in writing and forward same to the Commissioner. If there is a failure in any respect to meet such requirements, the committee shall notify the applicant in writing of such deficiencies and the committee shall within a reasonable time to be determined by the Commissioner make a second inspection. If the specified defects are remedied, the committee shall thereupon certify its findings in writing to the Commissioner. Not more than two inspections shall be required of the committee under any one application. (1953, c. 732.)

§ 106-168.7. Issuance of license.

Upon receipt of the certificate of compliance from the committee, the Commissioner shall issue a license to the applicant to conduct rendering operations as specified in the application. A license shall be valid until revoked for cause as hereinafter provided. (1953, c. 732.)

§ 106-168.8. Minimum standards for conducting rendering operations.

The following minimum standards shall be required for all rendering operations subject to the provisions of this Article:

(1) Buildings utilized in connection with the rendering plant shall be of sufficient size and shape to accommodate all phases of actual or intended processing. Adequate partitions shall be installed therein so as to eliminate any contact between raw materials and finished products and so as to preclude contamination of finished products. The buildings shall be constructed in a manner and of materials which will insure adequate drainage and sanitation in all phases of operation.

(2) Raw material upon arrival at the rendering plant shall be unloaded into a building for processing. All raw material shall be processed by approved methods within 24 hours after delivery to the rendering plant.

(3) Processing equipment shall be airtight, except for proper escapes for vapors caused by the cooking process.

(4) Cooking vapors shall be controlled and disposed of by approved methods.

(5) Vehicles used to transport raw material shall be so constructed as to prevent any drippings or seepings from such material from escaping from the truck. Such vehicles shall have body sides of sufficient height that no portion of any raw material transported therein shall be visible. All vehicles shall be provided with suitable top or covering to prevent the spread of disease by flies or other agents during the transportation of raw material.

(6) All vehicles and containers used in transporting raw material shall be disinfected at the earliest practicable time after unloading, and shall, in any event, be disinfected before again being taken upon a public highway or before leaving the rendering plant. Approved facilities and materials for disinfection shall be carried on vehicles transporting carcasses. Employees shall be required to wear rubber boots which shall be disinfected prior to entry to a farm.

(7) Approved facilities, means and methods for disinfection shall be available at the rendering plant at all times. Employees and employees' clothing coming in contact with raw material shall be disinfected before coming in contact with any finished products, or any portion of the plant in which the same are located. Rodent and fly control measures shall be practiced as a further means of prevention of the spread of disease.

(8) Proof of general liability insurance of one million dollars ($1,000,000) shall be made in a manner satisfactory to the Commissioner. (1953, c. 732; 2012-127, s. 4.)

§ 106-168.9. Transportation by licensee.

Any person holding a license under the provisions of this Article, or acting as a collector as herein defined, may haul and transport raw material, except such material as may be specifically prohibited by law or by the rules and regulations promulgated by the Commissioner, when such transporting and hauling is done in accordance with the provisions of this Article. (1953, c. 732.)

§ 106-168.10. Disposal of diseased animals.

Any person holding a license under the provisions of this Article is authorized to kill diseased, sick, old or crippled animals on the premises of the owner upon his request; provided that no animal known to have tuberculosis, Bang's disease, anthrax, or any other disease for which quarantine may be imposed, shall be removed from any premises placed under quarantine without permission of the State Veterinarian, or his authorized agent. The licensee shall keep and make available to the Commissioner, upon request, such records as the Commissioner may require with respect to the collection and disposal of dead animals. (1953, c. 732.)

§ 106-168.11. Authority of agents of licensee.

Authority granted to any person holding a valid license under the provisions of this Article shall extend also to the agents and employees of such person while acting within the scope of their authority. All such agents and employees shall comply with the provisions of this Article and rules and regulations not inconsistent therewith, and shall display evidence of such employment or agency upon proper request at any time while so acting. (1953, c. 732.)

§ 106-168.12. Commissioner authorized to adopt rules and regulations.

The Commissioner of Agriculture is hereby authorized to make and establish reasonable rules and regulations, not inconsistent with the provisions of this Article, after consulting the committee, for the proper administration and enforcement thereof. (1953, c. 732.)

§ 106-168.13. Effect of failure to comply.

Failure to comply with the provisions of this Article or rules and regulations not inconsistent therewith shall be cause of revocation of license, if such failure shall not be remedied within a reasonable time after notice to the licensee. Any person whose license is revoked may reapply for a license in the manner provided in this Article for an initial application, except that the Commissioner shall not be required to cause the rendering plant and equipment of the applicant to be inspected by the committee until the expiration of 30 days from the date of revocation. (1953, c. 732.)

§ 106-168.14. Collectors subject to certain provisions.

Any collector, as defined in this Article, shall be subject to the provisions of subdivision (5) and subdivision (6) of G.S. 106-168.8 and the provisions of G.S. 106-168.9, and any rules and regulations adopted by the Commissioner pursuant thereto. (1953, c. 732.)

§ 106-168.14A. Collectors of waste kitchen grease subject to certain provisions.

(a) For purposes of this section, "collector of waste kitchen grease" means any person who collects waste kitchen grease for the purpose of selling the same to any renderer or other person for further processing.

(b) Any collector of waste kitchen grease who sells the waste kitchen grease collected shall provide the purchaser with a statement of ownership setting forth the lawful ownership of the waste kitchen grease sold to such purchaser. (2012-127, s. 5.)

§ 106-168.15. Violation a misdemeanor.

Any person conducting rendering operations or collecting raw material in violation of the provisions of this Article shall be guilty of a Class 1 misdemeanor. (1953, c. 732; 1993, c. 539, s. 745; 1994, Ex. Sess., c. 24, s. 14(c).)

§ 106-168.16. Civil penalties.

The Commissioner may assess a civil penalty of not more than five thousand dollars ($5,000) against any person who violates a provision of this Article or any rule promulgated thereunder. In determining the amount of the penalty, the Commissioner shall consider the degree and extent of harm caused by the violation.

The clear proceeds of civil penalties assessed pursuant to this section shall be remitted to the Civil Penalty and Forfeiture Fund in accordance with G.S. 115C-457.2. (1995, c. 516, s. 7; 1998-215, s. 8.)

Article 15.

Inspection of Meat and Meat Products by Counties and Cities.

§§ 106-169 through 106-173: Repealed by Session Laws 1997-74, s. 8.

Article 15A.

Meat Grading Law.

§§ 106-173.1 through 106-173.16. Repealed by Session Laws 1983, c. 248, s. 2.

Article 16.

Bottling Plants for Soft Drinks.

§§ 106-174 through 106-184.1: Repealed by Session Laws 1975, c. 614, s. 42.

Article 17.

Marketing and Branding Farm Products.

§ 106-185. Scope of Article; federal-State cooperation.

(a) Scope. - This Article gives the Department of Agriculture and Consumer Services the authority to investigate marketing conditions for and establish and maintain standard grades, packages, and State brands for farm products. As used in this Article, the term "farm products" means farm crops, horticultural crops, and animal products.

(b) Cooperation. - The Commissioner of Agriculture may enter into agreements with the United States Department of Agriculture that require State and federal cooperation in performing the duties imposed by this Article. (1919, c. 325, s. 1; C.S., s. 4781; 1921, c. 140; 1993, c. 223, s. 1; 1997-261, s. 36.)

§ 106-186. Power to employ agents and assistants.

The Board of Agriculture is charged with the execution of the provisions of this Article, and has authority to employ such agents and assistants as may be necessary, fix their compensation and define their duties, and may require bonds in such amount as they may deem advisable, conditioned upon the faithful performance of duties by any employee or agent. (1919, c. 325, s. 2; C.S., s. 4782.)

§ 106-187. Board of Agriculture to investigate marketing of farm products.

It shall be the duty of the Board of Agriculture to investigate the subject of marketing farm products, to diffuse useful information relating thereto, and to furnish advice and assistance to the public in order to promote efficient and economical methods of marketing farm products, and authority is hereby given to gather and diffuse timely information concerning the supply, demand, prevailing prices, and commercial movement of farm products, including quantities in common and cold storage, and may interchange such information with the United States Department of Agriculture. (1919, c. 325, s. 3; C.S., s. 4783.)

§ 106-188. Promulgation of standards for receptacles, etc.

After investigation, and from time to time as may be practical and advisable, the Board shall have authority to establish and promulgate standards of opened and closed receptacles for, and standards for the grade and other classification of farm products, by which their quantity, quality, and value may be determined, and prescribe and promulgate rules and regulations governing the marks, brands, and labels which may be required for receptacles for farm products, for the purpose of showing the name and address of the producer or packer; the quantity, nature and quality of the product, or any of them, and for the purpose of preventing deception in reference thereto, and for the purpose of establishing a State brand for any farm product produced in North Carolina: Provided, that any standard for any farm product or receptacle therefor, or any requirement for marking receptacles for farm products, now or hereafter established under authority of the Congress of the United States, shall forthwith, as far as applicable, be established or prescribed and promulgated as the official standard or requirement in this State: Provided, that no standard established or requirement for marking prescribed under this Article shall become effective until the expiration of 30 days after it shall have been promulgated. (1919, c. 325, s. 4; C.S., s. 4784.)

§ 106-189. Sale and receptacles of standardized products must conform to requirements.

Whenever any standard for the grade or other classification of any farm product becomes effective under this Article no person thereafter shall pack for sale, offer to sell, or sell within this State any such farm product to which such standard is applicable, unless it conforms to the standard, subject to such reasonable variations therefrom as may be allowed in the rules and regulations made under this Article: Provided, that any farm product may be packed for sale, offered for sale, or sold, without conforming to the standard for grade or other classification applicable thereto, if it is especially described as not graded or plainly marked as "Not graded." This proviso shall not apply to peaches. (It is the intent and purpose of this exemption to exempt peaches from the requirements of Article 17 of Chapter 106 that ungraded peaches, when sold or offered for sale, shall be marked "ungraded," "field run," "not graded," "grade not determined" or "unclassified," or words of similar import.) The Board of Agriculture, or the Commissioner of Agriculture, and their authorized agents, are authorized to issue "stop-sale" orders which shall prohibit further sale of the products if they have reason to believe such products are being offered, or exposed, for sale in violation of any of the provisions of this Article until the law has been complied with or said violations otherwise legally disposed of.

Whenever any standard for an open or closed receptacle for a farm product shall be made effective under this Article no person shall pack for sale in and deliver in a receptacle, or sell in and deliver in a receptacle, any such farm product to which such standard is applicable, unless the receptacle conforms to the standard, subject to such variations therefrom as may be allowed in the rules and regulations made under this Article, or unless the receptacle be of a capacity twenty-five percent (25%) less than the capacity of the minimum standard receptacle for the product: Provided, that any receptacle for such farm product of a capacity within twenty-five percent (25%) of, or larger than, the minimum standard receptacle for the product may be used if it be specifically described as not a standard size, or be conspicuously marked with the phrase, "Not standard size," in addition to any other marking which may be prescribed for such receptacles under authority given by this Article.

Whenever any requirement for marking a receptacle for a farm product shall have been made effective under this Article no person shall sell and deliver in this State any such farm product in a receptacle to which such requirement is applicable unless the receptacle be marked according to such requirements. (1919, c. 325, s. 5; C.S., s. 4785; 1943, c. 483; 1969, c. 849.)

§ 106-189.1: Repealed by Session Laws 1983, c. 248, s. 3.

§ 106-189.2. Sale of immature apples.

(a)　　Notwithstanding any other provision of law, the Board of Agriculture shall adopt requirements for apple grade standards. The apple grade standards shall include the requirements for maturity of the United States standards for grades of apples and may employ the use of the refractometer to determine the sugar content and maturity of apples and the pressure test to determine the maturity of apples. All apples sold, offered for sale, or shipped into this State shall meet these requirements.

(b)　　Any person, firm or corporation violating the provisions of this section shall be guilty of a Class 3 misdemeanor and shall be punished only by a fine of not less than one hundred dollars ($100.00). Each day on which apples are sold or offered for sale in violation of the provisions of this section shall constitute a separate violation. (1973, c. 973; 1985, c. 585; 1993, c. 539, s. 746; 1994, Ex. Sess., c. 24, s. 14(c).)

§ 106-190. Inspectors or graders authorized; revocation of license.

The Board is authorized to employ, license, or designate persons to inspect and classify farm products and to certify as to the grade or other classification thereof, in accordance with the standards made effective under this Article, and shall fix, assess and collect, or cause to be collected, fees for such services. Whenever, after opportunity for a hearing is afforded to any person employed, licensed, or designated under this section, it is determined that such person has failed to classify farm products correctly in accordance with the standards established therefor under this Article, or has violated any provision of this Article, or of the rules and regulations made hereunder, the Board may suspend or revoke the employment, license, or designation of such person. Pending investigation the person in charge of this work may suspend or revoke any such appointment, license, or designation temporarily without hearing. (1919, c. 325, s. 6; C.S., s. 4786.)

§ 106-190.1. Aggregate State service credit for graders.

All fruit, vegetable, grain, poultry, egg and egg products graders employed by the Board in positions in fact permanent and full-time, but who were inadvertently or incorrectly classified as temporary until January 1, 1974, shall be given aggregate State service credit for the period of employment before January 1, 1974. This credit shall be given only to persons employed on a full-time, year-round basis during which time they were classified as temporary. Credit shall be given for purposes of determining the amount of leave earned by the employee, eligibility for and amount of longevity pay, and any other determinations for which the length of State service is relevant. Employees given retroactive aggregate State service credit under this section shall receive retroactive longevity pay, to the extent for which they would have been eligible for longevity pay if they had been correctly classified from the date of their initial employment, for all service beginning January 1, 1974, until August 1, 1977, with any longevity pay actually paid to be subtracted therefrom. (1977, c. 1038, s. 1.)

§ 106-191. Appeal from classification.

The owner or person in possession of any farm product classified in accordance with the provisions of this Article may appeal from such classification under such rules and regulations as may be prescribed. (1919, c. 325, s. 7; C.S., s. 4787.)

§ 106-192. Certificate of grade prima facie evidence.

A certificate of the grade or other classification of any farm product issued under this Article shall be accepted in any court of this State as prima facie evidence of the true grade or other classification of such farm product at the time of its classification. (1919, c. 325, s. 8; C.S., s. 4788.)

§ 106-193. Unwholesome products not classified; health officer notified.

Any person employed, licensed, or designated shall neither classify nor certify as to the grade or other classification of any farm product which, in his judgment, is unwholesome or unfit for food of man or other animal. If, in the performance of his official duties, he discovers any farm product which is unwholesome or unfit for food of man or for other animal for which it is intended, he shall promptly report the fact to a health officer of the State or of any county or municipality thereof. (1919, c. 325, s. 9; C.S., s. 4789.)

§ 106-194. Inspection and sampling of farm products authorized.

Agents and employees are authorized from time to time to ascertain the amount of any farm products in this State, to inspect the same in the possession of any person engaged in the business of marketing them in this State, and to take samples of such products. In carrying out these purposes agents and employees are authorized to enter on any business day, during the usual hours of business, any storehouse, warehouse, cold storage plant, packing house, stockyard, railroad yard, railroad car, or any other building or place where farm products are kept or stored by any person engaged in the business of marketing farm products. (1919, c. 325, ss. 10, 11; C.S., s. 4790.)

§ 106-194.1. Farm Product Inspection Account.

The Farm Product Inspection Account is established as a nonreverting account within the Department of Agriculture and Consumer Services. Interest and other investment income earned by the Account shall be credited to it.

Fees collected under this Article shall be credited to the Account and applied to the costs of administering this Article. Fees credited to the Account from grading and inspection services provided under a cooperative agreement with the United States Department of Agriculture are subject to any restrictions on use set out in the cooperative agreement. (1993, c. 223, s. 2; 1997-261, s. 109.)

§ 106-195. Rules and regulations; how prescribed.

The Board of Agriculture is authorized to make and promulgate such rules and regulations as may be necessary to carry out the provisions of this Article. Such rules and regulations shall be made to conform as nearly as practicable to the rules and regulations of the Secretary of Agriculture of the United States, prescribed under any act of Congress of the United States relating to the marketing of farm products. (1919, c. 325, s. 12; C.S., s. 4791.)

§ 106-196. Violation of Article or regulations a misdemeanor.

Any person who violates any provision of this Article, or of the rules and regulations made under the Article for carrying out its provisions, or fails or refuses to comply with any requirement thereof, or who wilfully interferes with agents or employees in the execution, or on account of the execution, of his or their duties, shall be guilty of a Class 3 misdemeanor. (1919, c. 325, ss. 13, 14; C.S., s. 4792; 1993, c. 539, s. 747; 1994, Ex. Sess., c. 24, s. 14(c).)

Article 18.

Shipper's Name on Receptacles.

§ 106-197: Repealed by Session Laws 1997-74, s. 9.

Article 19.

Trademark for Standardized Farm Products.

§§ 106-198 through 106-202: Repealed by Session Laws 1987, c. 244, s. 1(g).

§§ 106-202.1 through 106-202.5. Reserved for future codification purposes.

Article 19A.

Records of Sales of Farm Products.

§ 106-202.6. Dated sales confirmation slips; inapplicable to consumers.

(a) In every sales transaction of farm or horticultural crops, or animal products, the buyer, broker, or authorized agent shall give to the seller a sales confirmation slip bearing the date of the sales transaction.

(b) This section shall not apply if the buyer is a natural person and/or the farm or horticultural crops, or animal products are purchased primarily for a personal, family, or household purpose. (1979, c. 363.)

§§ 106-202.7 through 106-202.11. Reserved for future codification purposes.

Article 19B.

Plant Protection and Conservation Act.

§ 106-202.12. Definitions.

As used in this Article, unless the context requires otherwise:

(1)   "Board" means the North Carolina Plant Conservation Board as provided in this Article.

(2)   "Commissioner" means the Commissioner of Agriculture.

(3)   "Conserve" and "conservation" mean to use, and the use of, all methods and procedures for the purposes of increasing the number of individuals of resident species of plants up to adequate levels to assure their continuity in their ecosystems. These methods and procedures include all activities associated with scientific resource conservation such as research, census, law enforcement, habitat protection, acquisition and maintenance, propagation, and transplantation into unoccupied parts of historic range. With respect to endangered and threatened species, the terms mean to use, and the use of, methods and procedures to bring any endangered or threatened species to the point at which the measures provided for the species are no longer necessary.

(4)   "Endangered species" means any species or higher taxon of plant whose continued existence as a viable component of the State's flora is determined to be in jeopardy by the Board; also, any species of plant determined to be an "endangered species" pursuant to the Endangered Species Act.

(5)   "Endangered Species Act" means the Endangered Species Act of 1973, Public Law 93-205 (87 Stat. 884), as it may be subsequently amended.

(6)   "Exotic species" means a species or higher taxon of plant not native or naturalized in North Carolina but appearing in the Federal Endangered and Threatened Species List or in the appendices to the International Treaty on Endangered and Threatened Species.

(7)   "Plant" means any member of the plant kingdom, including seeds, roots and other parts or their propagules.

(8)   "Protected plant" means a species or higher taxon of plant adopted by the Board to protect, conserve, and/or enhance the plant species and includes those the Board has designated as endangered, threatened, or of special concern.

(9)   "Resident plant or resident species" means a native species or higher taxon of plant growing in North Carolina.

(10) "Scientific committee" means the North Carolina Plant Conservation Scientific Committee.

(11) "Special concern species" means any species of plant in North Carolina which requires monitoring but which may be collected and sold under regulations adopted under the provisions of this Article.

(12) "Threatened species" means any resident species of plant which is likely to become an endangered species within the foreseeable future throughout all or a significant portion of its range, or one that is designated as threatened by the Federal Fish and Wildlife Service. (1979, c. 964, s. 1.)

§ 106-202.13. Declaration of policy.

The General Assembly finds that the recreational needs of the people, the interests of science, and the economy of the State require that threatened and endangered species of plants and species of plants of special concern be protected and conserved, that their numbers should be enhanced and that propagative techniques be developed for them; however, nothing in this Article shall be construed to limit the rights of a property owner, without his consent, in the management of his lands for agriculture, forestry, development or any other lawful purpose. (1979, c. 964, s. 1.)

§ 106-202.14. Creation of Board; membership; terms; chairman; quorum; board actions; compensation.

(a) The North Carolina Plant Conservation Board is created within the Department of Agriculture and Consumer Services.

(b) The Board shall consist of seven members who are residents of North Carolina, one of whom represents each of the following:

(1) The North Carolina Botanical Garden of The University of North Carolina at Chapel Hill;

(2) The botanical, scientific community in North Carolina;

(3) The North Carolina Forest Service of the Department of Agriculture and Consumer Services;

(4) A North Carolina citizens conservation organization;

(5) The commercial plant production industry in North Carolina;

(6) The Department of Agriculture and Consumer Services;

(7) The North Carolina public at large.

The Governor shall appoint the first four members enumerated above; the Commissioner shall appoint the remaining three members.

(c) Initial appointments to the Board shall be made by October 1, 1979. Of the terms of initial appointees, the representatives of the North Carolina Botanical Garden of The University of North Carolina at Chapel Hill, the commercial plant production industry in North Carolina, and a North Carolina citizens conservation organization shall serve two-year terms; all other members shall serve four-year terms. All subsequent terms shall be for four-year terms.

(d) All members shall hold their offices until their successors are appointed and qualified. Any vacancy occurring in the membership of the Board prior to the expiration of the term shall be filled for the remainder of the unexpired term. The Commissioner may at any time remove any member from the Board for cause. Each appointment to fill a vacancy in the membership of the Board shall be of a person having the proper credentials for that vacancy and appointed by the proper appointing agency.

(e) The Board shall select its chairman from its own membership to serve for a term of two years. The chairman shall have a full vote. Any vacancy occurring in the chairmanship shall be filled by the Board for the remainder of the term. The Board may select other officers as it deems necessary.

(f) Any action of the Board shall require at least four concurring votes.

(g) Members of the Board who are not State employees shall receive per diem, subsistence and travel allowances authorized by G.S. 138-5; members who are State employees shall receive the subsistence and travel allowances authorized by G.S. 138-6; and members who are also members of the General Assembly shall receive subsistence and travel allowances authorized by G.S.

120-3.1. (1979, c. 964, s. 1; 1989, c. 727, s. 218(45); 1997-261, ss. 37, 38; 1997-443, s. 11A.119(a); 2011-145, s. 13.25(qq); 2013-155, s. 9.)

§ 106-202.15. Powers and duties of the Board.

The Board shall have all of the following powers and duties:

(1) To adopt and maintain a list of protected plant species for North Carolina, identifying each entry by the common name and scientific name, along with its status as endangered, threatened, or of special concern, as provided under G.S. 106-202.16.

(2) To reconsider and revise the lists from time to time in response to public proposals and as the Board deems necessary.

(3) To conserve and to regulate the collection and shipment of those plant species or higher taxa that are of such similarity to endangered and threatened species that they cannot be easily or readily distinguished from an endangered or threatened species.

(4) To regulate within the State any exotic species, in the same manner as a resident species if the exotic species is on the Federal Endangered and Threatened Species List or it is listed in the Appendices to the International Treaty to Conserve Endangered and Threatened Species.

(5) To determine that certain plant species growing in North Carolina, whether or not they are on the endangered or threatened species list, are of special concern and to limit, regulate or forbid sale or collection of these plants.

(6) To conduct investigations to determine whether a plant should be on the protected plant lists and the requirements for survival of resident species of plants.

(7) To adopt regulations to protect, conserve and enhance resident and exotic species of plants on the lists, or to otherwise affect the intent of this Article.

(8) To develop, establish and coordinate conservation programs for endangered species and threatened species of plants, consistent with the

policies of the Endangered Species Act, including the acquisition of rights to land or aquatic habitats.

(9) To enter into and administer cooperative agreements through the Commissioner of Agriculture, in concert with the North Carolina Botanical Garden and other agencies, with the U.S. Department of Interior or other federal, State or private organizations concerning endangered and threatened species of plants and their conservation and management.

(10) To cooperate or enter into formal agreements with any agency of any other state or of the federal government for the purpose of enforcing any of the provisions of this Article.

(11) Through the Commissioner, to receive funds, donations, grants or other moneys, issue grants, enter contracts, employ personnel and purchase supplies and materials necessary to fulfill its duties.

(12) To adopt rules under which the Department of Agriculture and Consumer Services may issue permits to licensed nurserymen, commercial growers, scientific supply houses and botanical gardens for the sale or distribution of plants on the protected list provided that the plants are nursery propagated or grown horticulturally.

(13) To stop the sale of or to seize any endangered, threatened, or special concern plant species, or part thereof possessed, transported, or moved within this State or brought into this State from any place outside the State if such is found by the Board or its duly authorized agent to be in violation of this Article or rules adopted pursuant to this Article. Such plants shall be moved or disposed of at the direction of the Board or its agent or by court order.

(14) To establish fees for permits authorized in this Article. (1979, c. 964, s. 1; 1989, c. 508, s. 1; 1997-261, s. 39; 2007-456, s. 1.)

§ 106-202.16. Criteria and procedures for placing plants on protected plant lists.

(a) All native or resident plants which are on the current federal lists of endangered or threatened plants pursuant to the Endangered Species Act have the same status on the North Carolina Protected Plants lists.

(b)   The Board, the Scientific Committee, or any resident of North Carolina may propose to the Department of Agriculture and Consumer Services that a plant be added to or removed from a protected plant list.

(c)   If the Board, with the advice of the Scientific Committee, finds that there is any substance to the proposal, it shall publish notice of the proposal in a Department of Agriculture and Consumer Services news release.

(d)   The Board shall collect relevant scientific and economic data, concerning any substantial proposal, necessary to determine:

(1)   Whether or not any other State or federal agency or private entity is taking steps to protect the plant under consideration;

(2)   The present or threatened destruction, modification or curtailment of its habitat;

(3)   Over-utilization for commercial, scientific, educational or recreational purposes;

(4)   Critical depletion from disease or predation;

(5)   The inadequacy of existing regulatory mechanisms; or

(6)   Other natural or man-made factors affecting its continued existence in North Carolina.

If the Board, with the advice of the Scientific Committee, finds that the plant should be added to or removed from a protected plant list the Board shall instigate rule-making procedures to add or remove the plant from the list.

(e), (f) Repealed by Session Laws 1987, c. 827, s. 31. (1979, c. 964, s. 1; 1987, c. 827, s. 31; 1997-261, s. 109.)

§ 106-202.17. Creation of committee; membership; terms; chairman; meetings; committee action; quorum; compensation.

(a)   The North Carolina Plant Conservation Scientific Committee is created within the Department of Agriculture and Consumer Services.

(b) The Scientific Committee shall consist of the Directors of The University of North Carolina at Chapel Hill Herbarium, the North Carolina State University Herbarium, the North Carolina Botanical Garden of The University of North Carolina at Chapel Hill, the North Carolina State Museum of Natural Sciences and the North Carolina Natural Heritage Program of the Department of Environment and Natural Resources or their designees, a representative of the North Carolina Association of Nurserymen, Inc., appointed by the Commissioner, and a representative of a conservation organization, appointed by the Commissioner. Members shall serve for three-year terms and may succeed themselves.

(c) The Board shall select a chairman of the Scientific Committee from the Scientific Committee's membership to serve for three years.

(d) The Scientific Committee may hold its meetings at the North Carolina Botanical Garden of The University of North Carolina at Chapel Hill.

(e) Any action of the Scientific Committee shall require at least four concurring votes.

(f) Members of the Scientific Committee who are not State employees may receive per diem, subsistence and travel allowances authorized by G.S. 138-5 if they so request; members who are State employees may receive the subsistence and travel allowances authorized by G.S. 138-6 if they so request; and members who are also members of the General Assembly may receive subsistence and travel allowances authorized by G.S. 120-3.1 if they so request. (1979, c. 964, s. 1; 1989, c. 727, s. 218(46); 1993, c. 561, s. 116(i); 1997-261, s. 109; 1997-443, s. 11A.119(a); 2007-456, s. 2.)

§ 106-202.18. Powers and duties of the Scientific Committee.

The Scientific Committee shall have all of the following powers and duties:

(1) To gather and provide information and data and advise the Board with respect to all aspects of the biology and ecology of endangered and threatened plant species.

(2) To develop and present to the Board management and conservation practices for preserving endangered or threatened plant species.

(3) To recommend habitat areas for acquisition to the extent that funds are available or expected.

(4) To investigate and make recommendations to the Board as to the status of endangered, threatened plant species, or species of special concern.

(5) To make recommendations to the Board concerning regulation of the collection and shipment of endangered or threatened plant species within North Carolina.

(6) To review and comment on environmental impact statements prepared by State agencies on projects that may affect protected plants; and

(7) To advise the Board on matters submitted to the Scientific Committee by the Board or the Commissioner which involve technical questions and the development of pertinent rules and regulations, and make any recommendations as deemed by the Scientific Committee to be worthy of the Board's consideration. (1979, c. 964, s. 1; 2007-456, s. 3.)

§ 106-202.19. Unlawful acts; penalties; enforcement.

(a) Unless the conduct is covered under some other provision of law providing greater punishment, it is unlawful to engage in any of the following conduct:

(1) To uproot, dig, take or otherwise disturb or remove for any purpose from the lands of another, any plant on a protected plant list without a written permit from the owner which is dated and valid for no more than 180 days and which indicates the species or higher taxon of plants for which permission is granted; except that the incidental disturbance of protected plants during agricultural, forestry or development operations is not illegal so long as the plants are not collected for sale or commercial use.

(2) To sell, barter, trade, exchange, export, offer for sale, barter, trade, exchange or export or give away for any purpose including advertising or other promotional purpose any plant on a protected plant list, except as authorized according to the rules and regulations of the Board.

(3) To violate any rule of the Board promulgated under this Article.

(4) Repealed by Session Laws 2012-200, s. 18, effective October 1, 2012.

(5) To buy ginseng outside of a buying season as provided by the Board without obtaining the required documents from the person selling the ginseng.

(6) To buy ginseng for the purpose of resale or trade without holding a currently valid permit as a ginseng dealer.

(6a) To uproot, dig, take, or otherwise disturb or remove for any purpose from another person's land ginseng, galax, or Venus flytrap without a written permit from the owner that is dated and valid for no more than 180 days. A person in lawful possession of the land who has a recorded lease which allows for the disturbance or removal of any vegetation on the land is not subject to this subdivision.

(6b) To buy galax outside of a buying season as provided by the Board without obtaining the required documents from the person selling the galax.

(6c) To buy Venus flytrap outside of a buying season as provided by the Board without obtaining the required documents from the person selling the Venus flytrap.

(6d) To buy more than five pounds of galax for the purpose of resale or trade without a copy of the landowner's written permission and confirmation of the collection date.

(6e) To buy more than 50 Venus flytrap plants for the purpose of resale or trade unless fully compliant with applicable regulations.

(7) To fail to keep records as required under this Article, to refuse to make records available for inspection by the Board or its agent, or to use forms other than those provided for the current year or harvest season by the Department of Agriculture and Consumer Services.

(8) To provide false information on any record or form required under this Article.

(9) To make false statements or provide false information in connection with any investigation conducted under this Article.

(10) To possess any protected plant, or part thereof, which was obtained in violation of this Article or any rule adopted under this Article.

(11) To violate a stop sale order issued by the Board or its agent.

(a1) Any person convicted of violating this Article, or any rule of the Board adopted pursuant to this Article shall be guilty of a Class 2 misdemeanor. Each illegal movement or distribution of a protected plant shall constitute a separate violation. In addition, if any person continues to violate or further violates any provision of this Article after written notice from the Board, the court may determine that each day during which the violation continued or is repeated constitutes a separate violation subject to the foregoing penalties.

(a2) A civil penalty of not more than two thousand dollars ($2,000) may be assessed by the Board against any person guilty of violating this Article a second or subsequent time. The clear proceeds of civil penalties assessed pursuant to this subsection shall be remitted to the Civil Penalty and Forfeiture Fund in accordance with G.S. 115C-457.2.

(b) The Commissioner or any employee or agent of the Department of Agriculture and Consumer Services designated by the Commissioner to enforce the provisions of this Article, may enter any place within the State at all reasonable times where plant materials are being grown, transported, or offered for sale and require the presentation for inspection of all pertinent papers and records relative to the provisions of this Article, after giving notice in writing to the owner or custodian of the premises to be entered. If he refuses to consent to the entry, the Commissioner may apply to any district court judge and the judge may order, without notice, that the owner or custodian of the place permit the Commissioner to enter the place for the purposes herein stated and failure by any person to obey the order may be punished as for contempt.

(c) The Commissioner of Agriculture is authorized to apply to the superior court for, and the court shall have jurisdiction upon hearing and, for cause shown, to grant a temporary or permanent injunction restraining any person from violating any provision of G.S. 106-202.19(a), regardless of whether there exists an adequate remedy at law. (1979, c. 964, s. 1; 1989, c. 508, s. 2; 1993, c. 539, s. 749; 1994, Ex. Sess., c. 24, s. 14(c); 1997-261, ss. 40, 41; 1998-215, s. 9; 2001-487, s. 43(b); 2007-456, ss. 4, 5; 2012-200, s. 18.)

§ 106-202.20. Forfeiture of illegally possessed plants; disposition of plants.

Upon conviction of any defendant for a violation of G.S. 106-202.19, the court, in its discretion, may order the defendant to forfeit any plant or plant parts which he possesses in violation of G.S. 106-202.19. The court shall direct disposition of any forfeited plant or plant part by destruction or sale. The clear proceeds of forfeitures and sales pursuant to this section shall be remitted to the Civil Penalty and Forfeiture Fund in accordance with G.S. 115C-457.2. (1989, c. 508, s. 3; 1997-261, s. 109; 1998-215, s. 10.)

§ 106-202.21. Ginseng dealer permits.

(a)   No person shall act in the capacity of a ginseng dealer, or shall engage, or offer to engage in the business of, advertise as, or assume to act as a ginseng dealer unless that person holds a currently valid permit as provided in this Article.

(b)   Applications for a ginseng dealer permit shall be on a form and shall contain information as prescribed by the Board. All permits issued under this section shall expire on 30 June of the fiscal year for which they are issued.

(c)   A ginseng dealer permit may be renewed annually upon application to the Board.

(d)   A ginseng dealer shall notify the Board of any change of address or business location within 30 days of such change.

(e)   The Board shall issue to each applicant who satisfies the requirements of this Article a permit which entitles the applicant to conduct the business described in the application during the harvest season for which the permit is issued, unless the permit is suspended or revoked. (1989, c. 508, s. 3.)

§ 106-202.22. Denial, suspension, or revocation of permit.

(a)   The Board may deny, suspend, revoke, or modify any permit issued under this Article if it finds that the applicant or permit holder has violated this Article or rules adopted pursuant to this Article.

(b) Suspension of any permit under this Article shall be for not less than one year. Any permit holder whose permit has been revoked shall not be eligible to reapply until two years after the final decision of the Board or two years after his permit is surrendered pursuant to such revocation, whichever is earlier. The expiration or voluntary surrender of a permit shall not deprive the Board of jurisdiction to suspend, revoke or modify such permit. A person whose permit has been suspended or revoked shall not engage in business as an employee, partner, or associate of another permit holder during the period of such revocation or suspension.

(c) If a permit is suspended or revoked, the permit holder shall, within five days of such suspension or revocation, surrender such permit to the Commissioner or his authorized representative. (1989, c. 508, s. 3.)

Article 20.

Standard Weight of Flour and Meal.

§§ 106-203 through 106-209. Repealed by Session Laws 1945, c. 280, s. 2.

Article 21.

Artificially Bleached Flour.

§§ 106-210 through 106-219. Repealed by Session Laws 1975, c. 614, s. 42.

Article 21A.

Enrichment of Flour, Bread, Cornmeal and Grits.

§§ 106-219.1 through 106-219.9. Repealed by Session Laws 1975, c. 614, s. 42.

Article 22.

Inspection of Bakeries.

§§ 106-220 through 106-232. Repealed by Session Laws 1975, c. 614, s. 42.

Article 23.

Oleomargarine.

§ 106-233. Repealed by Session Laws 1975, c. 614, s. 42.

§ 106-234. Repealed by Session Laws 1949, c. 978, s. 2.

§ 106-235. Repealed by Session Laws 1963, c. 1135.

§§ 106-236 through 106-238. Repealed by Session Laws 1975, c. 614, s. 42.

Article 24.

Excise Tax on Certain Oleomargarines.

§ 106-239. Repealed by Session Laws 1975, c. 614, s. 42.

Article 25.

North Carolina Egg Law.

§§ 106-240 through 106-245. Repealed by Session Laws 1955, c. 213, s. 14.

§§ 106-245.1 through 106-245.12. Repealed by Session Laws 1965, c. 1138, s. 3.

Article 25A.

North Carolina Egg Law.

§ 106-245.13. Short title; scope; rule of construction.

This Article is named and may be cited as the North Carolina Egg Law and relates to eggs sold in the State of North Carolina. Words used in the singular form in this Article shall include the plural, and vice versa as the cause may require. (1965, c. 1138, s. 1.)

§ 106-245.14. Definitions.

The following words, terms, and phrases shall be construed for the purpose of this Article as follows:

(1) "Authorized representative" means the Commissioner or any duly authorized agent or employee who is assigned to carry out the provisions of this Article.

(2) "Candling and grading" means selecting eggs as to their conformity to the standards of quality and size or weight class preparatory to marketing them as a specific grade and size or weight class.

(3) "Commissioner" means the North Carolina Commissioner of Agriculture.

(4) "Consumer" means any person who purchases eggs for his or her use or his or her own family use or consumption and not for resale.

(5) "Container" means any box, case, basket, carton, sack, bag, or other receptacle containing eggs. "Subcontainer" means any container used within another container.

(6) "Distributor" means any person, producer, firm or corporation offering for sale or distributing eggs in the State to a retailer, cafe, restaurant, or any other establishment offering for sale to consumers, including but not limited to institutional consumers as defined in this Article. Distributors also shall include any person, producer, firm or corporation distributing eggs to his or its own retail outlets or stores but shall not include any person, firm or corporation engaged only to haul or transport eggs.

(7) "Eggs" means product of a domesticated chicken in the shell or as further processed egg products.

(8) "Facilities" means any room, compartment, refrigerator or vehicle used in handling eggs in any manner.

(9) "Grades" shall mean and include specifications defining the limit of variation in quality of two or more eggs.

(10) "Institutional consumer" means a restaurant, hotel, licensed boarding house, commercial bakery or any other institution in which eggs are prepared as food for use by its patrons, residents or patients.

(11) "Law" means the provisions of this Article and all rules and regulations issued hereunder.

(12) "Lots" means a physical grouping of eggs or containers with eggs therein, as determined by the North Carolina Department of Agriculture and Consumer Services.

(13) "Marketing of eggs" or "market" means the sale, offer for sale, gift, barter, exchange, advertising, branding, marking, labeling, grading, or other preparatory operation or distribution in any manner of eggs or containers of eggs as defined in this Article.

(14) "Packer" means any person that is engaged in grading, shell treating or packing eggs for sale to consumers, direct or through distribution outlets of stores.

(15) "Person" means and includes any individual, producer, firm, partnership, exchange, association, trustee, receiver, corporation, or any other business organization and any member, officer, or employee thereof.

(16) "Retailer" means any person who markets eggs to consumers.

(17) "Size or weight class" means a classification of eggs based on weight at the rate per dozen.

(18) "Standards for quality" means specifications of the physical characteristics of any or all of the component parts or the individual egg. (1965, c. 1138, s. 1; 1997-261, s. 42.)

§ 106-245.15. Designation of grade and class on containers required; conformity with designation; exemption.

No person shall market to consumers, institutional consumers or retailers or expose for that purpose any eggs unless there is clearly designated therewith on the container the grade and size or weight class established in accordance with the provisions of this Article and such eggs shall conform to the designated grade and size or weight class (except when sold on contract to a United States governmental agency); provided, however, a producer marketing eggs of his own production shall be exempt from this section when such marketing occurs on the premises where the eggs are produced, processed, or when ungraded sales do not exceed 30 dozen per week. (1955, c. 213, s. 7; 1965, c. 1138, s. 1; 1973, c. 739, s. 1.)

§ 106-245.16. Standards, grades and weight classes.

The Board of Agriculture shall establish and promulgate such standards of quality, grades and weight classes for eggs sold or offered for sale in this State as will protect the consumer and the institutional consumer from eggs which are injurious or likely to be injurious to health by reason of the condition of the shell, or contents thereof, or by reason of the manner in which eggs are processed, handled, shipped, stored, displayed, sold or offered for sale. Such standards of quality, grades and weight classes as are promulgated and established by the Board shall also promote honesty and fair dealings in the poultry industry. Such standards, grades and weight classes may be modified or altered by the Board whenever it deems it necessary. (1955, c. 213, s. 9; 1965, c. 1138, s. 1; 1969, c. 139, s. 1.)

§ 106-245.17. Stop-sale orders.

If an authorized representative of the North Carolina Department of Agriculture and Consumer Services shall determine, after inspection, that any lot of eggs is in violation of this Article, he may issue a "stop-sale order" as to such lot or lots of eggs and forthwith notify the owner or custodian of such eggs. Such order shall specify the reason for its issuance. A stop-sale order shall prohibit the further marketing of the eggs subject to it until such eggs are released by the State agency. (1965, c. 1138, s. 1; 1997-261, s. 109.)

§ 106-245.18. Container labeling.

(a) Any container or subcontainer in which eggs are marketed shall bear on the outside portion of the container, but not be limited to, the following:

(1) The applicable consumer grade provided for in this Article.

(2) The applicable size or weight class provided for in this Article.

(3) The word "eggs."

(4) The numerical count of the contents.

(5) The name and address of the packer or distributor. Words and numerals used to designate the grade and size shall be in clearly legible bold-faced type at least three-eighths inch in height. Any person intending to reuse a container shall obscure any inappropriate labeling thereon and relabel the container in accordance with this section prior to refilling the container with eggs. In any case, the address of the packer or distributor shall be shown in letters not exceeding three-eighths inch in height.

(b) The term "fresh" may only be applied to eggs conforming to the specifications for Grade A or better. No other descriptive term other than applicable grade and size may be applied. (1965, c. 1138, s. 1; 1973, c. 739, s. 2.)

§ 106-245.19. Invoices.

(a) Any person, except a producer marketing eggs to another person for candling and grading, when marketing eggs to a retailer, institutional consumer, or other person shall furnish to the purchaser at the time of delivery an invoice showing date of sale, name and address of the seller, name of purchaser, quantity, grade and size-weight classification.

(b) A copy of such invoice shall be kept on file by both the person selling and the purchaser at their respective places of business for a period of at least 30 days. (1955, c. 213, s. 7; 1965, c. 1138, s. 1.)

§ 106-245.20. Advertisements.

No person shall advertise eggs for sale at a given price unless the unabbreviated grade or quality and size-weight are conspicuously designated in block letters at least half as high as the tallest letter in the word "eggs" or the tallest figure in the price, whichever is larger. The provisions of this section shall not apply to retailers who (i) display egg prices in the same manner as other products sold by the retailer at the retail establishment, excluding any items on sale or subject to a promotion, and (ii) comply with G.S. 106-245.15. (1955, c. 213, s. 7; 1965, c. 1138, s. 1; 2013-265, s. 11.)

§ 106-245.21. Rules and regulations.

The North Carolina Board of Agriculture is authorized to make and amend, from time to time, such rules and regulations as may be necessary to administer and enforce the provisions of this Article. Such rules and regulations shall be published and copies thereof made available to interested parties upon request therefor. (1955, c. 213, s. 8; 1965, c. 1138, s. 1.)

§ 106-245.22. Sanitation.

(a) Any person engaged in the marketing of or the processing of eggs for marketing shall, in addition to maintaining egghandling facilities in a manner commensurate with laws governing food establishments, keep the eggs in a proper environment, in accordance with regulations promulgated by the North Carolina Board of Agriculture, to maintain quality. In addition, any container, including the packaging material therein, when used for the marketing of eggs shall be clean, unbroken and free from foreign odor. In all instances eggs shall, so far as possible and by use of all reasonable means, be protected from being soiled or dirtied by foreign matter. When cleaning is necessary a sanitary method approved by the Commissioner shall be employed.

(b) Repealed by Session Laws 1973, c. 739, s. 3. (1965, c. 1138, s. 1; 1973, c. 739, s. 3.)

§ 106-245.23. Power of Commissioner.

The Commissioner, or his authorized agents or representatives, may enter, during the regular business hours, any establishment or facility where eggs are bought, stored, offered for sale, or processed, in order to inspect and examine eggs, egg containers, and the premises, and to examine the records of such establishments or facilities relating thereto. (1955, c. 213, s. 10; 1965, c. 1138, s. 1.)

§ 106-245.24. Penalties for violations; enjoining violations; venue.

(a) Any person who violates any provision of this Article shall be guilty of a Class 3 misdemeanor.

(b) In addition to the criminal penalties provided for above, the Commissioner of Agriculture may apply by equity to a court of competent jurisdiction, and such court shall have jurisdiction and for cause shown to grant temporary or permanent injunction, or both, restraining any person from violating, or continuing to violate, any provisions of this Article.

(c) Any proceeding for a violation of this Article may be brought in the county where the violator resides, has a place of business or principal office or where the act or omission or part thereof, complained of occurred. (1955, c. 213, s. 12; 1965, c. 1138, s. 1; 1993, c. 539, s. 750; 1994, Ex. Sess., c. 24, s. 14(c).)

§ 106-245.25. Warnings in lieu of criminal prosecutions.

Nothing in this Article shall be construed as requiring the Commissioner to report for criminal prosecution violations of this Article whenever he believes that the public interest will be adequately served and compliance with the Article obtained by a suitable written notice or warning. (1965, c. 1138, s. 1.)

§ 106-245.26. Remedies cumulative.

Each remedy provided in this Article shall be in addition to and not exclusive of any other remedy provided for in this Article. (1965, c. 1138, s. 1.)

§ 106-245.27. Persons punishable as principals.

(a) Whoever commits any act prohibited by any section of this Article or aids, abets, induces, or procures its commission, is punishable as a principal.

(b) Whoever causes an act to be done which if directly performed by him or another would be a violation of the provisions of this Article, is punishable as a principal. (1965, c. 1138, s. 1.)

§ 106-245.28. Act of agent as that of principal.

In construing and enforcing the provisions of this Article, the act, omission, or failure, of any agent, officer or other person acting for or employed by an individual, association, partnership, corporation, or firm, within the scope of his employment or office shall be deemed to be the act, omission, or failure to [of] the individual, association, partnership, corporation, or firm as well as that of the person. (1965, c. 1138, s. 1.)

§ 106-245.29. Reserved for future codification purposes.

Article 25B.

Egg Promotion Tax.

§ 106-245.30 Legislative findings; purpose of Article.

The General Assembly finds and declares that eggs are important to the prosperity of this State and are a major source of income to a large segment of the State's population. Additional research, education, publicity, advertising and other means of promoting the sale and use of eggs are required to enhance the economical production and marketing of eggs and will be beneficial to the State as a whole. (1987, c. 815, s. 1.)

§ 106-245.31. Definitions.

As used in this Article:

(1)   "Board" means the North Carolina Board of Agriculture.

(2)   "Commissioner" means the Commissioner of Agriculture.

(3)   "Department" means the North Carolina Department of Agriculture and Consumer Services. (1987, c. 815, s. 1; 1997-261, s. 43.)

§ 106-245.32. Levy of tax; rules.

An excise tax is levied on eggs and processed eggs sold for use in this State. The tax on eggs is five cents (5¢) for each case of 30 dozen eggs. The tax on processed eggs is eleven cents (11¢) for each 100 pounds of processed eggs sold for use in this State. The tax imposed by this section is payable only once on the same eggs or processed eggs.

Processed eggs include frozen eggs, liquid eggs, and hard-cooked eggs. "Use" means consumption by the consumer. The Board may adopt rules necessary to administer this tax. (1987, c. 815, s. 1; 1989 (Reg. Sess., 1990), c. 1001, s. 1.)

§ 106-245.33. Report and payment of tax by handler; definition and functions of handler.

(a)   The tax imposed by this Article is payable monthly to the Department by the handler of eggs or processed eggs. The tax is due when a report is required to be filed. A handler shall file a report with the Department on a form provided by the Department within 20 days after the end of each month. The report shall state the volume of eggs or processed eggs handled by the handler during the preceding month.

(b) The term "handler" means any person who operates a grading station in North Carolina, a packer, huckster, or distributor who handles eggs in North Carolina, a farmer who packs, processes, or otherwise performs the functions of a handler in North Carolina, or a distributor or seller of processed eggs. The term "handler" includes any person in North Carolina who purchases eggs for sale or distribution or any farmer in North Carolina who sells or distributes eggs to anyone other than a registered handler.

For purposes of this Article, the functions of a handler of eggs or processed eggs include the sale, distribution, or other disposition of eggs or processed eggs in North Carolina regardless of where the eggs or processed eggs were produced or purchased.

The term "registered handler" means any person who has registered with the Department to receive monthly return forms for reporting the tax levied by this Article.

Every person, whether inside or outside the State, who engages in business in North Carolina as a handler is required to register and to collect and pay the tax due on all eggs or processed eggs sold for use in this State. A handler shall maintain a certificate of registration, file returns, and perform all other duties required of handlers. (1987, c. 815, s. 1; 1989 (Reg. Sess., 1990), c. 1001, s. 2.)

§ 106-245.34. Exemptions.

Eggs sold by a handler who sells less than 500 cases a year are exempt from the tax levied under this Article. Processed eggs sold by a handler who sells less than 1,000 pounds of processed eggs a year are exempt from the tax levied under this Article. The Board shall establish a procedure for returning taxes paid on exempt eggs or processed eggs. (1987, c. 815, s. 1; 1989 (Reg. Sess., 1990), c. 1001, s. 3.)

§ 106-245.34A. Additional exemption.

The tax provided for herein shall not be levied upon any eggs which are assessed under the Agricultural Marketing Agreement Act of 1937 (7 USC 601 et seq.). (1987, c. 815, s. 2.)

§ 106-245.35. Records to be kept by handler.

The handler shall keep a complete record of the eggs or processed eggs handled by him for a period of not less than two years from the time the eggs or processed eggs were handled. These records shall be open for inspection by the Commissioner or his duly authorized agents and shall be established and maintained as required by the Commissioner. (1987, c. 815, s. 1; 1989 (Reg. Sess., 1990), c. 1001, s. 4.)

§ 106-245.36. Interest on tax; collection of delinquent tax.

The tax imposed under the provisions of this Article and unpaid on the date on which the tax was due and payable shall bear interest at the rate determined in accordance with G.S. 105-241.21 from and after such due date until paid. If any person defaults in any payment of the tax or interest thereon, the amount shall be collected by a civil action in the name of the State and the person adjudged in default shall pay the cost of such action. The Attorney General, at the request of the Commissioner, shall institute such action in the proper court for the collection of the amount of any tax past due under this Article including interest thereon. (1987, c. 815, s. 1; 2007-491, s. 44(1)a.)

§ 106-245.37. North Carolina Egg Fund.

All moneys levied and collected under the provisions of this Article shall be deposited with the State Treasurer to a fund to be known as the "North Carolina Egg Fund". All moneys credited to the "North Carolina Egg Fund" are hereby appropriated to the North Carolina Egg Association, a North Carolina nonprofit corporation, for research, education, publicity, advertising, and other promotional activities for the benefit of producers of eggs sold in North Carolina. Moneys in the North Carolina Egg fund are held in trust for the benefit of producers of eggs sold in North Carolina and such moneys shall not be or become part of the General Fund. (1987, c. 738, s. 138(a); c. 815, s. 1.)

§ 106-245.38. Violations.

(a) It shall be a Class 1 misdemeanor for any handler knowingly to report falsely to the Department the quantity of eggs or processed eggs handled by him during any period, to falsify the records of the eggs or processed eggs handled by him, to fail to keep a complete record of the eggs or processed eggs handled by him, or to fail to preserve the records for a period of not less than two years from the time the eggs or processed eggs are handled.

(b) It shall be a violation of the North Carolina Egg Law, Article 25A of this Chapter, for a handler to fail to register as required by this Article. Any eggs transported, sold, or offered for sale by a handler who is not a registered handler shall be subject to the stop-sale and penalty provisions of the North Carolina Egg Law. (1987, c. 815, s. 1; 1989 (Reg. Sess., 1990), c. 1001, s. 5; 1993, c. 539, s. 751; 1994, Ex. Sess., c. 24, s. 14(c).)

§ 106-245.39. Effect on Article 50 of Chapter 106.

After October 1, 1987 no egg assessment shall be collected under Article 50 of Chapter 106 of the General Statutes. (1987, c. 815, s. 3.)

Article 26.

Inspection of Ice Cream Plants, Creameries, and Cheese Factories.

§ 106-246: Repealed by Session Laws 2013-265, s. 13, effective July 17, 2013.

§ 106-247. Cleaning and sterilization of vessels and utensils.

Suitable means or appliances shall be provided for the proper cleaning or sterilizing of freezers, vats, mixing cans or tanks, conveyors, and all utensils, tools and implements used in making or handling cream, ice cream, butter or cheese and all such apparatus shall be thoroughly cleaned as promptly after use as practicable. (1921, c. 169, s. 2; C.S., s. 7251(b).)

§ 106-248: Repealed by Session Laws 2013-265, s. 14, effective July 17, 2013.

§ 106-249. Receivers of products to clean utensils before return.

Every person, company, or corporation who shall receive milk, cream, or ice cream which is delivered in cans, bottles, or other receptacles, shall thoroughly clean same as soon as practicable after the contents are removed and before the said receptacles are returned to shipper or person from whom the same was received or before such receptacles are delivered to any carrier to be returned to shipper. (1921, c. 169, s. 4; C.S., s. 7251(d).)

§ 106-250. Correct tests of butterfat; tests by Board of Agriculture.

Creameries and factories that purchase milk and cream from producers of same on a butterfat basis, and pay for same on their own test, shall make and pay on correct test, and any failure to do so shall constitute a violation of this Article. The Board of Agriculture, under regulations provided for in G.S. 106-253, shall have such test made of milk and cream sold to factories named herein that will show if dishonest tests and practices are used by the purchasers of such products. (1921, c. 169, s. 5; C.S., s. 7251(e).)

§ 106-251. Department of Agriculture and Consumer Services to enforce law; examinations.

It shall be the duty of the Department of Agriculture and Consumer Services to enforce this Article, and the Board of Agriculture shall cause to be made by the experts of the Department such examinations of plants and products named herein as are necessary to insure the compliance with the provisions of this Article. For the purpose of inspection, the authorized experts of the Department shall have authority, during business hours, to enter all plants or storage rooms where cream, ice cream, butter, or cheese or ingredients used in the same are made, stored, or kept, and any person who shall hinder, prevent, or attempt to prevent any duly authorized expert of the Department in the performance of his duty in connection with this Article shall be guilty of a violation of this Article. (1921, c. 169, s. 6; C.S., s. 7251(f); 1997-261, s. 44.)

§ 106-252. Closure of plants for violation of Article; certificate to district attorney of district.

If it shall appear from the examinations that any provision of this Article has been violated, the Commissioner of Agriculture shall have authority to order the plant or place of manufacture closed until the law is complied with. If the owner or operator of the place refuses or fails to comply with the order, law or regulations, the Commissioner shall then certify the facts in the case to the district attorney in the district in which the violation was committed. (1921, c. 169, s. 7; C.S., s. 7251(g); 1973, c. 47, s. 2.)

§ 106-253. Standards of purity and sanitation; regulating trade or brand names of frozen or semifrozen desserts.

The Board of Agriculture is authorized to make such definitions and to establish such standards of purity for products and sanitation for plants or places of manufacture named herein with such regulations, not in conflict with this Article, as shall be necessary to make provisions of this Article effective and insure the proper enforcement of same, and the violation of said standards of purity or regulations shall be deemed to be a violation of this Article. The Board is authorized to require the posting of inspection certificates. It shall be unlawful for any person, firm or corporation to use the words "cream," "milk," or "ice cream," or either of them, or any similar sounding word or terms, as a part of or in connection with any product, trade name or brand of any frozen or semifrozen dessert manufactured, sold or offered for sale and not in fact made from dairy products under and in accordance with regulations, definitions or standards approved or promulgated by the Board of Agriculture. (1921, c. 169, s. 8; C.S.,

s. 7251(h); 1933, c. 431, s. 3; 1945, c. 846; 1959, c. 707, s. 3; 1981 (Reg. Sess., 1982), c. 1359, s. 1.)

§ 106-254. Inspection fees; wholesalers; retailers and cheese factories.

For the purpose of defraying the expenses incurred in the enforcement of this Article, the owner, proprietor or operator of each ice cream factory where ice cream, milk shakes, milk sherbet, sherbet, water ices, mixes for frozen or semifrozen desserts and other similar frozen or semifrozen food products are made or stored, or any cheese factory or butter-processing plant that disposes of its products at wholesale to retail dealers for resale in this State shall pay to the Commissioner of Agriculture each year an inspection fee of forty dollars ($40.00). Each maker of ice cream, milk shakes, milk sherbet, sherbet, water ices and/or other similar frozen or semifrozen food products who disposes of his product at retail only, and cheese factories, shall pay to the Commissioner of Agriculture an inspection fee of ten dollars ($10.00) each year. The inspection fee of ten dollars ($10.00) shall not apply to conventional spindle-type milk-shake mixers, but shall apply to milk-shake dispensing and vending machines, which operate on a continuous or automatic basis. (1921, c. 169, s. 9; C.S., s. 7251(i); 1933, c. 431, s. 4; 1959, c. 707, s. 4; 1961, c. 791; 1989, c. 544, s. 15.)

§ 106-255. Violation of Article a misdemeanor; punishment.

Any person, firm, or corporation who shall violate any of the provisions of this Article shall be guilty of a Class 3 misdemeanor, and upon conviction thereof shall only be fined not to exceed twenty-five dollars ($25.00) for the first offense, and for each subsequent offense in the discretion of the court. (1921, c. 169, s. 10; C.S., s. 7251(j); 1993, c. 539, s. 752; 1994, Ex. Sess., c. 24, s. 14(c).)

Article 27.

Records of Purchases of Milk Products.

§§ 106-256 through 106-259: Repealed by Session Laws 1987, c. 244, s. 1(h).

Article 28.

Records and Reports of Milk Distributors and Processors.

§ 106-260. "Milk" defined.

Wherever the word "milk" appears hereinafter in this Article, it shall be construed to include all whole milk, cream, chocolate milk, buttermilk, skim milk, special milk and all flavored milk, including flavored drinks, skim condensed, whole condensed, dry milks and evaporated. (1941, c. 162, s. 1; 1951, c. 1133, s. 1.)

§ 106-261. Reports to Commissioner of Agriculture as to milk purchased and sold.

Every person, firm or corporation that purchases milk for processing or distribution or sale, or that purchases milk for processing and distribution and sale, in North Carolina shall, not later than the twentieth of each month following the month such business is carried on, furnish information to the Commissioner of Agriculture, upon blanks to be furnished by him which will show a detailed statement of the quantities of the various classifications of milk purchased and the class in which milk was distributed or sold. Such report shall include all milk purchased from the producers and other sources, imported, all milk sold to consumers, sold or transferred between plants, distributors, affiliates and subsidiaries, and all milk used in the manufacture of other dairy products; provided, however, that every person, firm or corporation engaged in purchasing milk and/or dairy products as defined in G.S. 106-260, for processing and manufacturing purposes only and who is not engaged in distributing and/or selling milk or milk products in fluid form, shall be required to report only the receipts of such milk or milk products and the quantities of dairy products manufactured. Provided, further, that the provisions of this section shall not apply to retail stores unless the same are owned, controlled or operated by milk processors and/or distributors. (1947, c. 162, s. 2; 1951, c. 1133, s. 2.)

§ 106-262. Powers of Commissioner of Agriculture.

The Commissioner of Agriculture is hereby authorized and empowered:

(1) To require such reports as will enable him to determine the quantities of milk purchased and the classification in which it was used or disposed;

(2) To designate any area of the State as a natural marketing area for the sale or use of milk or milk products;

(3) To set up classifications for the sale or use of milk or milk products for each marketing area after full, complete and impartial hearing. Due notice of such hearing shall be given.

(4) To make rules and regulations and issue orders necessary to carry out and enforce the provisions of this Article, including the supervision of producer bases and other production incentive plans; methods of uniform and equitable payments to all producers selling milk to the same firm, person or corporation; uniform methods of computing weights of milk and/or milk products; and maximum handling and transportation charges for milk sold and/or transferred between plants. (1941, c. 162, s. 3; 1951, c. 1133, s. 3.)

§ 106-263. Distribution of milk in classification higher than that in which purchased.

It shall be unlawful for any operator of a milk processing plant or any milk distributor, required to make reports under this Article, or their affiliates or subsidiaries, to sell, use, transfer, or distribute any milk in a classification higher than the classification in which it was purchased, except in an emergency declared and approved in writing by the local board of health having supervision of operators and distributors on such market for a period of two weeks, and such period may be extended if, in the opinion of the local board of health, an emergency still exists at the end of such two weeks' period. (1941, c. 162, s. 4.)

§ 106-264. Inspections and investigations by Commissioner.

For the purpose of administering this Article the Commissioner of Agriculture or his agent is hereby authorized to enter at all reasonable hours all places where milk is being stored, bottled, or processed, or where milk is being bought, sold, or handled, or where books, papers, records, or documents relating to such transactions are kept, and shall have the power to inspect and copy the same in any place within the State, and may take testimony for the purpose of ascertaining facts which in the judgment of the Commissioner are necessary to administer this Article. The Commissioner shall have the power to determine the truth and accuracy of said books, records, papers, documents, accounts, and reports required to be furnished by milk distributors, their affiliates or subsidiaries in accordance with the provisions of this Article. (1941, c. 162, s. 5.)

§ 106-265. Failure to file reports, etc., made unlawful.

It shall be unlawful for any person, firm or corporation engaged in the business herein regulated to fail to furnish the information and file the reports required by this Article, and each day's failure to furnish the reports required hereunder shall constitute a separate offense. (1941, c. 162, s. 6.)

§ 106-266. Violation made misdemeanor.

Any person, firm, or corporation violating any of the provisions of this Article and/or any rule, regulation or order promulgated in accordance with the provisions of this Article shall be guilty of a Class 1 misdemeanor. (1941, c. 162, s. 7; 1951, c. 1133, s. 4; 1993, c. 539, s. 753; 1994, Ex. Sess., c. 24, s. 14(c).)

Article 28A.

Regulation of Milk Brought into North Carolina

§§ 106-266.1 through 106-266.5: Repealed by Session Laws 1979, c. 157, s. 1.

§ 106-266.6. Reserved for future codification purposes.

Article 28B

Regulation of Production, Distribution, etc., of Milk and Cream.

§ 106-266.7: Repealed by Session Laws 2004-199, s. 27(a), effective August 17, 2004.

§ 106-266.8: Repealed by Session Laws 2004-199, s. 27(a), effective August 17, 2004.

§ 106-266.9: Repealed by Session Laws 2004-199, s. 27(a), effective August 17, 2004.

§ 106-266.10: Repealed by Session Laws 2004-199, s. 27(a), effective August 17, 2004.

§ 106-266.11: Repealed by Session Laws 2004-199, s. 27(a), effective August 17, 2004.

§ 106-266.12: Repealed by Session Laws 2004-199, s. 27(a), effective August 17, 2004.

§ 106-266.13: Repealed by Session Laws 2004-199, s. 27(a), effective August 17, 2004.

§ 106-266.14: Repealed by Session Laws 2004-199, s. 27(a), effective August 17, 2004.

§ 106-266.15: Repealed by Session Laws 2004-199, s. 27(a), effective August 17, 2004.

§ 106-266.16: Repealed by Session Laws 2004-199, s. 27(a), effective August 17, 2004.

§ 106-266.17: Repealed by Session Laws 2004-199, s. 27(a), effective August 17, 2004.

§ 106-266.18: Repealed by Session Laws 2004-199, s. 27(a), effective August 17, 2004.

§ 106-266.19: Repealed by Session Laws 2004-199, s. 27(a), effective August 17, 2004.

§§ 106-266.20 through 106-266.21: Repealed by Session Laws 1971, c. 779, s. 1.

Article 28C.

Grade "A" Milk Sanitation.

§ 106-266.30. Definitions.

The following definitions shall apply throughout this Article:

(1) "Grade 'A' milk" means fluid milk and milk products which have been produced, transported, handled, processed and distributed in accordance with the provisions of the rules adopted by the Board of Agriculture.

(2) "Milk" means the lacteal secretion practically free from colostrum obtained by the milking of one or more cows, goats, or other lactating animals. (1983, c. 891, s. 2; 2004-195, s. 6.1; 2011-145, s. 13.3(l), (m).)

§ 106-266.31. Board to adopt rules.

The Board of Agriculture shall adopt rules relating to the sanitary production, transportation, processing and distribution of Grade "A" milk. The rules, in order to protect and promote the public health, shall provide definitions and requirements for: (i) the sanitary production and handling of milk on Grade "A" dairy farms; (ii) the sanitary transportation of Grade "A" raw milk for processing; (iii) the sanitary processing of Grade "A" milk; (iv) the sanitary handling and distribution of Grade "A" milk; (v) the requirements for the issuance, suspension and revocation of permits; and (vi) the establishment of quality standards for Grade "A" milk. The rules shall be no less stringent than the 1978 Pasteurized Milk Ordinance recommended by the U.S. Public Health Service/Food and Drug Administration as amended effective January 1, 1982. The Board of Agriculture may adopt by reference the U.S. Public Health Service/Food and Drug

Administration 1978 Pasteurized Milk Ordinance, as amended. (1983, c. 891, s. 2; 1985, c. 462, s. 15; 2011-145, s. 13.3(l), (n).)

§ 106-266.32. Permits required.

No person shall produce, transport, process, or distribute Grade "A" milk without first having obtained a valid permit from the Department of Agriculture and Consumer Services. (1983, c. 891, s. 2; 2011-145, s. 13.3(l), (o).)

§ 106-266.33. Duties of the Department.

The Department of Agriculture and Consumer Services shall enforce the rules of the Board of Agriculture governing Grade "A" milk by making sanitary inspections of Grade "A" dairy farms, Grade "A" processing plants, Grade "A" milk haulers and Grade "A" distributors; by determining the quality of Grade "A" milk; and by evaluating methods of handling Grade "A" milk to insure compliance with the provisions of the rules of the Board of Agriculture. The Department of Agriculture and Consumer Services shall issue permits for the operation of Grade "A" dairy farms, processing plants and haulers in accordance with the provisions of the rules of the Board of Agriculture and shall suspend or revoke permits for violations in accordance with the rules. (1983, c. 891, s. 2; 1995, c. 123, s. 3; 2011-145, s. 13.3(l), (p).)

§ 106-266.34. Certain other authorities of Department of Agriculture and Consumer Services not replaced.

This Article shall not repeal or limit the Department of Agriculture and Consumer Services' authority to carry out labeling requirements, required butterfat testing, aflatoxin testing, pesticide testing, other testing performed by the Department of Agriculture and Consumer Services, and any other function of the Department of Agriculture and Consumer Services concerning Grade "A" milk under any other Article under this Chapter that is not inconsistent with this Article. (1983, c. 891, s. 2; 1997-261, s. 87; 2011-145, s. 13.3(l), (q).)

§ 106-266.35. Sale or dispensing of milk.

Only milk that is Grade "A" pasteurized milk may be sold or dispensed directly to consumers for human consumption. Raw milk and raw milk products shall be sold or dispensed only to a permitted milk hauler or to a processing facility at which the processing of milk is permitted, graded, or regulated by a local, State, or federal agency. The Board of Agriculture may adopt rules to provide exceptions for dispensing raw milk and raw milk products for nonhuman consumption. Any raw milk or raw milk product dispensed as animal feed shall include on its label the statement "NOT FOR HUMAN CONSUMPTION" in letters at least one-half inch in height. Any raw milk or raw milk product dispensed as animal feed shall also include on its label the statement "IT IS NOT LEGAL TO SELL RAW MILK FOR HUMAN CONSUMPTION IN NORTH CAROLINA." "Sale" or "sold" shall mean any transaction that involves the transfer or dispensing of milk and milk products or the right to acquire milk and milk products through barter or contractual arrangement or in exchange for any other form of compensation including, but not limited to, the sale of shares or interest in a cow, goat, or other lactating animal or herd. (1983, c. 891, s. 2; 2004-195, s. 6.2; 2008-88, s. 2; 2011-145, s. 13.3(l), (r).)

§ 106-266.36. Milk embargo.

If the Commissioner of Agriculture or a local health director has probable cause to believe that any milk designated as Grade "A" milk is misbranded or does not satisfy the milk sanitation rules adopted pursuant to G.S. 106-266.31, the Commissioner of Agriculture or a local health director may detain or embargo the milk by affixing a tag to it and warning all persons not to remove or dispose of the milk until permission for removal or disposal is given by the official by whom the milk was detained or embargoed or by the court. It shall be unlawful for any person to remove or dispose of the detained or embargoed milk without that permission.

The official by whom the milk was detained or embargoed shall petition a judge of the district or superior court in whose jurisdiction the milk is detained or embargoed for an order for condemnation of the article. If the court finds that the milk is misbranded or that it does not satisfy the milk sanitation rules adopted pursuant to G.S. 106-266.31, either the milk shall be destroyed under the supervision of the petitioner or the petitioner shall ensure that the milk will not be used for human consumption as Grade "A" milk. All court costs and fees, storage, expenses of carrying out the court's order and other expense shall be taxed against the claimant of the milk. If, the milk, by proper labelling or processing, can be properly branded and will satisfy the milk sanitation rules adopted pursuant to G.S. 106-266.31, the court, after the payment of all costs, fees, and expenses and after the claimant posts an adequate bond, may order that the milk be delivered to the claimant for proper labelling and processing under the supervision of the petitioner. The bond shall be returned to the claimant after the petitioner represents to the court either that the milk is no longer mislabelled or in violation of the milk sanitation rules adopted pursuant to G.S. 106-266.31, or that the milk will not be used for human consumption, and that in either case the expenses of supervision have been paid. (1983, c. 891, s. 2; 1997-443, s. 11A.63A; 2011-145, s. 13.3(s), (t).)

Article 29.

Inspection, Grading and Testing Milk and Dairy Products.

§ 106-267. Inspection, grading and testing dairy products; authority of State Board of Agriculture.

The State Board of Agriculture shall have full power to make and promulgate rules and regulations for the Department of Agriculture and Consumer Services in its inspection and control of the purchase and sale of milk and other dairy products in North Carolina; to make and establish definitions, not inconsistent with the laws pertaining thereto; to qualify and determine the grade and contents of milk and of other dairy products sold in this State; to regulate the manner of testing the same and the handling, treatment and sale of milk and dairy products, to require processors of fortified milk and milk products to pay all costs for assays of vitamin-fortified products, to provide for the issuance of permits upon compliance with this Article and the rules and regulations promulgated thereunder and to promulgate such other rules and regulations not inconsistent with the law as may be necessary in connection with the authority hereby given to the Commissioner of Agriculture on this subject. (1933, c. 550, ss. 1-3; 1951, c. 1121, s. 1; 1981, c. 338; c. 495, s. 5; 1997-261, s. 109.)

§ 106-267.1. License required; fee; term of license; examination required.

Every person who shall test milk or cream in this State by, or sample milk for, the Babcock method or otherwise for the purpose of determining the percentage of butterfat or milk fat contained therein, where such milk or cream is bought and paid for on the basis of the amount of butterfat contained therein, shall first obtain a license from the Commissioner of Agriculture. Any person applying for such license or renewal of license shall make written and signed application on blanks to be furnished by the Commissioner of Agriculture. The granting of a license shall be conditioned upon the passing by the applicant of an examination, to be conducted by or under the direction of the Commissioner of Agriculture. All licenses so issued or renewed shall expire on December 31 of each year, unless sooner revoked, as provided in G.S. 106-267.3. A license fee of five dollars ($5.00) for each license so granted or renewed shall be paid to the Commissioner of Agriculture by the applicant before any license is granted. (1951, c. 1121, s. 1; 1959, c. 707, s. 5; 1989, c. 544, s. 14.)

§ 106-267.2. Rules and regulations.

The Commissioner of Agriculture shall establish and promulgate rules and regulations not inconsistent with this Article that shall govern the granting of licenses under this Article and shall establish and promulgate rules and regulations not inconsistent with this Article that shall govern the manner of testing, including, but not in limitation thereof, the taking of samples, location where the testing of said samples shall be made and the length of time samples of milk or cream shall be held after testing. (1951, c. 1121, s. 1.)

§ 106-267.3. Revocation of license; hearing.

The Commissioner of Agriculture shall have power to revoke any license granted under the provisions of this Article, upon good and sufficient evidence that the provisions of this Article or the rules and regulations of the Commissioner of Agriculture are not being complied with: Provided, that before any license shall be revoked, an opportunity shall be granted the licensee, upon being confronted with the evidence, to show cause why such license should not be revoked. (1951, c. 1121, s. 1.)

§ 106-267.4. Representative average sample; misdemeanor, what deemed.

In taking samples of milk or cream from any milk can, cream can or any container of milk or cream, the contents of such milk can, cream can, or container of milk and cream shall first be thoroughly mixed either by stirring or otherwise, and the sample shall be taken immediately after mixing or by any other method which gives a representative average sample of the contents, and it is hereby made a Class 2 misdemeanor to take samples by any method or to fraudulently manipulate such samples so as not to give an accurate and representative average sample where milk or cream is bought or sold and where the value of said milk or cream is determined by the butterfat contained therein. (1951, c. 1121, s. 1; 1993, c. 539, s. 755; 1994, Ex. Sess., c. 24, s. 14(c).)

§ 106-267.5. Standard Babcock testing glassware; scales and weights.

In the use of the Babcock test all persons shall use the "standard Babcock testing glassware, scales, and weights." The term "standard Babcock testing glassware, scales and weights" shall apply to glassware, scales and weights. It shall be unlawful for any person, firm, company, association, corporation or agent thereof to falsely manipulate, underread or overread the Babcock test or any other contrivance used for determining the quality of value of milk or cream where the value of said milk or cream is determined by the percentage of butterfat contained in the same or to make a false determination by the Babcock test or otherwise, or to falsify the record of such test or to pay on the basis of any test, measurement or weight except the true test, measurement or weight. (1951, c. 1121, s. 1.)

§ 106-268. Definitions; enforcement of Article.

(a) The definitions set forth in this section shall apply to milk, dairy products, ice cream, frozen desserts, frozen confections or any other products which purport to be milk, dairy products or frozen desserts for which a definition and standard of identity has been established and when any of such products heretofore enumerated shall be sold, offered for sale or held with intent to sell by a milk producer, manufacturer or distributor, and insofar as practicable and applicable, the definitions contained in Article 12 of Chapter 106 of the General

Statutes, as amended, shall be effective as to the products enumerated in this Article and section.

(b)   The term "adulteration" means:

(1)   Failure to meet definitions and standards as established by the Board of Agriculture.

(2)   If any valuable constituent has been in whole or in part omitted or abstracted therefrom.

(3)   If any substance has been substituted wholly or in part thereof.

(4)   If it is adjudged to be unfit for human consumption.

(c)   The term "misbranded" means:

(1)   If its labeling is false or misleading in any particular.

(2)   If it is offered for sale under the name of another dairy product or frozen dessert.

(3)   If it is sold in package form unless it bears a prominent label containing the name of the defined product, name and address of the producer, processor or distributor and carries an accurate statement of the quantity of contents in terms of weight or measure.

(d)   The Department of Agriculture and Consumer Services, through its agents or inspectors, shall have free access during business hours to all places of business, buildings, vehicles, cars, storage places, containers and vessels used in the production, testing, processing and distribution of milk, cream, butter, cheese, ice cream, frozen dessert or any dairy product for which standards of purity and of identity have been established, as well as any substance which purports to be milk, dairy products, frozen dessert or confection for which a definition and standard of purity has been established; the Department acting through its duly authorized agents and inspectors, may open any box, carton, parcel, package or container holding or containing, or supposed to hold or contain any of the above-enumerated dairy products, as well as related products, and may take therefrom samples for analysis, test or inspection. If it appears that any of the provisions of this Article or of this section have been violated, or whenever a duly authorized agent of the Department has cause to believe that any milk, cream, butter, cheese, ice cream, frozen dessert or any dairy product for which standards of purity and of identity have been established or any substance which purports to be milk, a dairy product or a frozen dessert for which a definition and standard of identity has been established, is adulterated or misbranded or by reason of contamination with microorganisms has become deleterious to health during production, processing or distribution, and such products, or any of them, are in a stage of production, or are being exposed for sale, or are being held for processing or distribution or such products are being held with intent to sell the same, such agent or inspector is hereby authorized to issue a "stop-sale" order which shall prohibit further sale of any of the products above enumerated or which shall prohibit further processing, production or distribution of any of the products above enumerated. The agent or inspector shall affix to such product a tag or other appropriate marking giving notice that such product is, or is suspected of, being adulterated, misbranded or contaminated and that the same has been detained or embargoed, and warning all persons not to remove or dispose of such product, by sale or otherwise, until permission for removal or disposal is given by such agent or inspector, until the law or regulation has been complied with or said violation has otherwise been legally disposed of. It shall be unlawful for any person to remove or dispose of any embargoed product, by sale or otherwise, without such permission: Provided, that if such adulteration or misbranding can be corrected by proper labeling or processing of the products so that the products meet the definitions and standards of purity and identity, then with the approval of such agent or inspector, sale and removal may be made. Any milk, dairy products or any of the products enumerated in this Article or section not in compliance with this Article or section shall be subject to seizure upon complaint of the Commissioner of Agriculture, or any of the agents or inspectors of the Department of Agriculture and Consumer Services, to a court of competent jurisdiction in the area in which said products are located. In the event the court finds said products, or any of them, to be in violation of this Article or of this section, the court may order the condemnation of said products, and the same shall be disposed of in any manner consistent with the rules and regulations of the Board of Agriculture and the laws of the State and in such a manner as to minimize any loss or damage as far as possible: Provided, that in no instance shall the disposition of said products be ordered by the court without first giving the claimant or owner of same an opportunity to apply to the court for the release of said products or for permission to again process or relabel the same so as to bring the product in compliance with this Article or section. In the event any "stop-sale" order shall be issued under the provisions of this Article or section, the agents, inspectors or representatives of the Department of Agriculture and Consumer Services shall release the products, or any of them, so withdrawn from sale when the requirements of the provisions of this Article and section have been complied with and upon payment of all costs and expenses incurred in connection with the withdrawal. (1951, c. 1121, s. 1; 1997-456, s. 27; 1997-261, s. 46.)

§ 106-268.1. Penalties.

Any person, firm or corporation violating any of the provisions of this Article, or any of the rules, regulations or standards promulgated hereunder, shall be deemed guilty of a Class 2 misdemeanor. (1951, c. 1121, s. 1; 1993, c. 539, s. 756; 1994, Ex. Sess., c. 24, s. 14(c).)

Article 30.

Board of Crop Seed Improvement.

§ 106-269. Creation and purpose.

There is hereby created a Board of Crop Seed Improvement. It shall be the duty and function of this Board, in cooperation with the Agricultural Experiment Station of North Carolina State College of Agriculture and Engineering, and the Seed Testing Division of the North Carolina Department of Agriculture and Consumer Services, to foster and promote the development and distribution of pure strains of crop seeds among the farmers of North Carolina. (1929, c. 325, s. 1; 1955, c. 330, s. 1; 1997-261, s. 109.)

§ 106-270. Board membership.

The Board of Crop Seed Improvement shall consist of the Commissioner of Agriculture, the Dean of the School of Agriculture, President of the North Carolina Foundation Seed Producers Incorporated, and the Director of Research of the School of Agriculture of North Carolina State College of Agriculture and Engineering, the Head of the Seed Testing Division of the North Carolina Department of Agriculture and Consumer Services, and the President of the North Carolina Crop Improvement Association. (1929, c. 325, s. 2; 1955, c. 330, s. 2; 1997-261, s. 109.)

§ 106-271. Powers of Board.

The said Board shall have control, management and supervision of the production, distribution and certification of purebred crop seeds under the provisions of this Article. (1929, c. 325, s. 3.)

§ 106-272. Cooperation of other departments with Board; rules and regulations.

Insofar as any of the State departments or agencies shall have to do with the testing, development, production, certification and distribution of farm crop seeds, such departments or agencies shall actively cooperate with the said Board in carrying out the purposes of this Article. The said Board shall have authority to make, establish and promulgate all needful rules and regulations, for certification necessary for the proper exercise of the duties conferred upon said Board and for the carrying out the full purposes of this Article. (1929, c. 325, s. 4; 1983, c. 800, ss. 1, 2.)

§ 106-273. North Carolina Crop Improvement Association.

For the purpose of carrying out more fully the provisions of this Article and of fostering the development, certification and distribution of pure seeds the said Board shall have authority to promote the organization and incorporation of an association of farmers to be known as the North Carolina Crop Improvement Association, which said Association when so organized and incorporated shall, subject to the rules and regulations prescribed by said Board, adopt all necessary rules and regulations and collect from their members such fees as shall be necessary for the proper functioning of such organizations. (1929, c. 325, s. 5.)

§ 106-274. Certification of crop seeds.

For the purposes of this Article the certification of seed, tubers, plants, or plant parts hereunder shall be defined as being produced, conditioned, and distributed under the rules and regulations for certification. (1929, c. 325, s. 6; 1983, c. 800, s. 3.)

§ 106-275. False certification of purebred crop seeds made misdemeanor.

It shall be a Class 1 misdemeanor for any person, firm, association, or corporation, selling seeds, tubers, plants, or plant parts in North Carolina, to use any evidence of certification, such as a blue tag or the word "certified" or both, on any package of seed, tubers, plants, or plant parts, nor shall the word "certified" be used in any advertisement of seeds, tubers, plants, or plant parts, unless such commodities used for plant propagation shall have been duly inspected and certified by the agency of certification provided for in this Article, or by a similar legally constituted agency of another state or foreign country. (1933, c. 340, s. 1; 1993, c. 539, s. 757; 1994, Ex. Sess., c. 24, s. 14(c).)

§ 106-276. Supervision of certification of crop seeds.

Certification of crop seeds shall be subject to the supervision of the Board of Crop Seed Improvement. The North Carolina Crop Improvement Association is recognized as the official agency for seed certification. (1929, c. 325, s. 7; 1955, c. 330, s. 3.)

Article 31.

North Carolina Seed Law.

§ 106-277. Purpose.

The purpose of this Article is to regulate the labeling, possessing for sale, sale and offering or exposing for sale or otherwise providing for planting purposes of agricultural seeds and vegetable seeds; to prevent misrepresentation thereof; and for other purposes. (1963, c. 1182; 1987 (Reg. Sess., 1988), c. 1034, s. 1; 2009-455, s. 1.)

§ 106-277.1. Short title.

This Article shall be known by the short title of "The North Carolina Seed Law of 1963." (1941, c. 114, s. 1; 1945, c. 828; 1949, c. 725; 1963, c. 1182.)

§ 106-277.2. Definitions.

As used in this Article, unless the context clearly requires otherwise:

(1) The term "advertisement" means all representations, other than those required on the label, disseminated in any manner or by any means, relating to seed within the scope of this Article.

(2) The term "agricultural seeds" shall include the seed of grass, forage, cereal, fiber crops and any other kinds of seeds commonly recognized within this State as agricultural or field seeds, lawn seeds and mixtures of such seeds, and may include noxious-weed seeds when the Commissioner determines that such seed is being used as agricultural seed.

(2a) - (2e) Reserved.

(2f) The term "blend" means a mechanical combination of varieties identified by a blend designation in which each component variety is equal to or above the minimum standard germination for its class; which is always present in the same percentage in each lot identified by the same "blend" designation; and for which research data supports an advantage of the "blend" over the singular use of either component variety. "Blend" designations shall be treated as variety names.

(3) The term "Board" means the North Carolina Board of Agriculture as established under G.S. 106-2.

(3a) Reserved.

(3b) The term "brand" means an identifying numeral, letter, word, or any combination of these, used with the word "brand" to designate source of seeds.

(3c) The term "buyer" means a person who buys agricultural or vegetable seed for the purpose of planting and growing the seed.

(4)   The terms "certified seeds," "registered seeds" or "foundation seeds" mean seed that has been produced and labeled in accordance with the procedures and in compliance with the requirements of an official seed-certifying agency.

(5)   The term "clone" means all the individuals derived by vegetative propagation from a single, original individual.

(6)   The term "code designation" means a series of numbers or letters approved by the United States Department of Agriculture and used in lieu of the full name and address of the person who labels seeds, as required in this Article in G.S. 106-277.5(10).

(7)   The term "Commissioner" means the Commissioner of Agriculture of North Carolina or his designated agent or agents.

(7a) The term "conditioning" means cleaning, scarifying, or blending to obtain uniform quality and other operations that would change the purity or germination of the seed and therefore require retesting to determine the quality of the seed, but does not include operations such as packaging, labeling, blending together of uniform lots of the same kind, or kind and variety, without cleaning, or preparation of a mixture without cleaning, any of which would not require retesting to determine the quality of the seed.

(8)   The term "date of test" means the month and year the percentage of germination appearing on the label was obtained by laboratory test.

(9)   The term "dealer" or "vendor" shall mean any person, not classified as a grower, who buys, sells or offers for sale any seed for seeding purposes and shall include any person who has seed grown under contract for resale for seeding purposes.

(9a) The term "Department" means the Department of Agriculture and Consumer Services as established in G.S. 106-2.

(9b) The term "distribute" means to provide seed for seeding purposes to more than five persons, but shall not include seed provided for educational purposes.

(10) The term "germination" means the percentages by count of seeds under consideration, determined to be capable of producing normal seedlings in a given period of time and under normal conditions.

(11) The term "grower" shall mean any person who produces seed, directly as a landlord, tenant, sharecropper or lessee, which are offered or exposed for sale.

(12) The term "hard seeds" means seeds which, because of hardness or impermeability, do not absorb moisture and germinate but remain hard during the normal period of germination.

(13) The term "hybrid" means the first generation seed of a cross produced by controlling cross-fertilization within prescribed limits and combining (i) two or more inbred lines or clones, or (ii) one or more inbred lines or clones with an open-pollinated variety, or (iii) two or more varieties or species, clonal or otherwise, except open-pollinated varieties of normally cross-fertilized species. The second-generation or subsequent-generation seed from such crosses shall not be designated as hybrids. Hybrid designations shall be treated as variety names. The Board of Agriculture shall prescribe minimum limits of pollination control (percent hybridity) for each hybridized species which will qualify to be labeled "hybrid".

(14) The term "inbred line" means a relatively stable and pure breeding strain resulting from not less than four successive generations of controlled self-pollination or four successive generations of backcrossing in the case of male sterile lines or their genetic equivalent.

(15) The term "in bulk" refers to loose seed in bins, or open containers, and not to seed in bags or packets.

(16) The term "inert matter" means all matter not seeds, including broken seeds, sterile florets, chaff, fungus bodies, stones and other substances found not to be seed when examined according to procedures prescribed by rules and regulations promulgated pursuant to the provisions of this Article.

(17) The term "kind" means one or more related species or subspecies which singly or collectively is known by one common name, for example, corn, wheat, striate lespedeza, alfalfa, tall fescue.

(18) The term "labeling" includes all labels and other written, printed or graphic representations in any manner whatsoever accompanying and pertaining to any seed whether in bulk or in containers and includes representations on invoices.

(19) The term "lot" means a definite quantity of seed, identified by a lot number or other identification, which shall be uniform throughout for the factors which appear on the label.

(20) The term "mixture" means seeds consisting of more than one kind or kind and variety, each present in excess of five per centum (5%) of the whole.

(21) The term "North Carolina seed analysis tag" means the tag designed and prescribed by the Commissioner as the official North Carolina seed analysis tag.

(22) "Noxious-weed seeds" shall be divided into two classes:

a. "Prohibited noxious-weed seeds" are the seeds of weeds which, when established on the land, are highly destructive and are not controlled in this State by cultural practices commonly used, and shall include any crop seed found to be harmful when fed to poultry or livestock.

b. "Restricted noxious-weed seeds" are the seeds of weeds which are very objectionable in fields, lawns and gardens in this State and are difficult to control by cultural practices commonly used.

(23) The term "official certifying agency" means

a. An agency authorized under the laws of a state, territory, or possession to officially certify seed which has standards and procedures approved by the U.S. Secretary of Agriculture to assure the genetic purity and identity of the seed certified, or

b. An agency of a foreign country determined by the U.S. Secretary of Agriculture to adhere to procedures and standards for seed certification comparable to those adhered to generally by seed certifying agencies under a.

(24) The term "origin" means the state, District of Columbia, Puerto Rico, possession of the United States or the foreign country where the seed was grown.

(25) The term "other crop seeds" means seeds of kinds or varieties of agricultural or vegetable crops other than those shown on the label as the primary kind or kind and variety.

(26) The term "person" shall include any individual, partnership, corporation, company, society or association.

(27) Repealed by Session Laws 2009-455, s. 2, effective October 1, 2009.

(28) The term "pure seed" means agricultural or vegetable seeds, exclusive of inert matter, weed seeds and all other seeds distinguishable from the kind or kind and variety being considered when examined according to procedures prescribed by rules and regulations promulgated pursuant to the provisions of this Article.

(29) The term "purity" means the name or names of the kind, type or variety and the percentage or percentages thereof, the percentage of other crop seed; the percentage of weed seeds, including noxious-weed seeds; the percentage of inert matter; and the name and rate of occurrence of each noxious-weed seed.

(30) The terms "recognized variety name" and "recognized hybrid designation" mean the name or designation which was first assigned the variety or hybrid by the person who developed it or the person who first introduced it for production or sale after legal acquisition. Such terms shall be used only to designate the varieties or hybrids to which they were first assigned.

(31) Repealed by Session Laws 2009-455, s. 2, effective October 1, 2009.

(32) The term "seed offered for sale" means any seed or grain, whether in bags, packets, bins or other containers, exposed in salesrooms, storerooms, warehouses or other places where seed is sold or delivered for seeding purposes, and shall be subject to the provisions of the seed law, unless clearly labeled "not for sale as seed."

(33) The term "seizure" means a legal process carried out by court order against a definite amount of seed.

(34) The term "stop-sale" means an administrative order provided by law restraining the sale, use, disposition and movement of a definite amount of seed.

(35) The term "treated" means given an application of a substance or subjected to a process designed to reduce, control or repel disease organisms, insects or other pests which attack seeds or seedlings growing therefrom, or to improve the planting value of the seed.

(36) The term "variety" means a subdivision of a kind characterized by growth, plant, fruit, seed or other constant characteristics by which it can be differentiated in successive generations from other sorts of the same kind; for example, Knox Wheat, Kobe Striate Lespedeza, Ranger Alfalfa, Kentucky 31 Tall Fescue.

(37) The term "vegetable seeds" shall include the seeds of those crops which are grown in gardens or on truck farms and are generally known and sold under the name of vegetable seed in this State.

(38) The term "weed seeds" means the seeds, bulblets or tubers of all plants generally recognized as weeds within this State or which may be classified as weed seed by regulations promulgated under this Article.

(39) The term "wholesaler" shall mean a dealer engaged in the business of selling seed to retailers or jobbers as well as to consumers.

(40), (41) Repealed by Session Laws 1998, c. 210, s. 1. (1941, c. 114, s. 3; 1943, c. 203, s. 1; 1945, c. 828; 1949, c. 725; 1953, c. 856, ss. 1-3; 1963, c. 1182; 1971, c. 637, s. 1; 1987 (Reg. Sess., 1988), c. 1034, ss. 2-4; 1998-210, s. 1; 2009-455, s. 2.)

§ 106-277.3. Label or tag requirements generally.

Each container of agricultural and vegetable seeds which is sold, offered or exposed for sale, or transported within or into this State for seeding purposes shall bear thereon or have attached thereto in a conspicuous place a plainly written or printed label or tag in the English language giving the information required under G.S. 106-277.4 through 106-277.7, which information shall not be modified or denied in the labeling or on another label attached to the container. (1941, c. 114, s. 4; 1943, c. 203, s. 2; 1945, c. 828; 1949, c. 725; 1959, c. 585, s. 1; 1963, c. 1182.)

§ 106-277.4: Repealed by Session Laws 1987 (Reg. Sess., 1988), c. 1034, s. 5.

§ 106-277.5. Labels for agricultural seeds.

Agricultural seeds sold, offered or exposed for sale, transported for sale, or otherwise distributed within this State shall be labeled to show the following information:

(1) The commonly accepted name of the kind and the variety, or kind and the phrase "variety not stated" for each agricultural seed component, in excess of five percent (5%) of the whole, and the percentage by weight of each in order of its predominance. The Board of Agriculture may, pursuant to G.S. 106-277.15, require the variety to be stated on the labeling for certain kinds of agricultural seed, and the phrase "variety not stated" shall not be used on the labeling of such seed. When more than one component is required to be named, the word "mixture" or the word "mixed" shall be shown conspicuously on the label. Second generation from hybrid seeds, if sold, shall be labeled "second generation (of the parent), variety not stated." "F" designations on labels, unless used as a part of a variety name, will refer only to size and shape of corn seeds.

(2) Lot identification.

(3) Net weight.

(4) Origin, if known. If the origin is unknown, the fact shall be stated.

(5) Percentage by weight of inert matter.

(6) Percentage by weight of agricultural seeds and/or vegetable seeds (which shall be designated as "other crop seeds") other than those named on the label. Different varieties of the same kind of seed, when in quantities of less than five percent (5%) will be considered as other crop seed.

(7) Percentage by weight of all weed seeds, including noxious-weed seeds.

(8) For each named agricultural seed:

a. Percentage of germination, exclusive of hard seed.

b. Percentage of hard seeds, if present.

c. The calendar month and year the test was completed to determine such percentages.

In addition to the individual percentage statement of germination and hard seed, the total percentage of germination and hard seed may be stated as such, if desired.

(9) The name and number per pound of each kind of restricted noxious-weed seed present.

(10) Name and address of person who labeled said seed or who sells, offers or exposes said seed for sale within this State. If the seeds are labeled by the shipper for a consignee within this State, the shipper may use his approved code designation with the name and address of the consignee.

(11) Such other information as the Board shall prescribe by rule. (1941, c. 114, s. 4; 1943, c. 203, s. 2; 1945, c. 828; 1949, c. 725; 1959, c. 585, s. 1; 1963, c. 1182; 1971, c. 637, s. 3; 1987 (Reg. Sess., 1988), c. 1034, s. 6; 1995, c. 47, s. 1; 2009-455, s. 3.)

§ 106-277.6. Labels for vegetable seeds in containers of one pound or less.

Labels for vegetable seeds in containers of one pound or less shall show the following information:

(1) Name of kind and variety of seed.

(2) Repealed by Session Laws 2009-455, s. 4, effective October 1, 2009.

(2a) Lot identification.

(3) Repealed by Session Laws 2009-455, s. 4, effective October 1, 2009.

(3a) One of the following, as applicable:

a. The statement "Packed for (year)" or "Sell by (year)."

b. The statement "Sell by (month)(year)" where the month and year in which the germination test was complete is no more than 12 months from the date of the test, exclusive of the month and year of the test.

c. The percentage germination and the calendar month and year that the test was completed to determine the percentage, provided that the germination test was completed within 12 months, exclusive of the month and year of the test.

(4) For seeds which germinate less than the standards last established by the Commissioner and approved by the Board of Agriculture under the Article:

a. Percentage of germination, exclusive of hard seed.

b. Percentage of hard seed, if present.

c. The calendar month and year the test was completed to determine such percentage.

In addition to the individual percentage statement of germination and hard seed, the total percentage of germination and hard seed may be stated as such, if desired.

d. The words "Below Standard" in not less than eight-point type.

(5) Name and address of person who labeled said seed or who sells, offers or exposes said seed for sale within this State. If the seeds are labeled by the shipper for a consignee within this State, the shipper may use his approved code designation with the name and address of the consignee.

(6) Such other information as the Board shall prescribe by rule. (1941, c. 114, s. 4; 1943, c. 203, s. 2; 1945, c. 828; 1949, c. 725; 1959, c. 585, s. 1; 1963, c. 1182; 1971, c. 637, s. 4; 1995, c. 47, s. 2; 2009-455, s. 4.)

§ 106-277.7. Labels for vegetable seeds in containers of more than one pound.

Vegetable seeds in containers of more than one pound shall be labeled to show the following information:

(1) The name of each kind and variety present in excess of five percent (5%) and the percentage by weight of each in order of its predominance.

(2) Lot identification.

(3) Repealed by Session Laws 2009-455, s. 5, effective October 1, 2009.

(4) For each named vegetable seed:

a. The percentage of germination exclusive of hard seed.

b. The percentage of hard seed, if present.

c. The calendar month and year the test was completed to determine such percentages.

In addition to the individual percentage statement of germination and hard seed, the total percentage of germination and hard seed may be stated as such, if desired.

(5) Net weight, except when in bulk as defined in this Article.

(6) Name and address of persons who labeled said seed or who sells, offers or exposes said seed for sale within this State. If the seeds are labeled by the shipper for a consignee within this State, the shipper may use his approved code designation with the name and address of the consignee.

(7) No tag or label shall be required, unless requested, on seeds sold directly to and in the presence of the purchaser and taken from a bag or container properly labeled.

(8) Such other information as the Board shall prescribe by rule. (1941, c. 114, s. 4; 1943, c. 203, s. 2; 1945, c. 828; 1949, c. 725; 1959, c. 585, s. 1; 1963, c. 1182; 1971, c. 637, s. 5; 1995, c. 47, s. 3; 2009-455, s. 5.)

§ 106-277.8. Responsibility for presence of labels.

(a) The immediate vendor of any lot of seed which is sold, offered or exposed for sale shall be responsible for the presence of the labels required to be attached to any lots of seed whether he is offering for sale or selling seed which bears labels of a previous vendor, with or without endorsement, or bears his own label.

(b) The labeler of any original or unbroken lot of seed shall be responsible for the presence of and the information on all labels attached to said lot of seed at the time he sells or offers for sale such lot of seed. (1963, c. 1182.)

§ 106-277.9. Prohibitions.

It shall be unlawful for any person:

(1) To transport, to offer for transportation, to sell, distribute, offer for sale or expose for sale within this State agricultural or vegetable seeds for seeding purposes:

a. Unless a seed license has been obtained in accordance with the provisions of this Article.

b. Unless the test to determine the percentage of germination required by G.S. 106-277.5 through 106-277.7 shall have been completed (i) on agricultural seed within a nine-month period, exclusive of the calendar month in which the test was completed, (ii) on cool season lawn seeds and mixtures of cool season lawn seeds, including, but not limited to, Kentucky bluegrass, red fescue, chewings fescue, hard fescue, tall fescue, perennial ryegrass, intermediate ryegrass, annual ryegrass, colonial bent grass, and creeping bent grass, within a 15-month period, exclusive of the calendar month in which the test was completed, and (iii) on vegetable seed within a 12-month period, exclusive of the calendar month in which the test was completed, immediately prior to sale, exposure for sale, or offering for sale or transportation; provided, the North Carolina Board of Agriculture may adopt rules to designate a longer period for any kind of agricultural or vegetable seed which is packaged in such container materials (hermetically sealed), and under such other conditions prescribed, that will, during such longer period, maintain the viability of said seed under ordinary conditions of handling.

c. Not labeled in accordance with the provisions of this Article or having a false or misleading labeling or claim.

d. Pertaining to which there has been a false or misleading advertisement.

e. Consisting of or containing prohibited noxious-weed seeds.

f. Containing restricted noxious-weed seeds, except as prescribed by rules and regulations promulgated under this Article.

g. Containing weed seeds in excess of two percent (2%) by weight unless otherwise provided in rules and regulations promulgated under this Article.

h. That have been treated and not labeled as required in this Article, or treated and not conspicuously colored.

i. Repealed by Session Laws 2009-455, s. 6, effective October 1, 2009.

j. To which there is affixed names or terms that create a misleading impression as to the kind, kind and variety, history, productivity, quality or origin of the seeds.

k. Represented to be certified, registered or foundation seed unless it has been produced, processed and labeled in accordance with the procedures and in compliance with rules and regulations of an officially recognized certifying agency.

l. Represented to be a hybrid unless such seed conforms to the definition of a hybrid as defined in this Article.

m. Unless it conforms to the definition of a "lot."

n. Any variety, hybrid or blend of seeds not recorded with the Commissioner as required under rules and regulations promulgated pursuant to this Article.

o. Seed of any variety or hybrid that has been found by official variety tests to be inferior, misrepresented or unsuited to conditions within the State. The Commissioner may prohibit the sale or distribution of such seed by and with the advice of the director of research of the North Carolina agricultural experiment station.

p. Using a designation on seed tag in lieu of the full name and address of the person who labels or tags seed unless such designation qualifies as a code designation under this Article.

q. By variety name seed not certified by an official seed-certifying agency when it is a variety for which a certificate of plant variety protection under the Plant Variety Protection Act specifies sale only as a class of certified seed; provided, that seed from a certified lot may be labeled as to variety name when used in a mixture by, or with the approval of, the owner of the variety.

r. That employ a brand name on the label unless a variety or mixture of varieties is labeled as required in this Article. If a brand name other than a registered trademark is used, it must be a separate statement from the variety name or the statement of a mixture, or blend, of genetic variations.

s. Labeled as a "blend" unless the lot complies with the definition of "blend" in G.S. 106-277.2, and is registered with the Commissioner, as may be required in G.S. 106-277.9(1)n. Other mechanical combinations of varieties shall be labeled as a mixture according to the requirements in G.S. 106-277.5(1).

(2) To transport, offer for transportation, sell, offer for sale, or expose for sale seeds, whole grain not for seeding purposes unless labeled "not for seeding purposes."

(3) To detach, alter, deface, or destroy any label provided for in this Article or the rules and regulations promulgated hereunder, or to alter or substitute seed in any manner that defeats the purposes of this Article.

(4) To disseminate false or misleading advertisement in any manner concerning agricultural seeds or vegetable seeds.

(5) To hinder or obstruct in any manner an authorized agent of the Commissioner in the performance of his lawful duties.

(6) To fail to comply with or to supply inaccurate information in reply to a stop-sale order; or to remove tags attached to or to remove or dispose of seed or screenings held under a stop-sale order unless authorized by the Commissioner.

(7) To use the name of the Department of Agriculture and Consumer Services or the results of tests and inspections made by the Department for advertising purposes.

(8) To use the words "type" or "trace" in lieu of information required by G.S. 106-277.4 through 106-277.7.

(9) To label and offer for sale seed under the scope of this Article without keeping complete records as specified in G.S. 106-277.12. (1941, c. 114, s. 5; 1943, c. 203, s. 3; 1945, c. 828; 1949, c. 725; 1953, c. 856, s. 4; 1957, c. 263, s. 2; 1959, c. 585, s. 2; 1963, c. 1182; 1971, c. 637, s. 6; 1987 (Reg. Sess., 1988), c. 1034, ss. 7-9; 1997-261, s. 47; 2009-455, s. 6.)

§ 106-277.10. Exemptions.

(a) When the required analysis and other information regarding the seed is present on a seedman's label or tag which bears an official North Carolina seed stamp or is accompanied by the North Carolina seed analysis tag on which is written, stamped or printed the words "See Attached Tag for Seed Analysis," the provisions of G.S. 106-277.5 through 106-277.7 shall be deemed to have been complied with.

(b) The official tag or label of the North Carolina Crop Improvement Association shall be considered an "official North Carolina seed analysis tag" when attached to containers of seed duly certified by the said Association or when it refers to an accompanying tag which carries the same information required in G.S. 106-277.5 to 106-277.7 and when fees applicable to the North Carolina seed analysis tag have been paid to the Commissioner.

(c) The label requirements for peanuts, cotton and tobacco seed may be limited to:

(1) Lot identification.

(2) Origin, if known. If unknown, so stated.

(3) Commonly accepted name of kind and variety.

(4) Name and number per pound of noxious-weed seeds.

(5) Percentage of germination with month and year of tests.

(6) Name and address of person who labeled said seed or who sells, offers, or exposes said seed for sale.

(d) The provisions of G.S. 106-277.3 through 106-277.7 do not apply:

(1) To seed or grain sold or represented to be sold for purposes other than for seeding provided that said seed is labeled "not for seeding purposes" and that the vendor shall make it unmistakably clear to the purchaser of such seed or grain that it is not for seeding purposes.

(2) To seed for conditioning when consigned to, being transported to or stored in an approved conditioning establishment, provided that the invoice or labeling accompanying said seed bears the statement "seed for conditioning" and provided further that other labeling or representation which may be made with respect to the unlearned or unconditioned seed shall be subject to this Article.

(3) To seed sold by a farmer grower to a seed dealer or conditioner, or to seed in storage in or consigned to a seed-cleaning or conditioning plant; provided that any labeling or other representation which may be made with respect to the unlearned or unconditioned seed shall be subject to this Article.

(4) To any carrier in respect to any seed or screenings transported or delivered for transportation in the ordinary course of its business as a carrier; provided that such carrier is not engaged in producing, conditioning, or marketing agricultural or vegetable seeds subject to provisions of this Article.

(e) No person shall be subject to the penalties of this Article for having sold, offered or exposed for sale in this State any agricultural or vegetable seeds which were incorrectly labeled or represented as to origin, kind or variety when such seeds cannot be identified by examination thereof unless such person has failed to obtain an invoice or grower's declaration giving origin, kind and variety or to take such other precautions as may be necessary to insure the identity to be that stated. (1941, c. 114, s. 4; 1943, c. 203, s. 2; 1945, c. 828; 1949, c. 725; 1959, c. 585, s. 1; 1963, c. 1182; 2009-455, ss. 7, 8.)

§ 106-277.11. Disclaimers, nonwarranties and limited warranties.

The use of a disclaimer, nonwarranty or limited warranty clause in any invoice, advertising [or] written, printed or graphic matter pertaining to any seed shall not constitute a defense, or be used as a defense in any way, in any prosecution or in any proceedings for confiscation of seeds brought under the provisions of this Article or rules and regulations made and promulgated thereunder. (1945, c. 828; 1949, c. 725; 1963, c. 1182.)

§ 106-277.12. Records.

All persons transporting or delivering for transportation, selling, offering or exposing for sale agricultural or vegetable seeds if their name appears on the label shall keep for a period of two years a file sample and a complete record of such seed, including invoices showing lot number, kind and variety, origin, germination, purity, treatment, and the labeling of each lot. The Commissioner or his duly authorized agents shall have the right to inspect such records in connection with the administration of this Article at any time during customary business hours. (1945, c. 828; 1949, c. 725; 1963, c. 1182.)

§ 106-277.13. Tolerances to be established and used in enforcement.

Due to variations which may occur between the analyses or tests and likewise between label statements and the results of subsequent analyses and tests, recognized tolerances shall be employed in the enforcement of the provisions of this Article, except as otherwise established by appropriate rules and regulations promulgated under authority of this Article. (1963, c. 1182.)

§ 106-277.14. Administration.

The duty of enforcing this Article and its rules and regulations and carrying out its provisions and requirements shall be vested in the Commissioner of Agriculture. (1963, c. 1182.)

§ 106-277.15. Rules, regulations and standards.

The Board of Agriculture, in accordance with the Administrative Procedure Act, may adopt such rules, regulations and standards which they may find to be advisable or necessary to carry out and enforce the purposes and provisions of this Article, which shall have the force and effect of law. The Board of Agriculture shall adopt rules, regulations and standards as follows:

(1) Prescribing the methods of sampling, inspecting, analyzing, testing and examining agricultural and vegetable seed, and determining the tolerance to be followed in the administration of this Article.

(2) Declaring a list of prohibited and restricted noxious weeds, conforming with the definitions stated in this Article, and to add to or subtract therefrom, from time to time, after a public hearing following due public notice.

(3) Declaring the maximum percentage of total weed seed content permitted in agricultural seed.

(4) Declaring the maximum number of "restricted" noxious-weed seeds per pound of agricultural seed permitted to be sold, offered or exposed for sale.

(5) Declaring the minimum percentage of germination permitted for sale as "Agricultural Seeds."

(6) Declaring germination standards for vegetable seeds.

(7) Prescribing the form and use of tags or stamps to be used in labeling seed.

(8) Prescribing such other rules and regulations as may be necessary to secure the efficient enforcement of this Article.

(9) Establishing fees and charges for agricultural and vegetable seed testing and analysis.

(10) Prescribing minimum hybrid percentage for labeling for each species hybridized.

(11) Prescribing labeling and coloring requirements for treated seed.

(12) Establishing a Tobacco Seed Committee which shall approve flue-cured tobacco varieties prior to registration with the Department.

(13) Prescribing labeling requirements for agricultural and vegetable seed. (1941, c. 114, s. 6; 1943, c. 203, s. 4; 1945, c. 828; 1949, c. 725; 1953, c. 856, s. 5; 1957, c. 263, s. 3; 1963, c. 1182; 1981, c. 495, s. 6; 1987 (Reg. Sess., 1988), c. 1034, s. 10; 1995, c. 47, s. 4.)

§ 106-277.16. Seed-testing facilities.

The Commissioner is authorized to establish and maintain or make provision for seed-testing facilities, to employ educationally qualified persons, to make or provide for making purity and germination tests of seeds, upon request, for farmers or seedsmen, and to prescribe rules and regulations governing such testing, and to incur such expenses as may be necessary to comply with these provisions. (1941, c. 114, s. 6; 1943, c. 203, s. 4; 1945, c. 828; 1949, c. 725; 1953, c. 856, s. 5; 1957, c. 263, s. 3; 1963, c. 1182.)

§ 106-277.17. Registration and variety testing.

The Commissioner is authorized to require the registration, after field testing for performance and trueness-to-variety, of any variety, blend, or hybrid as a prerequisite to sale in this State and to promulgate rules and regulations pertaining to same. The Commissioner is further authorized to prohibit the sale of any variety, blend, or hybrid or any kind of crop, by and with the advice of the Director of the North Carolina Agricultural Research Service, that has been found by official field tests to be inferior, misrepresented or unsuited to conditions within the State. (1941, c. 114, s. 6; 1943, c. 203, s. 4; 1945, c. 828; 1949, c. 725; 1953, c. 856, s. 5; 1957, c. 263, s. 3; 1963, c. 1182; 1987 (Reg. Sess., 1988), c. 1034, ss. 11, 12; 1989, c. 770, s. 24.)

§ 106-277.18. Registration and licensing of dealers.

It shall be the duty of the Commissioner and he is hereby authorized to require each seed dealer selling, offering or exposing for sale in, or exporting from, this State any agricultural or vegetable seeds for seeding purposes, including packet or package seeds, to register with the Commissioner and to obtain a license annually. (1941, c. 114, s. 7; 1945, c. 828; 1947, c. 928; 1949, c. 725; 1963, c. 1182.)

§ 106-277.19. Revocation, suspension, or refusal of license for cause; hearing; appeal.

In accordance with Chapter 150B of the General Statutes, the Commissioner is authorized to suspend any seed license issued for a period not to exceed three years, revoke any seed license issued, or to refuse to issue a seed license to any person upon satisfactory proof that said person has repeatedly violated any of the provisions of this Article or any of the rules adopted thereunder. (1941, c. 114, s. 6; 1943, c. 203, s. 4; 1945, c. 828; 1949, c. 725; 1953, c. 856, s. 5; 1957, c. 263, s. 3; 1963, c. 1182; 2013-345, s. 1(a).)

§ 106-277.20. Right of entry for purposes of inspection; duty of vendors.

For the purpose of carrying out this Article the Commissioner or his agent is authorized to enter upon any public or private premises during regular business hours in order to have access to seeds subject to his Article and the rules and regulations thereunder. It shall be the duty of the dealer or vendor to arrange seed lots so as to be accessible for inspection, and to provide such information and records as may be deemed necessary. (1941, c. 114, s. 6; 1943, c. 203, s. 4; 1945, c. 828; 1949, c. 725; 1953, c. 856, s. 5; 1957, c. 263, s. 3; 1963, c. 1182.)

§ 106-277.21. Sampling, inspecting and testing; notice of violations.

It shall be the duty of the Commissioner, who may act through his authorized agents, to sample, inspect, make analysis of and test agricultural and vegetable seeds transported, held in storage, sold, offered or exposed for sale within this State for sowing purposes at such time and place and to such extent as he may deem necessary to determine whether said seeds are in compliance with the provisions of this Article, and to notify promptly the person or persons who transported, had in his possession, sold, offered or exposed the seeds for sale of any violation. (1941, c. 114, s. 6; 1943, c. 203, s. 4; 1945, c. 828; 1949, c. 725; 1953, c. 856, s. 5; 1957, c. 263, s. 3; 1963, c. 1182.)

§ 106-277.22. Stop-sale orders; penalty covering expenses; appeal.

The Commissioner is authorized to issue and enforce a written or printed "stop-sale" order to the owner or custodian of any lot of agricultural or vegetable seeds which the Commissioner, or his authorized agent, finds is in violation of any of the provisions of this Article or the rules and regulations promulgated thereunder, which order shall prohibit further sale or movement of such seed until such officer has evidence that the law has been complied with and a written release has been issued to the owner or custodian of said seed by the enforcement officer. Any person violating the labeling requirements of the law shall be subject to a penalty covering all costs and expenses incurred in connection with the withdrawal from sale and the release of said seed. With respect to seeds which have been denied sale as provided in this section, the owner, custodian or the person labeling such seeds shall have the right to appeal from such order to the superior court of the county in which the seeds are found, praying for judgment as to the justification of said order and for discharge of such seed from the order prohibiting the same in accordance with the findings of the court; and provided, further, that the provisions of this section shall not be construed as limiting the right of the enforcement officer to proceed as authorized by other sections of this Article. (1941, c. 114, s. 6; 1943, c. 203, s. 4; 1945, c. 828; 1949, c. 725; 1953, c. 856, s. 5; 1957, c. 263, s. 3; 1963, c. 1182.)

§ 106-277.23. Notice of violations; hearings, prosecutions or warnings.

It shall be the duty of the Commissioner to give notice of every violation of the provisions of this Article with respect to agricultural or vegetable seeds, or mixtures of such seeds, to the person in whose hands such seeds are found, and to send copies of such notice to the shipper of such seed and to the person whose "analysis tag or label" is attached to the container of such seeds, in which notice the Commissioner may designate a time and place for a hearing. The person or persons involved shall have the right to introduce evidence either in person or by agent or attorney. If, after hearing, or without such hearing in the event the person fails or refuses to appear, the Commissioner is of the opinion that the evidence warrants prosecution he may institute proceedings in a court of competent jurisdiction in the locality which the violation occurred or, if he believes the public interest will be adequately served thereby, he may direct to the alleged violator a suitable written notice or warning. (1941, c. 114, s. 8; 1945, c. 828; 1949, c. 725; 1963, c. 1182; 2009-455, s. 9.)

§ 106-277.24. Penalty for violations.

Any person, firm or corporation violating any provision of this Article or any rule or regulation adopted pursuant thereto shall be guilty of a Class 3 misdemeanor and upon conviction thereof shall pay a fine of not more than ten thousand dollars ($10,000). This fine shall not apply, however, to a retailer with respect to any transaction where the seed sold by the retailer was acquired by the retailer in a sealed container or package, or the retailer did not have reasonable knowledge that the seed sold was in violation of this Article. In determining the amount of the fine, the court shall consider the retail value of the seed sold in violation of the law, and in cases involving the unlawful sale of seed protected under the federal Plant Variety Protection Act, the court shall order the payment of restitution to any injured party for any losses incurred as a result of the unlawful sale. (1941, c. 114, s. 8; 1945, c. 828; 1949, c. 725; 1963, c. 1182; 1993, c. 539, s. 758; 1994, Ex. Sess., c. 24, s. 14(c); 2013-345, s. 1(b).)

§ 106-277.25. Seizure and disposition of seeds violating Article.

Any lot of agricultural or vegetable seeds, mixtures of such seeds being sold, exposed for sale, offered for sale or held with intent to sell in this State contrary to the provisions of this Article shall be subject to seizure on complaint of the Commissioner to the resident judge of the superior court in the county in which the seeds or mixtures of such seeds are located. In the event the court finds the seeds to be in violation of the provisions of this Article and orders the condemnation thereof, such seeds shall be denatured, processed, destroyed, relabeled, or otherwise disposed of in compliance with the laws of this State; provided that in no instance shall such disposition be ordered by the court without first having given the claimant an opportunity to apply to the court for the release of the seeds, with permission to process or relabel to bring them into compliance with the provisions of this Article. (1945, c. 828; 1949, c. 725; 1963, c. 1182; 2009-455, s. 10.)

§ 106-277.26. Publication of test results and other information.

The Commissioner is authorized to publish the results of analyses, tests, examinations, studies and investigations made as authorized by this Article, together with any other information he may deem advisable. (1941, c. 114, s. 6; 1943, c. 203, s. 4; 1945, c. 828; 1949, c. 725; 1953, c. 856, s. 5; 1957, c. 263, s. 3; 1963, c. 1182.)

§ 106-277.27. Cooperation with United States Department of Agriculture.

The Commissioner is authorized to cooperate with the United States Department of Agriculture in seed law enforcement and testing seed for trueness as to kind and variety. (1941, c. 114, s. 6; 1943, c. 203, s. 4; 1945, c. 828; 1949, c. 725; 1953, c. 856, s. 5; 1957, c. 263, s. 3; 1963, c. 1182.)

§ 106-277.28. License and inspection fees.

For the purpose of providing a fund to defray the expense of inspection, examination, and analysis of seeds and the enforcement of this Article:

(1)   Repealed by Session Laws 1991, c. 588, s. 1.

(2)   Each seed dealer who offers for sale any agricultural, vegetable, or lawn or turf seeds for seeding purposes shall register with the Commissioner and shall obtain an annual license, for each location where activities are conducted, by January 1 of each year and shall pay the following license fee:

a.   Wholesale or combined wholesale and retail

seed dealer.. $125.00

b......... Retail seed dealer.. $30.00.

c.,d.   Repealed by Session Laws 2009-455, s. 11, effective October 1, 2009.

(3)   Each seed dealer or grower who has seed, whether originated or labeled by the dealer or grower, that is offered for sale in this State shall report

the quantity of seed offered for sale and pay an inspection fee of four cents (4¢) for each container of seeds weighing 10 pounds or more. Seed shall be subject to the inspection fee and reporting requirements only once in any 12-month period. This fee does not apply to seed grown by a farmer and offered for sale by the farmer at the farm where the seed was grown.

Each seed dealer or grower shall keep accurate records of the quantity of seeds and container weights offered for sale from each distribution point in the State. These records shall be available to the Commissioner or an authorized representative of the Commissioner at any and all reasonable hours for the purpose of verifying the quantity of seed offered for sale and the fees paid. Each seed dealer or grower shall report quarterly on forms furnished by the Commissioner the quantity and container weight of seeds first offered for sale that quarter. The reports shall be made on the first day of January, April, July, and October, or within 10 days thereafter. Inspection fees shall be due and paid with the next quarterly report filed after the seed is first offered for sale. If the report is not filed and the inspection fees paid to the Department of Agriculture and Consumer Services by the tenth day following the date due, or if the report of the quantity or container weights is false, the Commissioner may issue a stop-sale order for all seed offered for sale by the dealer or grower. If the inspection fees are unpaid more than 15 days after the due date, the amount due shall bear a penalty of ten percent (10%) which shall be added to the inspection fees due. (1941, c. 114, s. 7; 1945, c. 828; 1947, c. 928; 1949, c. 725; 1963, c. 1182; 1969, c. 105; 1987 (Reg. Sess., 1988), c. 1034, s. 13; 1989, c. 37, s. 8; 1991, c. 98, s. 1; c. 588, s. 1; 1995, c. 47, s. 5; 1997-261, s. 48; 2005-276, s. 42.1(c); 2009-455, s. 11.)

§ 106-277.29: Repealed by Session Laws 1998-210, s. 2.

§ 106-277.30. Filing complaint; investigation; referral to Seed Board.

(a)   Complaint by Buyer. - When a buyer believes that he or she has suffered damages due to the failure of agricultural or vegetable seed to produce or perform as labeled or as warranted, or as the result of negligence, the buyer may make a sworn complaint against the dealer from whom the seeds were purchased, alleging the damages sustained or to be sustained, and file the complaint with the Commissioner within such time as to permit inspection of the seed, crops, or plants. The buyer shall send a copy of the complaint to the dealer by registered or certified mail. A filing fee of one hundred dollars ($100.00) shall be paid to the Department with each complaint filed. This fee may be used by the Commissioner to offset the expenses of the Seed Board incurred under G.S. 106-277.32. Within 10 days after receipt of a copy of the complaint, the dealer may file an answer to the complaint and, in that event, shall send a copy to the buyer by registered or certified mail.

(b)   Investigation Requested by Dealer. - Any dealer who has received notice, either orally or in writing, that a buyer believes that he or she has suffered damage due to the failure of agricultural or vegetable seed sold by the dealer to perform as labeled or as warranted, or as a result of negligence, may request an investigation by the Seed Board pursuant to G.S. 106-277.32. A filing fee of one hundred dollars ($100.00) shall be paid to the Department by the party requesting the investigation. The dealer shall send a copy of the request to the buyer by registered or certified mail. The buyer may file a response to the request with the Commissioner within 10 days of receipt of the request for an investigation.

(c)   Referral to Seed Board. - The Commissioner shall refer the complaint or request for investigation to the Seed Board to investigate and make findings and recommendations on the matters complained of pursuant to G.S. 106-277.32. (1998-210, s. 3.)

§ 106-277.31. Notice required.

Dealers shall legibly print or type on each seed container or affix a label on each seed container a notice in the following form or using reasonably equivalent language:

"Notice of Claims Procedure for Defective Seed

North Carolina provides an opportunity for persons who believe that they have suffered damage from the failure of agriculture or vegetable seeds to perform as labeled or warranted, or as a result of negligence, to have the matter investigated and heard before a special seed board as an alternative to filing a court action. To take advantage of this procedure, a purchaser of seed must file a complaint with the North Carolina Commissioner of Agriculture in time for the seed, crop, or plants to be inspected. Failure to follow this procedure will limit the amount of damages you may be able to recover. Please contact the Commissioner of Agriculture for information about this claims procedure." (1998-210, s. 3.)

§ 106-277.32. Seed Board created; membership; duties.

(a) The Commissioner shall appoint a Seed Board composed of five members, three of whom shall be appointed upon the recommendation of the following: Director of the Agricultural Research Service, North Carolina State University; Director of the North Carolina Cooperative Extension Service, North Carolina State University; and President of the North Carolina Seedsmen's Association. The other two members shall include: one farmer who is not connected in any way to selling seeds at retail or wholesale and one employee of the Department. An alternate for each member shall also be appointed in the same manner as that member was appointed to serve whenever that member is unable or unwilling to serve. Each member of the Board shall serve a four-year term at the discretion of the Commissioner. The Board shall elect a chairperson. The chairperson shall conduct all meetings and deliberations and direct all other activities of the Board. Three members of the Board shall constitute a quorum and at least three board members must vote affirmatively for the Board to take any action.

(b) A clerk shall be appointed to serve the Board. The clerk shall be an employee of the Department. The clerk shall keep accurate and correct records of all meetings and deliberations and perform other duties for the Board as directed by the chairperson.

(c) The Department shall provide administrative support for the investigation under this section. The Board shall adopt rules to govern investigations and hearings. A copy of the rules shall be mailed to each party to a dispute upon receipt of a complaint.

(d) Members of the Board appointed by the Commissioner who are not governmental employees shall be entitled to receive reimbursement for necessary travel and subsistence expenses pursuant to G.S. 138-5. Members of the Board who are State employees shall be entitled to receive reimbursement for necessary travel and subsistence expenses pursuant to G.S. 138-6.

(e) The Attorney General shall represent the Board in any and all legal proceedings that may arise concerning or against the Board. (1998-210, s. 3.)

§ 106-277.33. Duties of Seed Board.

(a) In conducting its investigation of claims referred by the Commissioner, the Seed Board may engage in the following activities:

(1) Examine the buyer regarding the buyer's use of the seed of which the buyer complains and examine the dealer on the dealer's packaging, labeling, and selling of the seed alleged to be faulty.

(2) Grow a representative sample of the alleged faulty seed to production when such action is deemed by the Board to be necessary.

(3) Hold informal hearings at a time and place directed by the chairperson upon reasonable notice to the buyer and the dealer.

(4) Seek evaluations from authorities in allied disciplines, when deemed necessary by the Board.

(5) Visit and inspect the affected site and take samples, make plant counts, and take pictures of affected and unaffected areas.

(b) The Board shall keep a record of its activities and reports on file in the Department. The Department shall transmit all findings and recommendations to the buyer and to the dealer within 30 days of completion of the investigation.

(c) No investigation shall be made by less than the whole membership of the Board unless the chairperson directs such investigation in writing. Such investigation shall be summarized in writing and considered by the Board in reporting its findings and making its recommendations.

(d) The report of the investigation and the recommendations of the Seed Board shall be binding upon all parties to the extent, if any, that they have so agreed in writing subsequent to the filing of the complaint pursuant to G.S. 106-277.30. (1998-210, s. 3.)

§ 106-277.34. Actions regarding defective seed claims; evidence.

(a) In any court action involving a complaint that has been the subject of an investigation under G.S. 106-277.32, any party may introduce evidence of seed quality, cultivation practices and procedures, and scientific opinion contained in the report of the Seed Board. Statements of the parties and recommendations of the Seed Board as resolution of the dispute are not admissible as evidence unless such evidence is otherwise discoverable.

(b) In any court action where a buyer alleges that he or she suffered damages due to the failure of agricultural or vegetable seed to produce or perform as labeled or warranted, or as the result of negligence, and the buyer failed to make a sworn complaint against the dealer as set forth in G.S. 106-277.30, the buyer's right to recover damages shall be limited to actual expenditures paid by the buyer to other persons for the cost of seed, labor, equipment, fertilizer, insecticide, herbicide, land rent, or other expenses incurred in connection with the cultivation of the seed alleged to be defective, less any value received by the buyer arising from the sale or transfer of any crops grown from the seed in question. (1998-210, s. 3.)

§§ 106-278 through 106-284.4. Reserved for future codification purposes.

Article 31A.

Seed Potato Law.

§§ 106-284.5 through 106-284.13: Repealed by Session Laws 1973, c. 294.

Article 31B.

Vegetable Plant Law.

§ 106-284.14. Title.

This Article shall be known as the "Vegetable Plant Law." (1959, c. 91, s. 1.)

§ 106-284.15. Purpose of Article.

The purpose of this Article is to improve vegetable production in North Carolina and to enable vegetable producers to secure vegetable plants for transplanting that are free from diseases and insects, and in order to prevent the spread of diseases and insects affecting the future stability of the vegetable industry and the general welfare of the public. (1959, c. 91, s. 2; 1973, c. 1370, s. 1.)

§ 106-284.16. Definitions.

For the purpose of this Article, the following terms shall be construed respectively to mean:

(1) "Certified vegetable plants for transplanting" shall mean plants which have been tagged or labeled so as to indicate that such plants have been inspected by an authorized agent of an officially recognized State inspecting or certifying agency of some state, and found to conform to the appropriate standards set by the North Carolina Board of Agriculture.

(2) "Vegetable plants" shall mean such plants as asparagus, pepper, eggplant, sweet potato, onion, cabbage and other cole crops, tomato plants, white seed potatoes and onion sets intended for transplanting purposes and such other vegetable plants intended for transplanting purposes as the North Carolina Board of Agriculture may designate by regulation in order to protect the vegetable industry.

(3) As applied to vegetable plants "standards" include the qualities of color, freshness, firmness, strength, straightness, unbroken and undamaged condition, uniformity of size, and freedom from injurious insects, diseases,

nematodes, snails, and other pests and means the standards with respect thereto as established and fixed in regulations adopted by the North Carolina Board of Agriculture. (1959, c. 91, s. 3; 1973, c. 1370, s. 2.)

§ 106-284.17. Unlawful to sell plants not up to standard and not appropriately tagged or labeled.

It shall be unlawful for any person, firm, or corporation to pack for sale, offer or expose for sale, or ship into this State any vegetable plants which do not meet the appropriate standards as set by the North Carolina Board of Agriculture and which have not been appropriately tagged or labeled as certified vegetable plants for transplanting. (1959, c. 91, s. 4; 1973, c. 1370, s. 3.)

§ 106-284.18. Rules and regulations.

The State Board of Agriculture is hereby authorized to adopt reasonable rules and regulations to carry out the intent, purposes and provisions of this Article. (1959, c. 91, s. 5; 1973, c. 1370, s. 4.)

§ 106-284.19. Inspection; interference with inspectors; "stop-sale" notice.

To enforce the provisions of this Article effectively, the Commissioner of Agriculture and his duly authorized agents are authorized to inspect vegetable plants, and may enter any place of business, warehouse, common carrier or other places where such vegetable plants are stored or being held, for the purpose of making such an inspection; and it shall be unlawful for any person, firm or corporation in custody of such vegetable plants or of the place in which the same are held to interfere with the Commissioner or his duly authorized agents in making such inspections. When the Commissioner or his authorized inspectors find vegetable plants being held, offered or exposed for sale in violation of any of the provisions of this Article or any rule or regulation adopted pursuant thereto, he may issue a "stop-sale notice" to the owner or custodian of any such vegetable plants and shall tag such plants as are in violation. It shall be unlawful for anyone after notice or receipt of such "stop-sale notice" to remove such notice from plants or from any location to which attached; or to plant, sell, give away, move or exchange for transplanting purposes any plants in respect to which such notice has been issued unless and until so authorized by the Commissioner or his agent or a court of competent jurisdiction. (1959, c. 91, s. 6; 1973, c. 1370, s. 5.)

§ 106-284.20. Interference with Commissioner, etc., or other violation a misdemeanor; penalties.

If anyone shall interfere with or attempt to interfere with the Commissioner or any of his agents, while engaged in the performance of his duties under this law or shall violate any provision of this law or any rule or regulation of the Board of Agriculture adopted pursuant to this law, he shall be guilty of a Class 1 misdemeanor. Each day's violation shall constitute a separate offense. (1959, c. 91, s. 7; 1973, c. 1370, s. 6; 1993, c. 539, s. 759; 1994, Ex. Sess., c. 24, s. 14(c).)

§ 106-284.21. Authority to permit sale of substandard plants.

Notwithstanding any other provision of this Article, the Commissioner of Agriculture is authorized when the public necessity, welfare, economy, or any emergency situation requires it, to permit for such periods of time as, in his discretion may seem necessary, the sale of vegetable plants for transplanting purposes which do not meet the standards referred to in G.S. 106-284.16. (1959, c. 91, s. 8.)

§ 106-284.22. When Article not applicable.

The provisions of this Article shall not apply:

(1) To the sale by a grower or retail merchant of vegetable plants grown within this State when such sale is made for home or garden or any noncommercial use; provided, however, the provisions shall apply to such sale when such plants are found to be infested with pests so that the exposure for sale or planting is deemed by the Commissioner or his agent to be a hazard to the commercial vegetable industry of North Carolina.

(2) To the sale of vegetable plants for commercial transplanting purposes in this State when grown within this State and sold by a plant producer to a planter having personal knowledge of the conditions under which such vegetable plants were grown or produced provided that such plants are transplanted within a 30-mile radius at which they were grown; but also provided, however, the provisions shall apply to such sale when such plants are found to be infested with pests so that the exposure for sale or planting is deemed by the Commissioner or his agent to be a hazard to the commercial vegetable industry of North Carolina. (1959, c. 91, s. 9; 1973, c. 1370, s. 7.)

§ 106-284.23. Not set out.

§§ 106-284.24 through 106-284.29. Reserved for future codification purposes.

Article 31C.

North Carolina Commercial Feed Law of 1973.

§ 106-284.30. Title.

This Article shall be known as the "North Carolina Commercial Feed Law of 1973." (1973, c. 771, s. 2.)

§ 106-284.31. Purpose.

The purpose of this Article is to regulate the manufacture and distribution of commercial feeds in the State of North Carolina and to protect a farmer-buyer from the manufacturer-seller of concentrated, commercial feed who might sell substandard or mislabeled feedstuff, and not to protect from himself a farmer who mixes his own feed. (1973, c. 771, s. 1.)

§ 106-284.32. Enforcing official.

This Article shall be administered by the Commissioner of Agriculture of the State of North Carolina, hereinafter referred to as the "Commissioner." (1973, c. 771, s. 3.)

§ 106-284.33. Definitions of words and terms.

When used in this Article:

(1)   The term "Board" means the North Carolina State Board of Agriculture.

(2)   The term "brand name" means any word, name, symbol, or device, or any combination thereof, identifying the commercial feed of a distributor or registrant and distinguishing it from that of others.

(3)   The term "canned pet food" means any commercial feed packed in cans or hermetically sealed containers, and used or intended for use as food for pets.

(4)   The term "commercial feed" means all materials, except whole unmixed seed such as corn, including physically altered entire unmixed seeds when not adulterated within the meaning of G.S. 106-284.38(1), which are distributed for use as feed or for mixing in feed; provided, that the Board by regulation may exempt from this definition, or from specific provisions of this Article, hay, straw, stover, silage, cobs, husks, hulls, unpasteurized milk, and individual chemical compounds or substances which are not intermixed or mixed with other materials, and are not adulterated within the meaning of G.S. 106-284.38(1).

(4a)   The term "contract feeder" means a person who, as an independent contractor, feeds commercial feed to animals pursuant to a contract between that person and a manufacturer of commercial feeds whereby such commercial feed is supplied, furnished, or otherwise provided to such person by the said manufacturer and whereby such person's remuneration is determined all or in part by feed consumption, mortality, profits, or amount or quality of product produced by the independent contractor.

(5)   The term "customer-formula feed" means commercial feed, each batch of which is mixed according to the formula of the customer, furnished in writing over the signature of the customer or his designated agent with each batch

moved directly from the manufacturer to the customer and not stocked or displayed in a dealer's warehouse or sales area and not resold or redistributed to any person.

(6)   The term "distribute" means to offer for sale, sell, exchange, or barter, commercial feed.

(7)   The term "distributor" means any person who distributes.

(8)   The term "drug" means any article intended for use in the diagnosis, cure, mitigation, treatment, or prevention of disease in animals other than man and articles other than feed intended to affect the structure or any function of the animal body.

(9)   The term "feed ingredient" means each of the constituent materials making up a commercial feed.

(10)   The term "label" means a display of written, printed, or graphic matter upon or affixed to the container in which a commercial feed is distributed, or on the invoice or delivery slip with which a commercial feed is distributed.

(11)   The term "labeling" means all labels and other written, printed, or graphic matter (i) upon a commercial feed or any of its containers or wrapper or (ii) accompanying such commercial feed, or advertisement, brochures, posters, television and radio announcements used in promoting the sale of such commercial feed.

(12)   The term "manufacture" means to grind, mix or blend, or further process a commercial feed for distribution.

(13)   The term "mineral feed" means a commercial feed intended to supply primarily mineral elements or inorganic nutrients.

(14)   The term "official sample" means a sample of feed taken by the Commissioner or his agent in accordance with the provisions of G.S. 106-284.42(a), (c) or (e).

(15)   The terms "percent" or "percentage" means percentage by weight, except in G.S. 106-284.42 where these terms refer to the retail value of the lot of commercial feed.

(16) The term "permitted analytical variation" means allowance for the inherent variability in sampling and laboratory analysis in guaranteed components. Manufacturing variations and their effect on the guaranteed components are not included in such values.

(17) The term "person" means an individual, a partnership, a corporation, an association, and any other legal entity.

(18) The term "pet" means any domesticated animal normally maintained in or near the household(s) of the owner(s) thereof.

(19) The term "pet food" means any commercial feed prepared and distributed for consumption by pets.

(20) The term "product name" means the name of the commercial feed which identifies it as to kind, class, or specific use.

(21) The term "specialty pet" means any domesticated animal pet normally maintained in a cage or tank, such as, but not limited to, gerbils, hamsters, canaries, psittacine birds, mynahs, finches, tropical fish, goldfish, snakes and turtles.

(22) The term "specialty pet food" means any commercial feed prepared and distributed for consumption by specialty pets.

(23) The term "ton" means a net weight of 2,000 pounds avoirdupois. (1973, c. 771, s. 4; 1975, c. 900, s. 1; c. 961, s. 1; 2008-88, s. 3.)

§ 106-284.34. Registration.

(a) No person shall manufacture or distribute a commercial feed in this State, unless he has filed with the Commissioner on forms provided by the Commissioner, his name, place of business, and location of each manufacturing facility in this State, if any, and made application to the Commissioner for a permit to report the quantity of commercial feed distributed in this State.

(b) Manufacturers of registered feeds may apply for, and the Commissioner at his discretion may issue, numbered permits authorizing manufacturers of registered feeds to purchase commercial feed as defined in G.S. 106-284.33(4), and the responsibility for the payment of the inspection fee assessed by the provisions of this Article will be assumed by the purchaser to whom such permit has been issued. The Commissioner may at his discretion, and without notice, cancel any permit issued under the provision of this section. The use of permits issued under the provisions of this section shall be governed by rules and regulations promulgated by the Commissioner.

(c) No person shall distribute in this State a commercial feed, except a customer-formula feed, which has not been registered pursuant to the provisions of this section. The application for registration shall be submitted in the manner prescribed by the Commissioner. Upon approval by the Commissioner or his duly designated agent the registration shall be issued to the applicant. All registrations expire on the thirty-first day of December of each year. An annual registration fee of five dollars ($5.00) for each commercial feed other than canned pet food shall accompany each request for registration. An annual registration fee of twelve dollars ($12.00) for each canned pet food shall accompany each request for registration.

(d) The Commissioner is empowered to refuse registration of any commercial feed not in compliance with the provisions of this Article and to cancel any registration subsequently found not to be in compliance with any provisions of this Article: Provided, that no registration shall be refused or canceled unless the registrant shall have been given an opportunity to be heard before the Commissioner or his duly designated agent and to amend his application in order to comply with the requirements of this Article.

(e) The manufacturer of commercial feed that has not been registered and is found being distributed in the State shall pay a thirty-dollar ($30.00) delinquent registration fee in addition to the regular registration fee. (1973, c. 771, s. 5; 1989, c. 544, s. 7; 2005-276, s. 42.1(a).)

§ 106-284.35. Labeling.

A commercial feed shall be labeled as follows:

(1) In case of commercial feed, except a customer-formula feed, it shall be accompanied by a label bearing the following information:

a. The net weight.

b. The product name and the brand name, if any, under which the commercial feed is distributed.

c. The guaranteed analysis stated in such terms as the Board by regulation determines is required to advise the users of the composition of the feed or to support claims made in the labeling. In all cases the substances or elements must be determinable by laboratory methods such as the methods published by the Association of Official Analytical Chemists.

d. The common or usual name of each ingredient used in the manufacture of the commercial feed: Provided, that the Board by regulation may permit the use of collective terms for a group of ingredients which perform a similar function, or the Board may exempt such commercial feeds, or any group thereof, from this requirement of an ingredient statement if it finds that such statement is not required in the interest of consumers.

e. The name and principal mailing address of the manufacturer or the person distributing the commercial feed.

f. Adequate directions for use for all commercial feeds containing drugs and for such other feeds as the Board may require by regulations as necessary for their safe and effective use.

g. Such precautionary statements as the Board by regulation determines are necessary for the safe and effective use of the commercial feed.

(2) In the case of a customer-formula feed, it shall be accompanied by a label, invoice, delivery slip, or other shipping document to be presented to the purchaser at time of delivery, bearing the following information:

a. Name and address of the manufacturer.

b. Name and address of the purchaser.

c. Date of delivery.

d. The product name and brand name, if any, and the net weight of each registered commercial feed used in the mixture, and the net weight of each other ingredient used.

e. Adequate directions for use for all customer-formula feeds containing drugs and for such other feeds as the Board may require by regulation as necessary for their safe and effective use.

f. Such precautionary statements as the Board by regulation determines are necessary for the safe and effective use of the customer-formula feed. (1973, c. 771, s. 6.)

§ 106-284.36. Bag weights.

All commercial feed, except that in bags or packages of five pounds or less, shall be in such standard-weight bags or packages as the Board by regulation shall prescribe. (1973, c. 771, s. 7.)

§ 106-284.37. Misbranding.

A commercial feed shall be deemed to be misbranded:

(1) If its labeling is false or misleading in any particular.

(2) If it is distributed under the name of another commercial feed.

(3) If it is not labeled as required in G.S. 106-284.35.

(4) If it purports to be or is represented as a commercial feed, or if it purports to contain or is represented as containing a commercial feed ingredient, unless such commercial feed or feed ingredient conforms to the definition, if any, prescribed by regulation by the Board.

(5) If any word, statement, or other information required by or under authority of this Article to appear on the label or labeling is not prominently placed thereon with such conspicuousness (as compared with other words, statements, designs, or devices in the labeling) and in such terms as to render it likely to be read and understood by the ordinary individual under customary conditions of purchase and use. (1973, c. 771, s. 8.)

§ 106-284.38. Adulteration.

A commercial feed shall be deemed to be adulterated:

(1)   a.   If it bears or contains any poisonous or deleterious substance which may render it injurious to health; but in case the substance is not an added substance, such commercial feed shall not be considered adulterated under this subdivision if the quantity of such substance in such commercial feed does not ordinarily render it injurious to health; or

b.   If it bears or contains any added poisonous, added deleterious, or added nonnutritive substance which is unsafe within the meaning of section 406 of the Federal Food, Drug and Cosmetic Act (other than one which is (i) a pesticide chemical in or on a raw agricultural commodity; or (ii) a food additive); or

c.   If it is, or it bears or contains, any food additive which is unsafe within the meaning of section 409 of the Federal Food, Drug and Cosmetic Act; or

d.   If it is a raw agricultural commodity and it bears or contains a pesticide chemical which is unsafe within the meaning of section 408(a) of the Federal Food, Drug and Cosmetic Act; provided, that where a pesticide chemical has been used in or on a raw agricultural commodity in conformity with an exemption granted or a tolerance prescribed under section 408 of the Federal Food, Drug and Cosmetic Act and such raw agricultural commodity has been subjected to processing such as canning, cooking, freezing, dehydrating, or milling, the residue of such pesticide chemical remaining in or on such processed feed shall not be deemed unsafe if such residue in or on the raw agricultural commodity has been removed to the extent possible in good manufacturing practice and the concentration of such residue in the processed feed is not greater than the tolerance prescribed for the raw agricultural commodity unless the feeding of such processed feed will result or is likely to result in a pesticide residue in the edible product of the animal, which is unsafe within the meaning of section 408(a), of the Federal Food, Drug and Cosmetic Act.

e.   If it is, or it bears or contains, any color additive which is unsafe within the meaning of section 706 of the Federal Food, Drug and Cosmetic Act.

(2)   If any valuable constituent has been in whole or in part omitted or abstracted therefrom or any less valuable substance substituted therefor.

(3) If its composition or quality falls below or differs from that which it is purported or is represented to possess by its labeling.

(4) If it contains a drug and the methods used in or the facilities or controls used for its manufacture, processing, or packaging do not conform to current good manufacturing practice regulations promulgated by the Board to assure that the drug meets the requirements of this Article as to safety and has the identity and strength and meets the quality and purity characteristics which its purports or is represented to possess. In promulgating such regulations, the Board shall adopt the current good manufacturing practice regulations for medicated feed premixes and for medicated feeds established under authority of the Federal Food, Drug and Cosmetic Act, unless it determines that they are not appropriate to the conditions which exist in this State.

(5) If it contains viable weed seeds in amounts exceeding the limits which the Board shall establish by rule or regulation. (1973, c. 771, s. 9.)

§ 106-284.39. Prohibited acts.

The following acts and the causing thereof within the State of North Carolina are hereby prohibited:

(1) The manufacture or distribution of any commercial feed that is adulterated or misbranded.

(2) The adulteration or misbranding of any commercial feed.

(3) The distribution of agricultural commodities such as whole seed, hay, straw, stover, silage, cobs, husks, and hulls, which are adulterated within the meaning of G.S. 106-284.38(1).

(4) The removal or disposal of a commercial feed in violation of an order under G.S. 106-284.43.

(5) The failure or refusal to register in accordance with G.S. 106-284.34.

(6) The violation of G.S. 106-284.44(f).

(7) Failure to pay inspection fees and file reports as required by G.S. 106-284.40.

(8) The use of metal fasteners as bag fasteners or for attaching labels to the containers of commercial feed. (1973, c. 771, s. 10.)

§ 106-284.40. Inspection fees and reports.

(a) An inspection fee at the rate of three cents (3¢) for each carton of 48 cans shall be paid on canned pet food distributed in this State by the person whose name appears on the label as the manufacturing distributor or guarantor subject to (b)(1), (2), (3), and (5) of this section.

(b) An inspection fee at the rate of twelve cents (12¢) per ton shall be paid on commercial feeds distributed in the State by the person whose name appears on the label of the commercial feed as the manufacturer, distributor or guarantor of the commercial feed, subject to the following:

(1) No fee shall be paid on a commercial feed if the payment has been made by a previous distributor.

(2) No fee shall be paid on customer-formula feeds if the inspection fee is paid on the commercial feeds which are used as ingredients therein.

(3) No fee shall be paid on commercial feeds which are used as ingredients or a base for the manufacture of commercial feeds which are registered, if the fee has already been paid. If the inspection fee has already been paid on such commercial feed, the amount paid shall be deducted from the gross amount due on the total feed produced.

(4) In the case of a commercial feed other than canned pet food which is distributed in the State only in packages of five pounds or less, an annual registration fee of forty dollars ($40.00) shall be paid in lieu of the inspection fee specified above.

(5) The minimum inspection fee shall be ten dollars ($10.00) per quarter unless no feed was sold in the State during the quarter.

(6) Manufacturers of commercial feeds may appear before the Board, and after finding there exists a contract feeder relationship between a manufacturer of commercial feeds and an independent contractor, the Board may issue annual numbered permits exempting that manufacturer of commercial feed from paying the inspection fee assessed by the provisions of this law for that feed delivered to the contract feeder. The manufacturer of ingredients who sells such ingredients to manufacturers of commercial feeds under this subdivision shall have in his possession the exemption number of the permit referred to in G.S. 106-284.34(b) and/or the permit issued by the Board under this subdivision before the supplier may be relieved of the responsibility for payment of the inspection fee. The holder of a valid contract feeder exemption permit shall be exempt from paying the inspection fee on all ingredients purchased for its own use, provided that at least one-half of the ingredients purchased in the previous calendar year were used in feed delivered to contract feeders.

The holder of said permit may voluntarily return said permit to the Commissioner for cancellation at which time said holder may not apply for or receive another exemption permit under this subdivision for a period of 12 months. The exemption permits under this subdivision shall be renewable automatically every year by the Board without additional findings of fact unless it is brought to the Board's attention by the Commissioner or his duly designated officer or employee that there no longer exists the relationship of a contract feeder between the manufacturer of commercial feeds and an independent contractor. In the event the Commissioner or his duly designated officer or employee notifies the Board when the permit is to be automatically renewed or anytime the permit is in effect, that there no longer exists a contract feeder relationship for the permit holder, the Board shall determine the veracity of the notification and revoke said permit if the facts are found to be true by the Board.

Commercial feeds exempt from inspection fees under this subdivision shall not be subject to sampling and analysis other than as may be necessary to determine compliance with good manufacturing practice regulations pertaining to medicated animal feed and medicated feed premixes established under G.S. 106-284.38(4) of this law.

(c) Each person who is liable for the payment of such fee shall:

(1) File, not later than the last day of January, April, July and October of each year, a quarterly statement setting forth the number of net tons of commercial feeds and/or cases of canned pet food distributed in this State during the preceding calendar quarter, and upon filing such statements shall pay

the inspection fee at the rate stated in subsections (a) and (b) of this section. Inspection fees which are due and owing and have not been remitted to the Commissioner within 15 days following the due date shall have a penalty fee of ten percent (10%) (minimum ten dollars ($10.00)) added to the amount due when payment is finally made. The assessment of this penalty fee shall not prevent the Commissioner from taking other actions as provided in this Chapter.

(2) Keep such records as may be necessary or required by the Commissioner to indicate accurately the tonnage of commercial feed distributed in this State, and the Commissioner or his duly designated agent shall have the right to examine such records during normal business hours, to verify statements of tonnage. Failure to make an accurate statement of tonnage or to pay the inspection fee or comply as provided herein shall constitute sufficient cause for the cancellation of all registrations on file for the distributor. (1973, c. 771, s. 11; 1975, c. 900, s. 2; c. 961, s. 2; 1987 (Reg. Sess., 1988), c. 1043; 1989, c. 544, s. 6; 2005-276, s. 42.1(b).)

§ 106-284.41. Rules and regulations.

(a) The Board is authorized to promulgate such rules and regulations for commercial feeds and pet foods as are specifically authorized in this Article and such other reasonable rules and regulations as may be necessary for the efficient enforcement of this Article. In the interest of uniformity the Board shall by regulation adopt, unless it determines that they are inconsistent with the provisions of this Article or are not appropriate to conditions which exist in this State, the following:

(1) The official definitions of feed ingredients and official feed terms adopted by the Association of American Feed Control Officials and published in the official publication of that organization, and

(2) Any regulations promulgated pursuant to the authority of the Federal Food, Drug and Cosmetic Act (21 U.S.C. section 301 et seq.).

(b) Before the issuance, amendment, or repeal of any rule or regulation authorized by this Article, the Board shall publish the proposed regulation, amendment, or notice to repeal an existing regulation in a manner reasonably calculated to give interested parties, including all current registrants, adequate notice and shall afford all interested persons an opportunity to present their views thereon, orally or in writing, within a reasonable period of time. After consideration of all views presented by interested persons, the Board shall take appropriate action to issue the proposed rule or regulation or to amend or repeal an existing rule or regulation. The provisions of this subsection notwithstanding, if the Board pursuant to the authority of this Article, adopts the official definitions of feed ingredients or official feed terms as adopted by the Association of American Feed Control Officials, or regulations promulgated pursuant to the authority of the Federal Food, Drug and Cosmetic Act, any amendment or modification adopted by said Association or by the Secretary of Health, Education and Welfare in the case of regulations promulgated pursuant to the Federal Food, Drug and Cosmetic Act, shall be deemed adopted automatically under this Article without regard to the publication of the notice required by this subsection (b), unless the Board by resolution specifically determines that said amendment or modification shall not be adopted. (1973, c. 771, s. 12; 1975, c. 19, s. 32.)

§ 106-284.42. Inspection, sampling, and analysis.

(a) For the purpose of enforcement of this Article, and in order to determine whether its provisions have been complied with, including whether or not any operations may be subject to such provisions, officers or employees duly designated by the Commissioner upon presenting appropriate credentials, to the owner, operator, or agent in charge, are authorized (i) to enter, during normal business hours or actual operation, any factory, warehouse, or establishment within the State in which commercial feeds are manufactured, processed, packed, or held for distribution and take samples therefrom or to enter any vehicle being used to transport or hold such feeds and take samples therefrom; and (ii) to inspect during normal business hours or while in operation, such factory, warehouse, establishment or vehicle and all pertinent equipment, finished or unfinished materials, containers, and labeling therein. The inspection may include the verification of such records, and production and control procedures as may be necessary to determine compliance with this Article.

(b) A separate presentation of appropriate credentials shall be given for each such inspection, but a presentation shall not be required for each entry made during the period covered by the inspection. Each such inspection shall be commenced and completed with reasonable promptness. Upon completion of the inspection, the person in charge of the facility or vehicle shall be so notified.

(c) If the officer or employee making such inspection of a factory, warehouse, or other establishment has obtained a sample(s) in the course of the inspection, upon completion of the inspection and prior to leaving the premises he shall give to the owner, operator, or agent in charge a receipt describing the sample(s) obtained.

(d) If the owner of any factory, warehouse or establishment described in subsection (a), or his agent, refuses to admit the Commissioner or his agent to inspect in accordance with subsections (a) and (b), the Commissioner or his agent is authorized to obtain without notice from any district or superior court judge within the county where the facility is located, an order directing such owner or his agent to submit the premises described in such order to inspection.

(e) Sampling and analysis shall be conducted in accordance with methods published by the Association of Official Analytical Chemists, or in accordance with other generally recognized methods.

(f) The results of all analyses of official samples shall be forwarded by the Commissioner to the person named on the label and to the dealer. When the inspection and analysis of an official sample indicates a commercial feed has been adulterated or misbranded, and upon written request within 30 days following receipt of the analysis, the Commissioner shall furnish to the registrant a portion of the sample concerned.

(g) The Commissioner, in determining for administrative purposes whether a commercial feed is deficient in any component, shall be guided by the official sample as defined in G.S. 106-284.33, subdivision (14), and obtained and analyzed as provided for in subsections (a), (c), and (e) of this section.

(h) The Board is authorized to adopt regulations establishing permitted analytical variation providing for reasonable deviation from the guaranteed analysis.

(i) The registrant of a commercial feed found to be in significant violative deviation from the guarantee shall be subject to a penalty for this deviation.

(j) If the analysis of a sample shows a deviation from permitted analytical variation established by the Board, the registrant or other responsible person shall be penalized according to the following schedule:

Component Deviating	Method of Penalty Assessment
Crude protein	Three times the relative percentage * of deviation from the guarantee times the retail value of the commercial feed.
Crude fat	Ten percent (10%) of retail value of the lot of commercial feed.
Crude fiber	Ten percent (10%) of retail value of the lot of commercial feed.
Vitamins	Ten percent (10%) of retail value of the lot of commercial feed.
Minerals	Ten percent (10%) of retail value of the lot of commercial feed.
Crude protein equivalent from nonprotein nitrogen	Ten percent (10%) of retail value of the lot of commercial feed.
Animal drugs	Twenty percent (20%) of retail value of the lot of commercial feed.
Antibiotics	Twenty percent (20%) of retail value of the lot of commercial feed.
Other analysis	Ten percent (10%) of retail value of the lot of commercial feed.

* Example, a feed guaranteed 16.0% protein and assaying only 14.0%, will be considered as 2.0%/16.0%, or 12.5% deficient in protein. The penalty will be computed as 3 x 0.125 x retail value of the feed, or 0.375 x retail value of the feed.

(k) Penalties for multiple deficiencies within a sample shall be additive; provided that in no case shall the penalty exceed the retail value of the product. The minimum penalty under any of the foregoing provisions shall be twenty-five dollars ($25.00) or the retail value of the product whichever is smaller, regardless of the value of the deficiency.

(l) Within 60 days from the date of written notice by the Commissioner or his duly designated agent to the manufacturer, guarantor, dealer or agent, all penalties assessed and collected under this section shall be paid to the purchaser of the lot of feed or canned pet food represented by the sample analyzed. When such penalties are paid, receipts shall be taken and promptly forwarded to the Commissioner of Agriculture. If said consumers cannot be found, the clear proceeds of the penalty assessed shall be remitted to the Civil Penalty and Forfeiture Fund in accordance with G.S. 115C-457.2. (1973, ch. 771, s. 13; 1997-261, s. 109; 1998-215, s. 11.)

§ 106-284.43. Detained commercial feeds.

(a) "Withdrawal from distribution" orders: When the Commissioner or his authorized agent has reasonable cause to believe any lot of commercial feed is being distributed in violation of any of the provisions of this Article or of any of the prescribed regulations under this Article, he may issue and enforce a written or printed "withdrawal from distribution" order, ordering the distributor not to dispose of the lot of commercial feed in any manner until written permission is given by the Commissioner or a court. The Commissioner shall release the lot of commercial feed so withdrawn when said provisions and regulations have been complied with. If compliance is not obtained within 30 days, the Commissioner may begin, or upon request of the distributor or registrant shall begin, proceedings for condemnation.

(b) "Condemnation and confiscation": Any lot of commercial feed not in compliance with said provisions and regulations shall be subject to seizure on complaint of the Commissioner to the superior court in the county in which said commercial feed is located. In the event the court finds the said commercial feed to be in violation of this Article, and orders the condemnation of said commercial feed, it shall be disposed of in any manner consistent with the quality of the commercial feed and the laws of the State, provided, that in no instance shall the disposition of said commercial feed be ordered by the court without first giving the claimant an opportunity to apply to the court for release of said commercial feed or for permission to process or relabel said commercial feed to bring it into compliance with this Article. All costs and expenses incurred by the Department of Agriculture and Consumer Services in any proceedings associated with such seizure and confiscation shall be paid by the claimant. (1973, c. 771, s. 14; 1997-261, s. 109.)

§ 106-284.44. Penalties; enforcement of Article; judicial review; confidentiality of information.

(a)   Any person who shall be adjudged to have violated any provision of this Article, or any regulation of the Board adopted pursuant to this Article, shall be guilty of a Class 2 misdemeanor. In addition, if any person continues to violate or further violates any provision of this Article after written notice from the Commissioner, or his duly designated agent, the court may determine that each day during which the violation continued or is repeated constitutes a separate violation subject to the foregoing penalties.

(b)   Nothing in this Article shall be construed as requiring the Commissioner or his representative to: (i) report for prosecution, or (ii) institute seizure proceedings, or (iii) issue a withdrawal from distribution order, as a result of minor violations of the Article, or when he believes the public interest will best be served by suitable notice of warning in writing.

(c)   It shall be the duty of each district attorney to whom any violation is reported to cause appropriate proceedings to be instituted and prosecuted in a court of competent jurisdiction without delay. Before the Commissioner reports a violation for such prosecution, an opportunity shall be given the distributor to present his view to the Commissioner or his designated agent.

(d)   The Commissioner is hereby authorized to apply for and the court to grant a temporary restraining order and a preliminary or permanent injunction restraining any person from violating or continuing to violate any of the provisions of this Article or any rule or regulation promulgated under the Article notwithstanding the existence of other remedies at law.

(e)   Any person adversely affected by an act, order, or ruling made pursuant to the provisions of this Article may within 30 days thereafter bring action in the Superior Court of Wake County for judicial review of such act, order or ruling according to the provisions of Chapter 150B of the General Statutes.

(f) Any person who uses to his own advantage, or reveals to other than the Board, or officers of the other State agencies whose requests are deemed justifiable by the Commissioner, or to the courts when relevant in any judicial proceeding, any information acquired under the authority of this Article, concerning any method, records, formulations, or processes which as a trade secret is entitled to protection, is guilty of a Class 2 misdemeanor; provided, that this prohibition shall not be deemed as prohibiting the Commissioner, or his duly authorized agent, from exchanging information of a regulatory nature with duly appointed officials of the United States government, or of the other states, who are similarly prohibited by law from revealing this information. (1973, c. 47, s. 2; c. 771, s. 15; c. 1331, s. 3; 1987, c. 827, s. 1; 1993, c. 539, ss. 760, 761; 1994, Ex. Sess., c. 24, s. 14(c).)

§ 106-284.45. Cooperation with other entities.

The Commissioner may cooperate with and enter into agreements with governmental agencies of this State, other states, agencies of the federal government, and private associations in order to carry out the purpose and provisions of this Article. (1973, c. 771, s. 16.)

§ 106-284.46. Publication.

The Commissioner shall publish at least annually, in such forms as he may deem proper, information concerning the sales of commercial feeds, together with such data on their production and use as he may consider advisable, and a report of the results of the analyses of official samples of commercial feeds sold within the State as compared with the analyses guaranteed in the registration and on the label; provided, that the information concerning production and use of commercial feed shall not disclose the operations of any person. (1973, c. 771, s. 17.)

Article 32.

Linseed Oil.

§§ 106-285 through 106-302. Repealed by Session Laws 1977, c. 42.

Article 33.

Adulterated Turpentine.

§ 106-303: Repealed by Session Laws 1987, c. 244, s. 1(i).

Article 34.

Animal Diseases.

Part 1. Quarantine and Miscellaneous Provisions.

§ 106-304. Proclamation of livestock and poultry quarantine.

Upon the recommendation of the Commissioner of Agriculture, it shall be lawful for the Governor to issue his proclamation forbidding the importation into this State of any and all kinds of livestock and poultry from any state where there is known to prevail contagious or infectious diseases among the livestock and poultry of such state. (1915, c. 174, s. 1; C.S., s. 4871; 1969, c. 606, s. 1.)

§ 106-305. Proclamation of infected feedstuff quarantine.

Upon the recommendation of the Commissioner of Agriculture, it shall be lawful for the Governor to issue his proclamation forbidding the importation into this State of any feedstuff or any other article or material dangerous to livestock and poultry as a carrier of infectious or contagious disease from any area outside the State. This shall also include any and all materials imported for manufacturing purposes or for any other use, which have been tested by any state or federal agency competent to make such tests and found to contain living infectious and contagious organisms known to be injurious to the health of man, livestock and poultry. (1915, c. 174, s. 2; C.S., s. 4872; 1953, c. 1328; 1969, c. 606, s. 1.)

§ 106-306. Rules to enforce quarantine.

Upon such proclamation being made, the Commissioner of Agriculture shall have power to make rules and regulations to make effective the proclamation and to stamp out such infectious or contagious diseases as may break out among the livestock and poultry in this State. (1915, c. 174, s. 3; C.S., s. 4873; 1969, c. 606, s. 1.)

§ 106-307. Violation of proclamation or rules.

Any person, firm, or corporation violating the terms of the proclamation of the Governor, or any rule or regulation made by the Commissioner of Agriculture in pursuance thereof, shall be guilty of a Class 2 misdemeanor. (1915, c. 174, s. 4; C.S., s. 4874; 1969, c. 606, s. 1; 1993, c. 539, s. 762; 1994, Ex. Sess., c. 24, s. 14(c).)

§ 106-307.1. Serums, vaccines, etc., for control of animal diseases.

The North Carolina Department of Agriculture and Consumer Services is authorized and empowered to purchase for resale serums, viruses, vaccines, biologics, and other products for the control of animal and poultry diseases. The resale of said serums, viruses, vaccines, biologics and other products shall be at a reasonable price to be determined by the Commissioner of Agriculture. (1943, c. 640, s. 1; 1969, c. 606, s. 1; 1997-261, s. 49.)

§ 106-307.2. Reports of infectious disease in livestock and poultry to State Veterinarian.

(a) All persons practicing veterinary medicine in North Carolina shall report promptly to the State Veterinarian the existence of any reportable contagious or infectious disease in livestock and poultry. The Board of Agriculture shall establish by rule a list of animal diseases and conditions to be reported and the time and manner of reporting.

(b)   The State Veterinarian shall notify the State Health Director and the Director of the Division of Public Health in the Department of Health and Human Services when the State Veterinarian receives a report indicating an occurrence or potential outbreak of anthrax, arboviral infections, brucellosis, epidemic typhus, hantavirus infections, murine typhus, plague, psittacosis, Q fever, hemorrhagic fever, virus infections, and any other disease or condition transmissible to humans that the State Veterinarian determines may have been caused by a terrorist act. (1943, c. 640, s. 2; 1969, c. 606, s. 1; 2002-179, s. 9; 2011-145, s. 13.3(oo).)

§ 106-307.3. Quarantine of infected or inoculated livestock.

Hog cholera and other contagious and infectious diseases of livestock are hereby declared to be a menace to the livestock industry and all livestock infected with or exposed to a contagious or infectious disease may be quarantined by the State Veterinarian or his authorized representative in accordance with regulations promulgated by the State Board of Agriculture. All livestock that are inoculated with a product containing a living virus or other organism are subject to quarantine at the time of inoculation in accordance with regulations promulgated by the State Board of Agriculture: Provided, nothing herein contained shall be construed as preventing anyone entitled to administer serum or vaccine under existing laws from continuing to administer same. (1943, c. 640, s. 3; 1969, c. 606, s. 1.)

§ 106-307.4. Quarantine of inoculated poultry.

All poultry that are inoculated with a product containing a living virus or other organism capable of causing disease shall be quarantined at the time of inoculation in accordance with regulations promulgated by the State Board of Agriculture. Provided nothing herein contained shall be construed as preventing anyone entitled to administer vaccines under existing laws from continuing to administer same. (1969, c. 606, s. 1.)

§ 106-307.5. Livestock and poultry brought into State.

All livestock and poultry transported or otherwise brought into this State shall be in compliance with regulations promulgated by the State Board of Agriculture. (1943, c. 640, s. 4; 1969, c. 606, s. 1.)

§ 106-307.6. Violation made misdemeanor.

Any person, firm or corporation who shall violate any provisions set forth in G.S. 106-307.1 to 106-307.5 or any rule or regulation duly established by the State Board of Agriculture shall be guilty of a Class 2 misdemeanor. (1943, c. 640, s. 6; 1969, c. 606, s. 1; 1993, c. 539, s. 763; 1994, Ex. Sess., c. 24, s. 14(c).)

§ 106-307.7. Diseased livestock running at large.

Whenever the State Veterinarian is informed or reasonably believes that certain livestock is infected with or has been exposed to any contagious or infectious disease, that such livestock is running at large and that such livestock cannot be captured with the exercise of reasonable diligence, the State Veterinarian shall have authority to direct the appropriate sheriff or other proper officer to destroy such livestock in a reasonable manner and such sheriff or other officer shall make diligent effort to destroy such livestock. (1971, c. 676.)

Part 2. Foot and Mouth Disease; Rinderpest; Fowl Pest; Newcastle Disease.

§ 106-308. Appropriation to combat animal and fowl diseases.

If the foot and mouth disease, rinderpest (cattle plague), fowl pest, or Newcastle disease (Asiatic or European types), or any other type of foreign infectious disease which may become a menace to livestock and poultry and so declared to be by the Secretary of Agriculture of the United States, Chief of the United States Bureau of Animal Industry and the Commissioner of Agriculture of North Carolina, seem likely to appear in this State and an emergency as to such disease or diseases is declared by the Secretary of Agriculture of the United States, or his authorized agents, and the North Carolina Department of

Agriculture and Consumer Services has no funds available to immediately meet the situation in cooperation with the United States Department of Agriculture, the Director of the Budget, upon approval of the Governor and Council of State, shall set aside, appropriate and make available out of the Contingency and Emergency Fund such sum as the Governor and Council of State shall deem proper and necessary, and the Budget Bureau shall place said funds in an account to be known as the Animal and Fowl Disease Appropriation and make same available to the North Carolina Department of Agriculture and Consumer Services, to be used by the North Carolina Department of Agriculture and Consumer Services in the work of preventing or eradicating the above diseases, or any of them. Funds from the above appropriation shall be paid only for work in this connection upon warrants approved by the Commissioner of Agriculture. The provisions of Part 4 of Article 34 of Chapter 106 of the General Statutes relating to the compensation for killing diseased animals shall be applicable to animals infected with or exposed to the diseases named and described in this section, as well as to the destruction of material contaminated by or exposed to the diseases described in this section, as well as the necessary cost of the disinfection of materials. In no event shall any of the above appropriation be spent for the purposes set forth in this section unless the funds appropriated by this State are matched in an equal amount by the federal government or one of its agencies to be spent for the same purposes. (1915, c. 160, s. 1; C.S., s. 4875; 1951, c. 799; 1997-261, s. 109.)

§ 106-309. Disposition of surplus funds.

If said disease shall have appeared and shall have been eradicated and work is no longer necessary in connection with it, the State Treasurer shall return such part of the appropriation as is not expended to the general fund, and the Commissioner of Agriculture shall furnish the Governor an itemized statement of the money expended, and all moneys set aside out of the State funds and used for the purpose of eradicating said disease under the provisions of this Article shall be paid back to the State funds by the Department of Agriculture and Consumer Services out of the first funds received by said agricultural Department available for such purpose. (1915, c. 160, s. 2; C.S., s. 4876; 1997-261, s. 109.)

Part 3. Hog Cholera

§ 106-310. Burial of hogs dying natural death required.

It shall be the duty of every person, firm, or corporation who shall lose a hog by any form of natural death to have the same buried in the earth to a depth of at least two feet within 12 hours after the death of the animal. Any person, firm, or corporation that shall fail to comply with the terms of this section shall be guilty of a Class 3 misdemeanor, and shall be fined not less than five dollars ($5.00) nor more than ten dollars ($10.00) for each offense, at the discretion of the court. (1915, c. 225; C.S., s. 4877; 1993, c. 539, s. 764; 1994, Ex. Sess., c. 24, s. 14(c).)

§ 106-311. Hogs affected with cholera to be segregated and confined.

If any person having swine affected with the disease known as hog cholera, or any other infectious or contagious disease, who discovers the same, or to whom notice of the fact shall be given, shall fail or neglect for one day to secure the diseased swine from the approach of or contact with other hogs not so affected, by penning or otherwise securing and effectually isolating them so that they shall not have access to any ditch, canal, branch, creek, river or other watercourse which passes beyond the premises of the owners of such swine, he shall be guilty of a Class 3 misdemeanor. (1889, c. 173, s. 1; 1891, c. 67, ss. 1, 3; 1899, c. 47; 1903, c. 106; Rev., s. 3297; 1913, c. 120; C.S., s. 4490; 1993, c. 539, s. 765; 1994, Ex. Sess., c. 24, s. 14(c).)

§ 106-312. Shipping hogs from cholera-infected territory.

It shall be unlawful for any person, firm or corporation in any district or territory infected by cholera to bring, carry, or ship hogs into any stock-law section or territory, unless such hogs have been certified to be free from cholera either by the farm demonstration agent of the county or some other suitable person to be designated by the clerk of the superior court. Any violation of this section shall constitute a Class 1 misdemeanor. (1917, c. 203; C.S., s. 4491; 1993, c. 539, s. 766; 1994, Ex. Sess., c. 24, s. 14(c).)

§ 106-313. Price of serum to be fixed.

The Department of Agriculture and Consumer Services shall fix the price of anti-hog-cholera serum at such an amount as will cover the cost of production. (1917, c. 275, s. 1; 1919, c. 6; C.S., s. 4878; 1997-261, s. 50.)

§ 106-314. Manufacture and use of serum and virus restricted.

It shall be unlawful for any person, firm, or corporation to distribute, sell, or use in the State anti-hog-cholera serum unless said anti-hog-cholera serum is produced at the serum plant of the State Department of Agriculture and Consumer Services, or produced in a plant which is licensed by the Biological Products Licensing Section, Animal Inspection and Quarantine Division, Agricultural Research Service of the United States Department of Agriculture, allowing said plant to do an interstate business.

It shall be unlawful for any person, firm, or corporation to distribute, sell, or use in the State of North Carolina, virulent blood from hog-cholera-infected hogs, or virus, unless said virulent blood, or virus, is produced at the serum plant of the State Department of Agriculture and Consumer Services or produced in a plant which is licensed by the Biological Products Licensing Section, Animal Inspection and Quarantine Division, Agricultural Research Service of the United States Department of Agriculture, allowing said plant to do an interstate business. No virulent blood from hog-cholera-infected hogs, or virus, shall be distributed, sold or used in the State unless and until permission has been given in writing by the State Veterinarian for such distribution, sale or use. Said permission to be cancelled by the State Veterinarian when necessary.

Any person, firm, or corporation guilty of violating the provisions of this section or failing or refusing to comply with the requirements thereof shall be guilty of a Class 1 misdemeanor. (1915, c. 88; 1919, c. 125, ss. 1, 2, 3; C.S., s. 4879; 1959, c. 576, s. 1; 1993, c. 539, s. 767; 1994, Ex. Sess., c. 24, s. 14(c); 1997-261, s. 109.)

§ 106-315. Written permit from State Veterinarian for sale, use or distribution of hog-cholera virus, etc.

No hog-cholera virus or other product containing live virus or organisms of animal diseases shall be distributed, sold, or used within the State unless permission has been given in writing by the State Veterinarian for such distribution, sale, or use, said permission to be cancelled by the State Veterinarian when he deems same necessary. (1939, c. 360, s. 5; 1959, c. 576, s. 2.)

§ 106-316. Counties authorized to purchase and supply serum.

If the county commissioners of any county in the State deem it necessary to use anti-hog-cholera serum to control or eradicate the disease known as hog cholera, they are authorized within their discretion to purchase from the State Department of Agriculture and Consumer Services sufficient anti-hog-cholera serum and virus for use in their county and supply same free of cost to the residents of the county, or pay for any portion of the cost of said serum, the remaining portion to be paid by the owners of the hogs.

The use of anti-hog-cholera serum and virus and the quarantine of diseased animals shall remain under the supervision of the State Veterinarian.

Nothing in this section shall in any way interfere with existing laws and regulations covering the use of anti-hog-cholera serum and virus and the quarantine and control of contagious diseases, or any laws or regulations that may become necessary in the future. (1919, c. 132; C.S., s. 4881; 1997-261, s. 109.)

§ 106-316.1. Purpose of §§ 106-316.1 to 106-316.5.

It is the purpose and intent of G.S. 106-316.1 to 106-316.5 to safeguard the swine industry in North Carolina through a program designed to prevent the spread of hog cholera by prohibiting and restricting the use of virulent hog-cholera virus; to provide for the use of modified live virus hog-cholera vaccines that have been licensed as such by the Biological Products Licensing Section, Animal Inspection and Quarantine Division, Agricultural Research Service of the United States Department of Agriculture; to empower the State Board of Agriculture to establish rules and regulations and the Commissioner of Agriculture to establish emergency rules and regulations governing the movement of hogs into the State from other states and within the State; to establish rules and regulations designating the minimum dosage of anti-hog-cholera serum and antibody concentrate that shall be used in combination with modified live-virus hog-cholera vaccines on swine vaccinated at public livestock markets and other places; and to establish such other rules and regulations and emergency rules and regulations as may be necessary for carrying out the purposes of G.S. 106-316.1 to 106-316.5. (1955, c. 824, s. 1; 1959, c. 576, s. 3.)

§ 106-316.2. Use of virulent hog-cholera virus prohibited without permit; virulent hog-cholera virus defined; use of modified live virus vaccines.

Notwithstanding any other provision of the law, either general, public-local, special or private, and except as herein provided, the possession, sale and use of virulent hog-cholera virus in North Carolina is hereby prohibited. Virulent hog-cholera virus referred to in this section means any unattended hog-cholera virus collected directly or indirectly from blood or other tissues of swine infected with hog cholera which has not been licensed as a modified live virus hog-cholera vaccine. The State Veterinarian may issue a permit authorizing the sale, possession and use of virulent hog-cholera virus only for the purpose of laboratory diagnosis; official research programs; production of anti-hog-cholera serum, antibody concentrate, modified live virus, killed virus vaccine, and similar biological products; and following a declaration that a state of emergency exists in a designated quarantined hog-cholera area or areas within the State by the Commissioner of Agriculture of North Carolina. The use of virulent hog-cholera virus during a declared state of emergency shall be under the direct supervision of the State Veterinarian or his authorized representative. Modified live-virus hog-cholera vaccines that have been licensed as such by the Biological Products Licensing Section, Animal Inspection and Quarantine Division, Agricultural Research Service of the United States Department of Agriculture may be sold and used in compliance with the General Statutes of North Carolina and the rules, regulations, definitions and standards adopted by the North Carolina Board of Agriculture and the emergency rules and regulations established by the Commissioner of Agriculture. (1955, c. 824, s. 2; 1959, c. 576, s. 4.)

§ 106-316.3. Unlawful to import hogs inoculated with virulent virus; exceptions for immediate slaughter; health certificate and permit required.

It shall be unlawful to bring hogs into North Carolina that have been inoculated with virulent hog-cholera virus less than 30 days prior to the date of entry, except for immediate slaughter, and in addition thereto the transportation or importation of such hogs that have been inoculated with virulent hog-cholera virus must be accompanied by the health certificate and permit as required by the rules and regulations of the North Carolina Board of Agriculture or emergency rules and regulations of the North Carolina Commissioner of Agriculture. The provisions of this section shall not be construed to be in conflict with or to repeal any provisions of G.S. 106-317 through 106-322 or any other statute or rule or regulation prohibiting, restricting or controlling the interstate movement of hogs for other reasons. (1955, c. 824, s. 3; 1959, c. 576, s. 5.)

§ 106-316.4. Penalties for violation of §§ 106-316.1 to 106-316.5.

Any person, firm or corporation violating the provisions of G.S. 106-316.1 to 106-316.5 shall be guilty of a Class 1 misdemeanor. (1955, c. 824, s. 4; 1993, c. 539, s. 768; 1994, Ex. Sess., c. 24, s. 14(c).)

§ 106-316.5. Repealed by Session Laws 1963, c. 1084, s. 2.

§ 106-317. Regulation of the transportation or importation of hogs and other livestock into State.

To prevent the spread of hog cholera, vesicular exanthema, vesicular stomatitis, foot-and-mouth disease, or any other contagious, infectious and communicable swine disease in North Carolina, the North Carolina Board of Agriculture is authorized and empowered to promulgate rules and regulations governing the transportation and importation of swine into North Carolina from any other state or territory: Provided, that following a proclamation by the Secretary of Agriculture of the United States and the Commissioner of Agriculture of North Carolina that a state of emergency exists, arising from the existence of a dangerous contagious and infectious disease of livestock which threatens the livestock industry of the country, the North Carolina Commissioner of Agriculture is empowered and authorized to immediately promulgate emergency rules and regulations governing the movement of swine and other livestock within the

State and prohibiting, restricting and/or controlling the transportation and importation of swine and other livestock into North Carolina for the duration of the emergency. The emergency rules and regulations promulgated by the North Carolina Commissioner of Agriculture shall be subject to approval, disapproval or change at the next regular or special meeting of the North Carolina Board of Agriculture. The North Carolina Board of Agriculture under the authority of this section may by regulation establish a system of health certificates and permits for the better protection of the swine and livestock of this State. (1941, c. 373, s. 1; 1955, c. 424, s. 1.)

§ 106-318. Issuance of health certificates for swine and livestock; inspection.

Such health certificates that may be required under the rules and regulations by the Board of Agriculture or the emergency rules and regulations of the Commissioner of Agriculture shall be issued by a State, federal or duly licensed veterinarian in the state of origin certifying that the swine or other livestock transported and imported are healthy and not infected with or exposed to a contagious, infectious or communicable swine or other livestock disease, and all permits required under such rules and regulations shall be in possession of the owner or agent in charge, at all times until delivery of such swine or other livestock, and upon request, the owner or agent in charge shall produce said required certificate and permit for inspection by any police or peace officer or inspection agent of this State or any county thereof. The burden shall be on the person transporting said swine or other livestock to prove the origin, identity and destination of such swine and other livestock. (1941, c. 373, s. 2; 1955, c. 424, s. 2.)

§ 106-319. Burial of hogs and other livestock dying in transit.

It shall be the duty of any owner or agent having in charge any swine or other livestock imported or transported into this State who shall, before delivery lose a hog or other livestock from natural or unnatural death to have the same delivered to a rendering plant or buried in the area to a depth of at least two feet within 12 hours after death of said swine or other livestock. (1941, c. 373, s. 3; 1955, c. 424, s. 3.)

§ 106-320. Repealed by Session Laws 1963, c. 1084, s. 2.

§ 106-321. Penalties for violation.

Any person, firm or corporation who shall violate any provision set forth in this Article or any rule or regulation duly established by the State Board of Agriculture or emergency rules and regulations established by the Commissioner of Agriculture shall be guilty of a Class 1 misdemeanor. (1941, c. 373, s. 5; 1955, c. 424, s. 4; 1993, c. 539, s. 769; 1994, Ex. Sess., c. 24, s. 14(c).)

§ 106-322. Effect of §§ 106-317 to 106-322.

Sections 106-317 to 106-322 shall not repeal Article 34, Chapter 106, but shall be complementary thereto. (1941, c. 373, s. 6.)

§ 106-322.1. State-federal hog-cholera cooperative agreements; establishment of hog-cholera eradication areas.

The Commissioner of Agriculture is authorized to enter into cooperative State-federal agreements with the United States Department of Agriculture for the purpose of State-federal programs for the control and eradication of hog cholera. The Commissioner of Agriculture may designate individual counties or two or more counties as hog-cholera eradication areas. (1963, c. 1084, s. 1.)

§ 106-322.2. Destruction of swine affected with or exposed to hog cholera; indemnity payments.

If it appears in the judgment of the State Veterinarian to be necessary for the control and eradication of hog cholera to destroy or slaughter swine affected with or exposed to such disease, the State Veterinarian is authorized to order said swine destroyed or slaughtered, notwithstanding the wishes of the owners of said swine, provided that if the owner contests the diagnosis of hog cholera he shall be entitled to a review of the case by a licensed practicing veterinarian, the State Veterinarian, or his authorized representative, and the federal inspector in charge, or his authorized representative, to determine that a diagnosis of hog cholera was arrived at by the use of accepted, standard diagnostic techniques. The State Veterinarian is authorized to agree on the part of the State, in the case of swine destroyed or slaughtered on account of being affected with hog cholera or exposure to same to pay one half of the difference between the appraised value of each animal destroyed or slaughtered and the value of the salvage thereof; provided, that the State indemnity shall not be in excess of the indemnity payments made by the federal cooperating agency; provided further, that State indemnity payments shall be restricted to swine located on the farm or feedlot of the owner or authorized representative of the owner; provided further, that in no case shall any payments by the State be more than twenty-five dollars ($25.00) for any grade swine nor more than one hundred dollars ($100.00) for any purebred swine and subject to available State funds. The procedure for appraisal, disposal and salvage of slaughtered or destroyed swine shall be carried out in the same manner as that required under the General Statutes of North Carolina governing compensation for killing other diseased animals provided, however, that the appraisal may be made by the owner, or his representative, and the State Veterinarian, or his authorized representative, when agreement on the appraised value of the swine can be made; provided, further, that swine which entered the State 30 days or more before developing symptoms of hog cholera may be appraised in the same manner as swine which originate in North Carolina.

For the purposes of this section, "purebred swine" shall mean any swine upon which a certificate of pure breeding has been issued by a purebred swine association, or swine not more than 12 months of age eligible to receive such a certificate. (1963, c. 1084, s. 1; 1967, c. 105; 1969, c. 525, ss. 1, 2.)

§ 106-322.3. When indemnity payments not to be made.

No payments shall be made for any swine slaughtered in the following cases:

(1) If the owner does not clean up and disinfect premises as directed by an inspector of the Animal Health Division, Agricultural Research Service, United States Department of Agriculture or the State Veterinarian or his authorized representative;

(2) Where the owner has not complied with the livestock disease control laws and regulations applicable to hog cholera;

(3) For swine in a herd in which hog-cholera vaccine has been used illegally on one or more animals in the herd;

(4) Swine involved in an outbreak in which the existence of hog cholera has not been confirmed by the State Veterinarian or his authorized representative;

(5) Swine belonging to the United States or the State of North Carolina;

(6) Swine brought into the State in violation of State laws or regulations;

(7) Swine which the claimant knew to be affected with hog cholera, or had notice thereof, at the time they came into his possession;

(8) Swine which have not been within the State of North Carolina for at least 30 days prior to discovery of the disease;

(9) Where the owner does not use reasonable care in protecting swine from exposure to hog cholera;

(10) Where the owner has failed to submit the reports required by the United States Department of Agriculture and the North Carolina Department of Agriculture and Consumer Services for animals on which indemnity is paid under Article 34.

(11) Swine purchased by a buying station for slaughter which are not slaughtered within 10 days of purchase. (1969, c. 525, s. 21/2; 1997-261, s. 51.)

Part 4. Compensation for Killing Diseased Animals.

§ 106-323. State to pay part of value of animals killed on account of disease; purchase by State of animals exposed to certain diseases.

If it appears to be necessary for the control or eradication of Bang's disease and tuberculosis and paratuberculosis in cattle, or glanders in horses and mules, to destroy such animals affected with such diseases and to compensate owners for loss thereof, the State Veterinarian is authorized, within his discretion, to agree on the part of the State, in the case of cattle destroyed for Bang's disease and tuberculosis, and paratuberculosis to pay one third of the difference between the appraised value of each animal so destroyed and the value of the salvage thereof: Provided, that in no case shall any payment by the State be more than twenty-five dollars ($25.00) for any grade animal nor more than one hundred dollars ($100.00) for any purebred animal; provided further, that the State indemnity shall not be in excess of the indemnity payments made by the federal government. In the case of horses or mules destroyed for glanders, to pay one half of the appraised value, said half not to exceed one hundred dollars ($100.00).

The State Veterinarian is also authorized, in his discretion, and subject to the maximum payment hereinabove provided, to purchase in the name of the State, cattle which have been exposed to Bang's disease, tuberculosis or paratuberculosis and horses and mules which have been exposed to glanders. (1919, c. 62, s. 1; C.S., s. 4882; 1929, c. 107; 1939, c. 272, ss. 1, 2; 1969, c. 525, s. 3; 1973, c. 1122.)

§ 106-324. Appraisal of cattle affected with Bang's disease and tuberculosis.

Cattle affected with Bang's disease and tuberculosis and paratuberculosis shall be appraised by three men - one to be chosen by the owner, one by the United States Bureau of Animal Industry, and one by the State Veterinarian. If the United States Bureau of Animal Industry is not represented, then the appraisers shall be chosen, one by the owner, one by the State Veterinarian, the third by the first two named. The finding of such appraisers shall be final. (1919, c. 62, s. 2; C.S., s. 4883; 1929, c. 107; 1939, c. 272, s. 1.)

§ 106-325. Appraisal of animals affected with glanders; report.

Animals affected with glanders shall be appraised by three men - one to be chosen by the owner, one to be chosen by the State Veterinarian, the third to be named by the first two chosen, the finding of such appraisers to be final. The report of appraisal to be made in triplicate on forms furnished by the State Veterinarian, and a copy sent to the State Veterinarian at once. (1919, c. 62, s. 3; C.S., s. 4884.)

§ 106-326. Report of appraisal of cattle affected with Bang's disease and tuberculosis to State Veterinarian; contents.

Appraisals of cattle affected with Bang's disease or tuberculosis shall be reported on forms furnished by the State Veterinarian, which shall show the number of animals, the appraised value of each per head, or the weight and appraised value per pound, and shall be signed by the owners and the appraisers. This report must be made in triplicate and a copy sent to the State Veterinarian: Provided, that the State Veterinarian may change the forms for making claims so as to conform to the claim forms used by the United States Department of Agriculture. (1919, c. 62, s. 4; C.S., s. 4885; 1939, c. 272, ss. 1, 3.)

§ 106-327. Marketing of cattle affected with Bang's disease and tuberculosis.

Each owner of cattle affected with Bang's disease or tuberculosis, which have been appraised, and which have been authorized by the State Veterinarian to be marketed, shall market the cattle within 30 days and shall obtain from the purchaser a report in triplicate. One copy to be sent by the State Veterinarian at once, certifying as to the amount of money actually paid for the animals, all animals to be identified on report. (1919, c. 62, s. 5; C.S., s. 4886; 1939, c. 272, s. 1.)

§ 106-328. Report on salvage.

When the appraised cattle have been slaughtered and the amount of salvage ascertained, a report, on forms furnished by the State Veterinarian, in triplicate shall be made, signed by the owner and the United States Bureau of Animal Industry or State inspector and the appraisers by which the animals were appraised and destroyed, showing the difference between the appraised value and salvage. Two copies are to be attached to the voucher in which compensation is claimed, and one copy to be furnished by the owner of cattle. (1919, c. 62, s. 6; C.S., s. 4887.)

§ 106-329. Compensation when killing ordered.

Compensation for animals destroyed on account of glanders will only be paid when such destruction is ordered by the State Veterinarian or his authorized representative. When the owner of the animals presents his claim he shall support same with the original report of the appraiser, together with the report of the inspector who destroyed the animal, to the State Veterinarian. (1919, c. 62, s. 7; C.S., s. 4888.)

§ 106-330. Ownership of destroyed animals; outstanding liens.

When animals have been destroyed pursuant to this Article the inspector shall take reasonable precautions to determine, prior to his approval of vouchers in which compensation is claimed, who is the owner of and whether there are any mortgages or other liens outstanding against the animals. If it appears that there are outstanding liens, a full report regarding same shall be made and shall accompany the voucher. Every such report shall include a description of the liens, the name of the person or persons having possession of the documentary evidence, and a statement showing what arrangements, if any, have been made to discharge the liens outstanding against the animals destroyed of which the inspector may have knowledge. (1919, c. 62, s. 8; C.S., s. 4889.)

§ 106-331. State not to pay for feed of animals ordered killed.

Expense for the care and feeding of animals held for slaughter shall not be paid by the State. (1919, c. 62, s. 9; C.S., s. 4890.)

§ 106-332. Disinfection of stockyards by owners.

Stockyards, pens, cars, vessels and other premises and conveyances will be disinfected whenever necessary for the control and eradication of disease by the owners at their expense under the supervision of an inspector of the United States Bureau of Animal Industry or State Veterinarian. (1919, c. 62, s. 10; C.S., s. 4891.)

§ 106-333. Payments made only on certain conditions.

No payments shall be made for any animal slaughtered in the following cases:

(1) If the owner does not disinfect premises, etc., as directed by an inspector of the United States Bureau of Animal Industry or the State Veterinarian.

(2) For any animals destroyed where the owner has not complied with all lawful quarantine regulations.

(3) Animals reacting to a test not approved by the State Veterinarian.

(4) Animals belonging to the United States.

(5) Animals brought into the State in violation of the State laws and regulations.

(6) Animals which the owner or claimant knew to be diseased, or had notice thereof, at the time they came into his possession.

(7) Animals which had the disease for which they were slaughtered or which were destroyed by reason of exposure to the disease, at the time of their arrival in the State.

(8) Animals which have not been within the State of North Carolina for at least 120 days prior to the discovery of the disease.

(9) Where owner does not use reasonable care in protecting animals from disease.

(10) Where owner has failed to submit the necessary reports as required by this Article.

(11) Any unregistered bull. (1919, c. 62, s. 11; C.S., s. 4892; 1939, c. 272, s. 4.)

§ 106-334. Owner's claim for indemnity supported by reports.

The owner must present his claim for indemnity to the State Veterinarian for approval, and the claim shall be supported with the original report of the appraisers, the original report of the sale of the animals in the case of cattle destroyed on account of Bang's disease and tuberculosis, the certificate of the State or United States Bureau of Animal Industry inspector, and a summary of the claim. All of which shall constitute a part of the claim.

The owner must state whether or not the animals are owned entirely by him or advise fully of any partnership, and describe fully any mortgages or other liens against animals. (1919, c. 62, s. 12; C.S., s. 4893; 1939, c. 272, s. 1.)

§ 106-335. State Veterinarian to carry out provisions of Article; how moneys paid out.

The State Veterinarian is authorized, himself or by his representative, to do all things specified in this Article. All moneys authorized to be paid shall be paid from the State treasury and the State Treasurer is hereby authorized to make such payment. (1919, c. 62, s. 13; C.S., s. 4894; 1983, c. 913, s. 13.)

Part 5. Tuberculosis.

§ 106-336. Animals reacting to tuberculin test.

All animals reacting to a tuberculin test applied by a qualified veterinarian shall be known as reactors and be forever considered as affected with tuberculosis. (1921, c. 177, s. 1; C.S., s. 4895(a).)

§ 106-337. Animals to be branded.

All veterinarians who, either by clinical examination or by tuberculin test, find an animal affected with tuberculosis, shall, unless the animal is immediately slaughtered, properly brand said animal for identification on the left jaw with the letter "T," not less than two inches high, and promptly report the same to the State Veterinarian. (1921, c. 177, s. 2; C.S., s. 4895(b).)

§ 106-338. Quarantine; removal or sale; sale and use of milk.

The owner or owners of an animal affected with tuberculosis shall keep said animal isolated and quarantined in such a manner as to prevent the spread of the disease to the other animals or man. Said animals must not be moved from the place where quarantined or sold, or otherwise disposed of except upon permission of the State Veterinarian, and then only in accordance with his instructions. The milk from said animals must not be sold, and if used shall be first boiled or properly pasteurized. (1921, c. 177, s. 3; C.S., s. 4895(c).)

§ 106-339. Seller liable in civil action.

Any person or persons who sell or otherwise dispose of to another an animal affected with tuberculosis shall be liable in a civil action to any person injured, and for any and all damages resulting therefrom. (1921, c. 177, s. 4; C.S., s. 4895(d).)

§ 106-340. Responsibility of owner of premises where sale is made.

When cattle are sold or otherwise disposed of in this State by a nonresident of this State, the person or persons on whose premises the cattle are sold or otherwise disposed of with his knowledge and consent shall be equally responsible for violation of this law and the regulations of the Department of Agriculture and Consumer Services. (1921, c. 177, s. 5; C.S., s. 4895(e); 1997-261, s. 109.)

§ 106-341. Sale of tuberculin.

No person, firm, or corporation shall sell or distribute or administer tuberculin, or keep the same on hand for sale, distribution, or administration, except qualified veterinarians, licensed physicians, or licensed durggists, or others lawfully engaged in the sale of biological products. (1921, c. 177, s. 6; C.S., s. 4895(f).)

§ 106-342. Notice to owner of suspected animals; quarantine.

When the State Veterinarian receives information, or has reason to believe, that tuberculosis exists in any animal or animals, he shall promptly notify the owner or owners, and recommend that a tuberculin test be applied to said animals, that diseased animals shall be properly disposed of, and the premises disinfected under the supervision of the State Veterinarian, or his authorized representative. Should the owner or owners fail or refuse to comply with the said recommendations of the State Veterinarian within 10 days after said notice, then the State Veterinarian shall quarantine said animals on the premises of the owner or owners. Said animals shall not be removed from the premises where quarantined and milk or other dairy products from same shall not be sold or otherwise disposed of. Said quarantine shall remain in effect until the said recommendations of the State Veterinarian have been complied with, and the quarantine canceled by the State Veterinarian. (1921, c. 177, s. 7; C.S., s. 4895(g).)

§ 106-343. Appropriations by counties; elections.

The several boards of county commissioners in the State are hereby expressly authorized and empowered to make such appropriations from the general funds of their county as will enable them to cooperate effectively with the state Department of Agriculture and Consumer Services and Federal Department of Agriculture in the eradication of tuberculosis in their respective counties: Provided, that if in 10 days after said appropriation is voted, one fifth of the qualified voters of the county petition the board of commissioners to submit the question of tuberculosis eradication or no tuberculosis eradication to the voters of the county, said commissioners shall submit such questions to said voters. Said election shall be held and conducted under G.S. 163-287. If at any such election a majority of the votes cast shall be in favor of said tuberculosis eradication, the said board shall record the result of the election upon its minutes, and cooperative tuberculosis eradication shall be taken up with the state Department of Agriculture and Consumer Services and Federal Department of Agriculture. If, however, a majority of the votes cast shall be adverse, then said board shall make no appropriation. (1921, c. 177, s. 8; C.S., s. 4895(h); 1997-261, s. 109; 2013-381, s. 10.15.)

§ 106-344. Petition for election if commissioners refuse cooperation; order; effect.

If the board of commissioners of any county should exercise their discretion and refuse to cooperate as set out in G.S. 106-343, then if a petition is presented to said board by one fifth of the qualified voters of the county requesting that an election be held as provided in G.S. 106-343 to determine the question of tuberculosis eradication in the county, the board of commissioners shall order said election to be held in the way provided in G.S. 106-343, and if a majority of the votes cast at such election shall be in favor of tuberculosis eradication, then said board shall cooperate with the State and federal governments as herein provided. (1921, c. 177, s. 9; C.S., s. 4895(i).)

§ 106-345. Importation of cattle.

Whenever a county board shall cooperate with the State and federal governments, whether with or without an election, no cattle except for immediate slaughter shall be brought into the county unless accompanied by a tuberculin test chart and health certificate issued by a qualified veterinarian. (1921, c. 177, s. 10; C.S., s. 4895(j).)

§ 106-346. Amount of appropriation.

When cooperative tuberculosis eradication shall be taken up in any county as provided for in G.S. 106-336 to 106-350, the county commissioners of such counties shall appropriate from the general county fund an amount sufficient to defray one half of the expense of said cooperative tuberculosis eradication. (1921, c. 177, s. 11; C.S., s. 4895(k).)

§ 106-347. Qualified veterinarian.

The words "qualified veterinarian" which appear in G.S. 106-336 to 106-350 shall be construed to mean a veterinarian approved by the State Veterinarian and the chief of the United States Bureau of Animal Industry for the tuberculin testing of cattle intended for interstate shipment. (1921, c. 177, s. 12; C.S., s. 4895(l).)

§ 106-348. Rules and regulations.

The Commissioner of Agriculture, by and with the consent of the State Board of Agriculture, shall have full power to promulgate and enforce such rules and regulations as may be necessary to control and eradicate tuberculosis. (1921, c. 177, s. 13; C.S., s. 4895(m).)

§ 106-349. Violation of law a misdemeanor.

Any person or persons who shall violate any provision set forth in G.S. 106-336 to 106-350, or any rule or regulation duly established by the State Board of Agriculture or any officer or inspector who shall willfully fail to comply with any provisions of this law, shall be guilty of a Class 1 misdemeanor. (1921, c. 177, s. 14; C.S., s. 4895(n); 1993, c. 539, s. 770; 1994, Ex. Sess., c. 24, s. 14(c).)

§ 106-350. Sale of tubercular animal a felony.

Any person or persons who shall willfully and knowingly sell or otherwise dispose of any animal or animals known to be affected with tuberculosis without permission as provided for in G.S. 106-338 shall be guilty of a Class I felony. (1921, c. 177, s. 15; C.S., s. 4895(o); 1993, c. 539, s. 1295; 1994, Ex. Sess., c. 24, s. 14(c).)

Part 6. Cattle Tick.

§ 106-351. Systematic dipping of cattle or horses.

Systematic dipping of all cattle or horses infested with or exposed to the cattle tick (Margaropus annulatus) shall be taken up in all counties or portions of counties that shall at any time be found partially or completely infested with the cattle tick (Margaropus annulatus) under the direction of the State Veterinarian acting under the authority as hereinafter provided in G.S. 106-351 to 106-363 and as provided in all other laws and parts of laws of North Carolina and the livestock sanitary laws and regulations of the State Board of Agriculture not in conflict with G.S. 106-351 to 106-363. (1923, c. 146, s. 1; C.S., s. 4895(p).)

§ 106-352. Counties not embraced in quarantine zones.

If it shall be determined by the State Veterinarian or an authorized quarantine inspector, that any county or counties shall be partially or completely infested with the cattle tick (Margaropus annulatus), the county commissioners of said counties which are partially or completely infested with the cattle tick (Margaropus annulatus) shall immediately take up the work of systematic tick eradication as hereafter provided and continue same until the cattle tick (Margaropus annulatus) is completely eradicated and notice in writing of same is given by the State Veterinarian. (1923, c. 146, s. 3; C.S., s. 4895(r).)

§ 106-353. Dipping vats; counties to provide; cost.

The county commissioners of the aforesaid counties shall provide such numbers of dipping vats as may be fixed by the State Veterinarian or his authorized representative, and provide the proper chemicals and other materials necessary to be used in the work of systematic tick eradication in such counties, which shall begin on said dates and continue until the cattle tick (Margaropus annulatus) is completely eradicated and notice in writing of same is given by the State Veterinarian. The cost of said vats and chemicals, or any other expense incurred in carrying out the provisions of G.S. 106-351 to 106-363, except G.S. 106-354 and 106-358, shall be paid out of the general county fund. (1923, c. 146, s. 4; C.S., s. 4895(s).)

Vision Books Order Form

Fax Orders:	1-980-299-5965
Phone Orders:	1-704-898-0770
E-mail Orders:	www.visionbooks.org
Mail Orders:	Vision Books. LLC P.O. Box 42406 Charlotte, NC 28215

Shipp To:
Name_____
Address_____
City_____State_____Zip_____
Phone_____Fax_____
Email_____@_____

Bill To: We can bill a third party on your behalf.
Name_____
Address_____
City_____State_____Zip_____
Phone____(_____)_____Fax_____
Email_____@_____

Pamphlet Number ($15.00 Each)	Qty	Total Cost
_____	_____	_____
_____	_____	_____
_____	_____	_____
_____	_____	_____
_____	_____	_____
_____	_____	_____
_____	_____	_____
_____	_____	_____
<u>Full Volume Set 1-92</u>	<u>92 Pamphlets</u>	<u>1,380.00</u>

Free Shipping Shipping & Handling on Full Volume Orders
Add $1.00 Shipping & Handling per pamphlet $_____

Total Cost $_____

Thank you for your support. Management!

DID YOU ENJOY THIS BOOK?

Vision Books, LLC would like to hear from you! If you or someone you know has been fasely imprisoned, we would like to hear your story. If the 'North Carolina Criminal Law and Procedure' has had an effect in your life or if you have suggestions, we would like to hear from you. Send your letters to:

Vision Books, LLC
Attn: Staff Writers
P.O. Box 42406
Charlotte, NC 28215
Email: staff@visionbooks.org

Order Additional Copies:

Fax Orders:	1-980-299-5965
Phone Orders:	1-704-898-0770
E-mail Orders:	www.visionbooks.org
Mail Orders:	Vision Books, LLC P.O. Box 42406 Charlotte, NC 28215

www.ingramcontent.com/pod-product-compliance
Lightning Source LLC
Chambersburg PA
CBHW051629170526
45167CB00001B/119